PRINCESS ISABEL
of Brazil

D. Isabel, Princess Imperial of Brazil, as a young woman

Courtesy of the Fundação Grão Pará, Petropolis

PRINCESS ISABEL
of Brazil

*Gender and Power in the
Nineteenth Century*

RODERICK J. BARMAN

A Scholarly Resources Inc. Imprint
Wilmington, Delaware

Scholarly Resources Inc.
104 Greenhill Avenue
Wilmington, DE 19805-1897
www.scholarly.com

Library of Congress Cataloging-in-Publication Data

Barman, Roderick J., 1937–
Princess Isabel of Brazil : gender and power in the nineteenth
  century / Roderick J. Barman.
     p. cm. — (Latin American silhouettes)
  Includes bibliographical references and index.
  ISBN 0-8420-2845-5 (alk. paper) — ISBN 0-8420-2846-3
(pbk. : alk. paper)
     1. Isabel, Princess of Brazil, 1846–1921. 2. Brazil—History—
Empire, 1822–1889. 3. Sex role—Political aspects—Brazil.
4. Equality—Brazil—History—19th century. 5. Power (Social
sciences) 6. Princesses—Brazil—Biography. I. Title. II. Series.

F2536.I8 B37 2002
981'.04'092—dc21   2001054175

To Jean

Fear not, sweet love, what time can do;
Though silver dims the gold
Of your soft hair, believe that you
Can change but not grow old

We will not weep that spring be past
And autumn shadows fall;
These years shall be, although the last,
The loveliest of all

June 29, 1963—June 29, 2001

About the Author

R oderick J. Barman encountered the Empire of Brazil in his first
doctoral seminar at the University of California, Berkeley, in 1964.
Being English by birth and upbringing, he was fascinated to find a
country of the New World that had a monarch, titled nobility, and a
parliamentary system. The close links between Brazil and France, where
he had spent a year learning the language, also intrigued him. Disserta-
tion research in Rio de Janeiro confirmed his interest in the Empire
and awoke a warm affection for Brazil and the Brazilians.

A member of the History Department at the University of British
Columbia since 1971, Professor Barman is the author of *Brazil: The
Forging of a Nation, 1798–1852* (Stanford, 1988) and *Citizen Emperor: Pedro II and the Making of Brazil, 1825–1891* (Stanford, 1999),
the winner of the 2001 Warren Dean Prize for the best book on Brazilian history. Researching the life of D. Isabel led him into the field
of gender history, which has opened up for him new ways to approach
the past. He is now busy writing *Brazil: The Burdens of Nationhood,
1852–1930.*

CONTENTS

LIST OF ILLUSTRATIONS

INTRODUCTION

Women have at last become visible in history. The past is no longer the monopoly of men, with females ignored or at best marginalized. The struggle to give women presence and voice has been slow, laborious, and fiercely contested. Much remains to be done. Many approaches to the past continue to be highly gendered, none more so than the study of politics and power, long the citadel of male privilege. This very quality has perhaps repelled or discouraged revisionist work. Nonetheless, women have always been involved, behind the scenes if not formally, in the political process. While most women have had to participate at a disadvantage and from the edges, a few have, due to special circumstances, occupied positions within the structures of rule. Such a privileged woman was Princess Isabel, heir to the Brazilian throne for almost forty years, from 1851 to 1889.

This book has three goals. First, the text allows D. Isabel to speak for herself by providing copious extracts from her letters and recollections, especially in the seven inserts named "In Her Own Voice." The second goal is to present, so far as it is possible for a male to do so, a "feminist" analysis of D. Isabel's life. The book is structured around the female life cycle. It sees women as having been, in the past, shaped by and living within cultural, social, and economic structures created by men and predicated on female subordination and exploitation. It seeks to explain why women have had such difficulty in challenging these structures and their premises and in creating a system that gives autonomy and equality to women.

The work's third and perhaps most important goal is to use the princess's life as a vehicle for understanding the interplay of gender and power in the nineteenth century. Gender is defined as the dynamic (historically disparate and exploitative) between women and men. Power can be defined narrowly as political authority and more broadly as control of material resources and of cultural belief. As one of only nine women who during the nineteenth century were regents or monarchs of their countries, D. Isabel held power. Within the structures of power, gender does not function in isolation. It is intertwined with race and class, nowhere more so than in imperial Brazil. In the first chapter of this work, gender, race, and class are discussed, as is the power structure that imperial Brazil inherited from the colonial period.

The idea of writing this book came to me during the composition of *Citizen Emperor: Pedro II and the Making of Brazil, 1825–1891*, published in 1999. My research into the personal papers of the imperial family, held in Petrópolis, made clear the importance of Pedro II's elder daughter, D. Isabel, as the subject for a broad-ranging book. I must once again express my deep thanks to D. Pedro d'Orléans e Bragança, great-grandson of Pedro II and grandson of D. Isabel, for his generosity in giving me unrestricted access to their letters and papers. In July 2000, D. Pedro's eldest son, D. Pedro Carlos d'Orléans e Bragança, most kindly gave me renewed access to these personal papers and to the family's photograph collection. Without this twofold assistance, neither book could have been written. I have also to record the kindness shown to me by the Comtesse de Paris, D. Isabel's eldest granddaughter. We met quite by chance at the Château d'Eu, her childhood home, at the opening on September 30, 2000, of the exhibition "Souvenirs du Brésil dans les bagages du Comte et de la Comtesse d'Eu (1889)." In February 2001 the countess talked with me at her Paris home about her grandparents and her family life as a child. The countess, who much resembles her grandmother, recounted for me several memories of her beloved "Vovó."

This book also draws on research undertaken in the course of thirty years in the archives of the Museu Imperial at Petrópolis, the Instituto Histórico e Geográfico Brasileiro, the Arquivo Nacional, the Biblioteca Nacional in Rio de Janeiro, and the Universidade Federal de Pernambuco at Recife. My sincere thanks go to the staff at these institutions who have helped me so often and so much. By gracious permission of Her Majesty Queen Elizabeth II, this book contains materials relating to D. Isabel and the count d'Eu from the Royal Archives at Windsor, and I have to express to Miss Pamela Clark, the deputy registrar, my appreciation for her assistance on several occasions. I must also express my gratitude to the Viscount Norwich for permission to reproduce the verses that his father (Duff Cooper) addressed to his mother (Lady Diana Cooper) in the autobiography, *Old Men Forget*.

Important to this book are the illustrations. This visual text elucidates the lives of D. Isabel and those around her. My warmest thanks are due to D. Pedro Carlos d'Orléans e Bragança, who showed and granted me permission to reproduce here photographs (including that on the front cover) belonging to his family and now held by the Fundação Grão Pará. I must also express my appreciation to the staff of the Museu Imperial of Petrópolis for permitting the copying of photographs in their collection and for authorizing their reproduction here. My gratitude is due to Sr. Sergio Burgi and Sr. Juca Morais for their skill in making the photographic reproductions.

Scholarly Resources proved very receptive when approached with the idea for this book. I much appreciate the interest and cooperation of the press. In the text, footnotes are restricted to documenting quotations. Should readers want to identify sources underlying the text, they can look for the same subject in *Citizen Emperor*, or, if that does not serve, they can contact me directly for information on the subject. I am happy to be of assistance. Words in Portuguese in this book follow modern orthography, with a few exceptions. During D. Isabel's lifetime the currency of Brazil was the milréis, literally one thousand réis, and so written as 1$000. A thousand milréis was a conto, written as 1:000$000. Worth fifty-five cents in 1846, the year of D. Isabel's birth, the milréis fluctuated considerably in value, its high being fifty-nine cents in 1851 and its low thirteen cents in 1921, the year of her death. Dollar equivalents given in the text are only approximate.

Several grants from Social Science and Humanities Research Council of Canada have funded the research on which this book and *Citizen Emperor* are based. I must express my gratitude both to the Council and to the Faculty of Arts at the University of British Columbia for sharing the cost of a release time stipend during the academic year 1999–2000. In preparing the final text I have been much helped by the comments of Dr. Jean Barman, Dr. James N. Green, Sra. Fernanda Selayzin Duarte de Sousa, and the two readers for Scholarly Resources. The views expressed in this book are, of course, entirely my own, and none of the entities mentioned here is in any way responsible for them.

RJB

1

GENDER AND POWER IN BRAZIL

A Brazilian upper-class family with household slaves

Jean Baptiste Debret, Voyage pittoresque et historique au Brésil. *Paris, 1834*

Historians rarely mention D. Isabel, the daughter of Pedro II, Brazil's last emperor. If they discuss her at all, it is for two achievements. In 1871 the princess presided over the enactment of the Law of Free Birth, which assured the eventual disappearance of slavery in Brazil. In 1888 she played a principal role in securing an immediate end to slavery. The supporters of abolition at once dubbed her *A Redentora* (the redemptress), and that designation has endured. As *A Redentora*, D. Isabel continues to be an iconic figure in the popular

1

culture of Brazil. Otherwise, the princess has commanded little or no attention. Since her death in 1921, only three biographies have appeared, all in Portuguese. The first two, by Pedro Calmon and Hermes Vieira, were published in 1941 and the third by Lourenço Lacombe in 1989. Articles on the princess are notable for their scarcity.

D. Isabel merits our attention. For nearly forty years (1851–1889), the princess was heir to the Brazilian Empire. On three occasions between 1871 and 1888, amounting in all to three and a half years, she governed the country during her father's absences abroad. As regent she exercised the considerable powers that the Constitution of 1824 gave to the monarch. In this same period the princess gave birth to three sons, the ultimate heirs to the Brazilian throne. D. Isabel's character and actions, historians agree, were factors contributing to the replacement of the imperial regime by a republic on November 15, 1889.

Viewed from a broader perspective, the princess also possesses considerable importance. She was one of only nine women around the world who during the nineteenth century occupied posts of supreme authority in their country, either as monarch (Maria II of Portugal, Victoria of Great Britain, Isabella II of Spain, Liliuokalani of Hawaii, Wilhelmina of the Netherlands) or as regent (Maria Christina of Bourbon-Naples, D. Isabel of Brazil, Maria Christina of Habsburg, Emma of Waldeck-Pyrmont). All these women were born into royal or princely families and so raised within a world of privilege. All nine were brought up to fulfill what were considered to be women's roles as daughter, bride, wife, and mother. They all did so (Queen Liliuokalani alone bearing no children), but they were also required to assume a further role, that of ruling their country.

Their posts as monarch or regent were in no way sinecures. Wielding substantial powers, they each exerted a considerable influence on the conduct of public affairs. The position they held was male by definition. The monarch was perceived as being warrior, father figure, and statesman. He stood at the pinnacle of a public world that belonged to men, and he received obedience because he was a man. The nine women, even if perceived as lacking the qualities innate to men, were nonetheless expected to behave in the same fashion and to perform to the same standards as their male predecessors. Four of the five queens (Liliuokalani again being the exception) assumed their powers as rulers before their twentieth year, and the four regents were aged from twenty-four to thirty-two when they were called to their post. When they began to act as rulers, eight of the nine women were at a period in their life course when they had also to assume and fulfill their multiple and cumulative female obligations. D. Isabel's life provides insights into the triangular relationship existing for all of these nineteenth-century women rulers between gender (existence as a woman), power (the exercise of agency), and the life course.

Of the three concepts, the life course is the easiest to understand. Each human being fulfills a number of roles during their lifetime. Tamara Hareven, a leading scholar of the subject, has pointed to "the recognition of life stage as an important determinant of the impact of historical events on individual lives." This approach enables us to understand "how people perceive the relationship of their lives to historical events and their own roles as actors."[1] In the nineteenth century the roles that women played over their life course were, as was the case with the nine monarchs and regents, cumulative, not sequential. Women did not, in other words, give up existing roles when they assumed a new one. The nature of each role over the life course is shaped by the individual's capacities and circumstances at the moment in question and also by the prevailing set of assumptions, which themselves change over the course of each person's life. Each person exists within and interacts with a larger and shifting historical context.

The concepts of power and gender are more complex and fluid in meaning. An exercise of power takes place when an individual or a group can get another one to do something that the other would not otherwise do or when an individual or group can prevent another one from doing what the other wants to do. Power is a process, not an innate quality that people possess. The key to the exercise of power lies in individuals' and groups' differential access to and control over resources, which are both material and human in form. Resources range from precious metals and physical force to computer technology and command of languages.

Power is exercised within the set of assumptions and understandings—including beliefs (religious and nonreligious), modes of thought,

laws, customs and conventions, and behavior patterns—that prevail
at a given moment in time. This set of assumptions and understandings can be labeled, for our convenience here, "culture." Culture shapes
both relations within a society and the ways in which individuals perceive their own identities. It thus provides guidelines as to the exercise
of power. Culture sanctions some uses and disapproves of other uses
of the same resource. For example, physical force when used by a
government body (armed forces or police) is sanctioned but not so its
use by private individuals for personal advantage. These constraints
and taboos on the exercise of power are not mandatory. Human beings can and do disregard them. However, individuals absorb both
consciously and unconsciously the culture in which they live. Some
aspects of the culture are consciously learned, as if it were a code of
belief and behavior. Such aspects often become so accepted and so
internalized that people lose the ability to act contrary to them. Other
aspects of the culture can be termed instinctive, having been absorbed
virtually unknowingly from earliest childhood. People comply with
them without realizing they are doing so.

Much of culture is conceptualized and structured through what
William H. Sewell Jr., a leading social historian, has termed "the array
of binary oppositions that make up a given society's fundamental tools
of thought."[2] One of these binaries is "man-woman," a basic distinc-
tion upon which the exercise of power rests. In her seminal article,
"Gender: A Useful Category of Historical Analysis," Joan Wallach
Scott has sketched out how this particular binary shapes culture.
First, it is expressed through symbols. In cultures within the Judeo-
Christian tradition, such as those of Brazil, western Europe, and North
America, one of these foundational symbols is the binary of Adam
and Eve. Adam was created by God; Eve was fashioned out of Adam's
rib. Eve succumbed to temptation; the couple's fall from innocence
and expulsion from the Garden of Eden followed. Adam was the first
father and Eve the first mother.

An array of "normative concepts," Scott has argued, "set forth
interpretations of the meaning of the symbols." "Expressed in religious, educational, scientific, legal, and political doctrines," these concepts "typically take the form of a fixed binary opposition, categorically
and unequivocally asserting the meaning of male and female, mascu-

line and feminine."[3] Such is the case in Judeo-Christian cultures. Being in physical terms "Adam's rib," women are viewed as biologically subordinate to and dependent upon men. Eve's succumbing to temptation signifies that female nature is less strong, less constant, and less trustworthy than that of males. As "Eve's daughters," women have the primary role of giving birth and raising children, the primary role of males being that of provider and protector. Women make their lives within the home, within what is termed "the private sphere," whereas men live in the world of action, what is termed "the public sphere." Men and women exist in tandem, except that men are defined as possessing the ideal qualities and roles. They are the norm, which women cannot aspire to be because they are not men. Autonomy and agency are seen as the prerogative of men, and human resources are perceived in ways that privilege male access and control. Aggressiveness, even when physical, is a "manly" quality; for the female sex to show aggression is to be "unfeminine."

As Scott observes, multiple arrays of normative concepts interpreting the basic symbols always exist, but in any given culture a single array dominates. It alone is accepted as valid. In cultures based on the Judeo-Christian tradition the array deriving from the binary of Adam and Eve possessed validity until very recently. This array, often termed "patriarchy," was viewed as ordained by God (defined, of course, as male) or, alternatively, as based upon the natural order as understood by reason and science. It permeated every aspect of culture and so shaped the entire workings of society. Politics, often defined in terms of power as "who gets what when and how," is concerned with access to and control of material and human resources. Politics was seen as belonging to the public sphere, in which women had no place.

The existence of this hegemonic array of normative interpretations played an important role in shaping the autonomy and agency available to women of the nineteenth century, both rulers and commoners. For an individual "to be an agent," Sewell has argued, "means to be capable of some degree of control over the social relations in which one is enmeshed, which in turn implies the ability to transform those social relations to some degree."[4] The patriarchal cultures in which women existed had the effect of restricting and regulating their spheres of action and forms of expression. So strong and so in-grained was this hegemonic array of normative interpretations that it was difficult to challenge and easy to internalize. The existence of patriarchy did not, it must be emphasized, mean that women lacked autonomy and agency. They were not passive and compliant, as most men assumed they were. Individual women sometimes openly ques-tioned patriarchy, just as did Simone de Beauvoir in 1949 with her classic, *The Second Sex*. None of this altered the reality that the hege-mony persisted, with men dominant and women subordinate.

Not until the last third of the twentieth century did a systematic and sustained assault call patriarchy into question and weaken (but not overthrow) the dominance of men. A crucial first step was to destroy the assumption that the differences between females and males are preordained, innate, and biologically determined. To use Simone de Beauvoir's famous phrase, "one is not born, but rather becomes, a woman."[5] Her book began the shift to regarding differences between women and men as cultural constructions. The differences are cre-ated rather than being produced by biology.

To this end the word "gender" has replaced "sex" as the preferred term when analyzing the relationship between women and men. Natalie Zemon Davis, a pioneer in women's history, explained in 1975 "that we should be interested in the history of both women and men, that we should not be working only on the subjected sex any more than a historian of class can focus entirely on peasants. Our goal is to understand the significance of the sexes, of gender groups in the his-torical past."[6] Used in this way, gender means the social and cultural divisions frequently based on, but not necessarily coincidental with, anatomical sex. Such divisions are relative; that is, they are constructed. The meaning, interpretation, and expression of these divisions vary between cultures and over time. Factors such as class, age, race, ethnicity, and sexual orientation influence the ways in which gender is constructed and understood.

Using gender as a category of analysis calls into question long-established, deeply entrenched assumptions regarding the basic orga-nization of human society, including the male-female binary. The very concepts of man and woman melt away. Women and men include a wide range of sexualities, identities, and behavioral and temperamental traits. "Femininities," not a single "femininity," and "masculinities," not a sole "masculinity," exist. The result is a world in which everything is relative, fluid, and decentered. Norms no longer exist. We can do and be as we will, provided, that is, that we are autonomous entities who know and act.

The drawback with such a complete deconstruction, with reducing everything to the relative and the conditional, is that gender in the workings of human societies is not neutral. Gender is fundamental to the exercise of power, resulting in domination and subordination. Gender as a category of analysis came into being as a result of the challenge to patriarchy mounted by female scholars. Their work questioned the whole array of normative assumptions based on the male-female binary. To detach the study of gender from the continuing struggle against patriarchy is, it can be argued, to condone and give tacit sanction to a system that continues to exploit and subordinate women. This realization provides a salutary reminder to all of us. Even though we may not be studying a topic specifically in terms of gender, we must always be conscious of the relations of domination and subordination that gender creates. We need to be sensitive not just to what the working of gender tells us about the topic under analysis but to our own assumptions.

Sensitivity to gender is particularly important when we study the past. We need to approach the past with what may be termed a double vision. We need first to understand and so respect the culture of the society under study, no matter how much we may disagree with it. In effect, we should let people and groups in the past speak to the present with their own voices. Our second task is to set the chosen topic within a larger historical context and then to employ a conceptual analysis sufficiently open and flexible to take into account and explain the workings of the society under study. Through this twofold approach we can avoid imposing our present-day assumptions on persons living in the past.

Biography provides, if properly handled, an excellent genre by which we can achieve this double vision. Study of an individual's roles over the life course, as expressed in writings, letters, and reminiscences, offers entry into the modes of thought of the period and allows the past to speak with its own voice. One person's voice is, of course, singular and partial, but it is not for that reason invalid. In any given period multiple viewpoints and voices existed and often competed. Any one of these voices has a story, provided we recognize that it is partial and set it within a context. In the case of D. Isabel, her personal correspondence reveals her particular attitudes and assumptions about power and gender at different points along her life course. These attitudes and assumptions may not coincide with those of our own day, but they must be respected and set within a larger historical analysis.

A study of the larger historical context into which D. Isabel was born must begin with Brazil, the land of her birth. Some 3 million square miles in size, the country stretches from the tropical forests of the Amazon basin in the far north through the dry savannahs known as the *sertão* (backlands) and the luxuriant lowlands along the Atlantic coast to the temperate grasslands in the far south. This vast country gained its political independence from Portugal in 1822. Educated Brazilians strove to make their country mirror the new nation-states of Europe. The Constitution of 1824 introduced an elected legislature, an independent judiciary, and a bill of citizens' rights but balanced these with a powerful monarch who acted as a guardian of the political system. Portuguese was the national language, and the Catholic Church continued to be the state religion, although the 1824 Constitution permitted freedom of worship. By the time of D. Isabel's birth in 1846, Brazil was finally achieving some coherence and stability as a nation-state, but the colonial heritage remained strong and influential in many ways.

From the time of the Portuguese colonizers' first arrival in the New World in 1500, they sought wealth, which meant exploiting the land and its resources. To provide the workers they needed, the Portuguese subdued the aboriginal inhabitants. When, through death and flight, the aboriginal peoples proved insufficient, the colonizers brought in millions of slaves from Africa to work plantations and mines. Throughout the entire colonial period and into the nineteenth century, violence remained the key to acquiring and retaining land and compulsion the means of securing labor. On the eve of Brazil's political independence in 1822, slaves formed about 40 percent of the population. Despite the law of 1830 banning the importation of slaves from Africa, an illegal slave trade continued unchecked. Not until 1851, five years after D. Isabel's birth, did the imperial government finally stamp out this trade. Slavery continued thereafter to be a central element in the labor system, of particular importance in the burgeoning production of coffee.

The existence of slavery did not produce, in contrast to the United States, a society of rigid racial castes. In the colonial period the vast majority of settlers from Portugal were men who took as sexual partners indigenous or African women. The offspring of these unions, usually not sanctified by the Catholic Church but sometimes long lasting, created an intermediate racial and social group that grew

rapidly in number. Males in this group took up the posts and occupa-
tions that the comparative paucity of immigrants from Portugal left
unfilled. Females played an even more critical role in influencing race
relations. They were *morena* (dark), possessed of a compelling sexual
attraction that often overrode racial and class preoccupations. Portuguese in language, culture, and outlook, this group served to blur
racial divisions and to blend the categories of race and class. By the
end of the eighteenth century being "white" referred as much to high
socioeconomic and cultural standing as it did to physical appearance.
Nonetheless, the ruling groups' desire to make their country a copy of
European nation-states meant that they saw Brazil as being racially
"white," thus marginalizing the majority of the population.

This attitude was encouraged by the system of gender relations
that the Portuguese brought with them to the New World, a system
that persisted into the nineteenth century. Gender relations were un-
relentingly patriarchal. At the center of social relations, based on the
binary of honor and shame, stood the family. The honor of a family
resided in the purity of its lineage, this purity being transmitted through
women. Since women were perceived as essentially passive and submissive, they could not personally defend their own honor but had to
depend on males to do so. Defense of a family's honor was entrusted
to its male head (husband and/or father). He held unchallenged authority over the family's members, an authority that was most visible
in his right to choose spouses for his children and dependent relatives. In families of impeccable lineage the honorific of Dom was given
to males and Dona to females, both being usually written as D., as
with D. Isabel. Increasingly, over time, the honorific Dona was given
to any female whose family could lay claim to honorable status.

The patriarchal nature of gender relations extended into public
life. All posts in the government save for that of monarch were reserved to men. Within the Catholic Church, single men alone could
be priests, endowed with divine authority and exercising spiritual powers. In the area of commerce, the only women who could run busi-
nesses without risking loss of their honor were widows. At every level
of Brazilian society, both before and after political independence,
women were subordinate to men. An American who visited Rio de
Janeiro City in 1846, the year of D. Isabel's birth, observed how "not

till within a few years have ladies begun to appear in the streets. The old Moorish seclusion of the sex has but lately been invaded."[7]

The colonial heritage deeply influenced Brazil in its emergence as a nation-state. Portugal never provided its American possessions with the institutions necessary for an effective system of government. It retained control of the colonies by preventing the creation in them of an autonomous public culture. The printing press was banned and the importation of reading materials censored. No institutions of higher learning were permitted, and support for primary and secondary education was minimal. Cultural institutions of any type were viewed with suspicion, and few were authorized. The Catholic Church, with its seminaries, its lay brotherhoods, and its charitable organizations, was the exception to this rule, but the Portuguese government denied the Church any independence. Inadequately staffed and underfunded, the Church conspicuously failed to show zeal, self-denial, and sanctity.

At the end of the eighteenth century the Portuguese colonies in the New World lacked most of the preconditions for becoming a nation-state. Despite the examples of the United States in 1776 and of France in 1789, no viable independence movement developed. The impetus came from the outside. In 1807 a French invasion of Portugal forced the royal government under D. João VI to flee to the city of Rio de Janeiro. The diverse colonies of Portuguese America were united into a single state, the kingdom of Brazil, in 1816. The economy was thrown open to direct trade with the outside world. Printing was permitted, and some institutions of higher learning were created. In 1820 a revolt in Portugal forced King João VI to return to Lisbon, leaving his elder son, D. Pedro, behind in Rio de Janeiro as regent of Brazil. There followed a period of mounting confrontation between the regime in Lisbon and the government in Rio de Janeiro. In September 1822, D. Pedro declared Brazil's political independence with himself as its emperor. Within a year the new Empire had established its authority throughout Brazil, and in 1825 Great Britain brokered a peace treaty whereby Portugal recognized Brazil's existence as a separate nation-state.

The pantheon that enshrines the heroes of Brazilian political independence contains only three women. The empress Leopoldina,

D. ISABEL'S GRANDMOTHER, EMPRESS D. LEOPOLDINA OF BRAZIL

Courtesy of the Museu Nacional Histórico, Rio de Janeiro

daughter of the emperor of Austria, encouraged her husband D. Pedro to defy the Lisbon government. Maria Quitéria, a native of Bahia province, donned a soldier's uniform in order to fight for the cause of political independence. Joana Angélica, a nun, was shot down at the doorway of her convent in Salvador da Bahia while resisting the intrusion of Portuguese troops. Participation by women was certainly more extensive and more significant than these three stories imply, but they do show how difficult it was for women to play autonomous roles. Sister Joana Angélica was a heroine due to an act of passive resistance appropriate to her gender. D. Leopoldina confined herself to supporting and encouraging her husband, as a wife should. To participate in the struggle, Maria Quitéria had to violate gender conventions by cross-dressing. A woman who went to fight in female clothing would have been rejected. In other words, political independence brought no change to gender relations or to existing assumptions about power.

One reason for the lack of change was the central role played in the independence struggle by Freemasonry, an exclusively male order or movement that embraced the worldview propagated by the Enlightenment. In Europe and the Americas, Freemasons organized themselves in lodges, separate units that met behind closed doors, used elaborate rituals, and maintained absolute secrecy as to their practices and beliefs. Masonic lodges (the model for college fraternities) were the ideal forum for free discussion of radical ideas and for organizing political action. Their exclusion of women reinforced the perception of politics and public affairs as a male preserve, no more so than in Brazil, where the Masonic lodges continued to play an important role in politics and to serve as centers for socialization among the members of the ruling class.

The constitution promulgated by Emperor Pedro I on March 24, 1824, defined Brazil as "the political association of all Brazilian citizens" and conferred citizenship on all those born in Brazil, both free and freed. Although the constitution nowhere denied to women the status of citizens, its provisions assumed that citizens were male. Article 145 proclaimed that "all Brazilians are required to bear arms in order to uphold the independence and integrity of the Empire." The

D. Isabel's grandfather, Emperor Pedro I of Brazil

Courtesy of the Museu Nacional Histórico, Rio de Janeiro

provisions of the constitution governing elections created a two-tiered franchise, based on levels of income and some other qualifications, which did not include being a man. Assumptions about women's dependence and incapacity were so ingrained and so axiomatic that there was no need to bar them explicitly from voting. "The mass of *active citizens* alone enjoy political rights and consequently citizens inactive in terms of public law do not enjoy such faculties," one commentary on the constitution asserted. "In this class are included female Brazilians, notwithstanding what their capacities and qualifications may be." Women were, moreover, but one of a number of groups to whom the vote was denied, despite their being freeborn or freed. "Reason and the public interest cannot fail of necessity to acknowledge the incapacity resulting from gender, lack of age, insanity, lack of culture and the absence of ability, which would turn the right to vote into a social peril."[8] Not until 1932 were literate women (a small minority of all females) awarded this basic right.

In withholding citizenship rights from women, the 1824 Constitution conformed to prevailing assumptions. Article 117, which regulated the line of succession to Emperor Pedro I, did, however, permit women to inherit the throne. This concession was in part a matter of tradition, continuing the practice of Portugal, and in part a question of necessity. In March 1824, when the constitution was promulgated, the only living children of D. Leopoldina and Pedro I were three daughters (Maria, Januária, and Paula), the first of their two sons having died shortly after birth and the other at eleven months. D. Leopoldina gave birth to a fourth daughter, Francisca, in 1824 and to a healthy son, named Pedro after his father, on December 2, 1825. A year later the empress died in childbirth. Pedro I married again in 1829, to D. Amélia of Leuchtenberg.

Pedro I's reign proved short and stormy. In personal terms he lacked the restraint and flexibility required of a constitutional monarch, and he was too dependent on a coterie of Portuguese-born advisers. He further suffered from his birth in Portugal that identified him with the colonial heritage of autocracy and dependence. The new class of politicians, overwhelmingly Brazilian-born, wished to rid the country of this heritage and to take direct control of its affairs. No compromise between the monarch and his opponents proved possible, particularly since Pedro I insisted on appointing as ministers only those men whom he trusted, not those who commanded the confidence of the legislature. Other factors intensified the confrontation that erupted into open crisis in April 1831. Rather than compromise his rights, the emperor abdicated the throne in favor of his son Pedro, just five years old, and withdrew to Europe. Before his death in 1834 the former emperor succeeded in restoring his eldest daughter Maria to the throne of Portugal (which her uncle D. Miguel had usurped).

The decade that followed Pedro I's abdication (1831–1840) was one of political unrest and social upheavals that caused Brazilians to view the young emperor as the key to maintaining national unity and internal order. In July 1840, when Pedro II was not yet fifteen years old, he was declared of age by a parliamentary coup, even though the 1824 Constitution had fixed the age of majority at eighteen. The British envoy at Rio de Janeiro commented, with smug condescension, on the reasons for this act:

> The Brazilian requires to see the central presence of a Sovereign at the head of the Govt. and to surround Him with a certain degree of splendor and demonstration of force and show without which the exercise of Power appears to him odious and illegitimate. Indeed one of the principal arguments used by the advocates for the immediate majority of the Emperor has ever been the necessity of putting forward the "Prestigio" or respect and veneration for the attributes of Royalty, in order to render an efficient Government in Brazil possible.[9]

Following the departure of his father for Europe in 1831, Pedro II had suffered a miserable childhood in which he experienced emotional deprivation and psychological manipulation. Suspicious of any person or policy that infringed on his personal autonomy, he sought above all else to avoid being under obligation. He found comfort and reassurance in the familiar and remained intensely loyal to it. He took refuge in the world of learning, particularly in books, which provided both pleasure and a sense of security. During his first years of rule after his premature majority in 1840, Pedro II displayed great personal self-control and poise in his public duties. As he grew to his adult height of over six feet, with fair skin and blond hair, he looked like what Brazilians thought an emperor should be. However, his reserve and surliness in personal relations and his lack of emotional maturity made him at first an ineffective ruler. The wife chosen for him, a sister of the king of Naples, did not improve matters. Instead of being the beautiful and intelligent princess of Pedro II's dreams, D. Teresa Cristina proved, when he first met her in September 1843, to be short, heavyset, plain of face, and with a pronounced limp. The emperor's first reaction was to reject her and send her back to Europe but, since the marriage ceremony was set for the next day, he was persuaded to submit to his fate. For several weeks he refused to have sexual intercourse with his wife and treated her with freezing indifference.

At the time the marriage was arranged, Pedro II had written to D. Teresa Cristina, expressing his "resolve to make you happy." She replied: "Be sure that I will do everything that duty demands of me to contribute to that of your Majesty; my only desire will be to please you."[10] This promise the new empress resolutely fulfilled, despite her husband's treatment of her. D. Teresa Cristina's kindness and consideration eventually softened him. Sexual relations were initiated, and in May 1844 she became pregnant. This first child, a son, was born in February 1845. In October of that year the couple embarked on a six-month visit to the far south of Brazil. Stimulated by his new experiences, Pedro II matured as both an individual and ruler. He became courteous in manner, constantly accessible, and adept at handling those he met. For the empress, being continuously in the company of the spouse whom she adored brought joy and happiness. Well before the year ended, it was certain that she was pregnant with her second child. The life of D. Isabel was about to begin.

2

DAUGHTER, 1846–1864

D. ISABEL (on the left) WITH HER FATHER, MOTHER, AND SISTER

Courtesy of the Museu Nacional Histórico, Rio de Janeiro

As day broke on July 29, 1846, D. Teresa Cristina, the empress of Brazil, felt the first pangs of childbirth. The pain and the danger before her she faced without complaint. She had been brought up to believe that a woman must expect trial and tribulation. Her main purpose in life was to marry the man chosen for her and to produce children, preferably sons. In 1843, D. Teresa Cristina had traveled from Italy to Brazil to wed Pedro II sight unseen. She had at once

EMPRESS D. TERESA CRISTINA, ABOUT THE TIME OF D. ISABEL'S BIRTH

Courtesy of the Museu Nacional Histórico, Rio de Janeiro

fallen deeply in love with him and could not bear being apart from
him. "I do nothing but think of you, my dear Pedro," she wrote to
him during a brief separation in July 1844. "It already seems a century since I last saw you."[1] She devoted her life to being a dutiful,
obedient wife. Her first child, the son expected of her, was born in
February 1845. D. Afonso, as the prince was named, was a healthy
baby. Now, eighteen months later, she was about to deliver again.

EMPEROR PEDRO II, ABOUT THE TIME OF D. ISABEL'S BIRTH

Courtesy of the Arquivo Nacional, Rio de Janeiro

The birth took place in the palace of São Cristóvão, standing on the northern outskirts of Rio de Janeiro City. An American visitor to the palace earlier that year described the imperial bedroom as "this delightful dormitory," "fitted up with French furniture" and "thirty feet above the ground, while its folding windows open upon forests, groves, and gardens in perpetual bloom."[2] Those present in this room during the empress's labor included a few ladies-in-waiting, in personal attendance on D. Teresa Cristina, and a larger number of female servants. The two men present were Pedro II and Dr. Cândido Borges Monteiro, who as a court physician was in charge of the actual delivery. The empress's labor was prolonged, the birth not occurring until half past six that evening. Pedro II immediately took the child into an adjoining room to be displayed to an awaiting assembly of cabinet ministers, councilors of state, presidents of the Senate and Chamber of Deputies, and court dignitaries, all of them male. The baby was, as those present observed, healthy, sound of body, and a girl. They immediately signed an official deposition, drawn up in triplicate, to this effect.

The witnesses must have felt disappointment that the empress had not produced a second son. That the birth had been without problems gave promise of further pregnancies, including more sons. What D. Teresa Cristina's reaction was we do not and cannot know, since she kept her thoughts to herself. She probably regretted her "failure" to produce a son, but the fact that she was the mother of both a girl and a boy must have given her private satisfaction.

After the formal presentation, the baby was at once washed and swaddled. D. Teresa Cristina did not have long to hold her child, much less to care for her. She was kept in bed, a semi-invalid in accord with the medical practice of the day. She did not breast-feed her daughter. A wet nurse was on hand, chosen with great care from among the Swiss German migrant community settled at Novo Friburgo in the north of Rio de Janeiro province. The baby was given her own *quarto* (chamber, or establishment), under the charge of D. Rosa de Santa Ana Lopes, one of the empress's ladies-in-waiting. D. Rosa did not personally take care of the princess but supervised the activities of the numerous servants and underservants, some of them slaves, who carried out the necessary tasks. D. Isabel's parents saw her frequently as a baby, but they played no role in her actual nurture. This system of upbringing was entirely in accord with practice in the royal and princely families of Europe in the early nineteenth century. It was a hierarchical order that was likely to produce in any child, male or female, a sense of superiority and an expectation of service and deference.

The pomp and ceremony surrounding D. Isabel's baptism made clear that she was different from others. On November 15, 1846, the baby was taken to the Imperial Chapel in the heart of Rio City. The bishop of Rio de Janeiro, who held the post of imperial chaplain, poured over her water obtained from the River Jordan in Palestine. Her godparents, represented by proxies in their absence, were her mother's mother, Maria Isabel, the dowager queen of Naples, and her father's brother-in-law, King Fernando of Portugal. Eight names were given to the baby—D. Isabel Cristina Leopoldina Augusta Micaela Gabriela Rafaela Gonzaga. The last four of these were by tradition given to members of the Bragança family, which reigned in Portugal and Brazil. The first two names, which honored her godmother and her mother, were what mattered. The princess during her childhood and adolescence signed her letters "Isabel Cristina" or "IC."

THE PALACE OF SÃO CRISTÓVÃO

Courtesy of the Biblioteca Nacional, Rio de Janeiro

A month after the baptism, D. Isabel's father informed his sister, Queen Maria II of Portugal: "No news here save the good state of health of myself, of the empress, and of the little ones, who are becoming increasingly cute, principally little Afonso, who is already walking and who says many words, still half incomprehensible, the which increases their charm."³ The greater age of Afonso, then twenty-two months old compared to D. Isabel's five months, explains in part why he captured his father's attention, but his gender was also a factor. As son and heir all eyes focused on him, whereas a daughter inevitably took second place. At the moment that Pedro II wrote to his sister in Portugal, D. Teresa Cristina was already two months pregnant with her third child. The hope was that she was carrying a boy, a second son to ensure the male succession to the throne.

The hopes were to be doubly disappointed. On July 11, 1847, Pedro II told his stepmother: "With the most piercing grief I tell you that my dear little Afonso, your godson, unfortunately died of convulsions, which he suffered during five hours on the 4th of last month; and a few days ago little Isabel was put at risk by a strong attack of convulsions that greatly frightened me."⁴ The empress's grief at her loss was heartrending to see and caused concern that she would miscarry and die. In fact, she was safely delivered on July 13 of a daughter, who was named Leopoldina Teresa.

D. Isabel, not quite one year old, retained no memory of either her brother's death or of the arrival of her sister. Nor did the arrival of a new brother, Pedro, on July 19, 1848, shortly before her second birthday, in all likelihood register on her mind. An ability to recall events usually does not come until a child's third year. D. Isabel's earliest memories seem to have involved not people but places, particularly the imperial residence of São Cristóvão. "The palace of São Cristóvão is situated in the suburbs of Rio on a slight rise, in the middle of a large and beautiful park," she remembered in old age. She recalled "the palace's beautiful façade. From the upper stories of this façade you could see a corner of the sea in the direction of Cajú, and from those of the other two facades the splendid panorama stretching from Tijuca to the Sugar Loaf."⁵ The estate had been given to D. João VI by a local merchant when the Portuguese government arrived in March 1808. Despite being extended and remodeled over the years, the building remained a vast and unlovely structure. In adulthood D. Isabel referred in one of her letters to "this solitude of São Cristóvão," an image that aptly catches the character both of the palace (now a museum) and of her childhood within it.⁶

The summer months, December to April in the Southern Hemi-sphere, were hot and unhealthy. Traditionally, the imperial family moved during these months from São Cristóvão palace to the *fazenda* (estate) of Santa Cruz, lying on a plain to the west of Rio de Janeiro. Santa Cruz was, however, almost as sultry as Rio City, and it offered few diversions. At the end of the 1820s, Pedro I had started to spend the summer at an estate in the mountains to the north of Rio. After his abdication in 1831, the property he had purchased fell into the hands of his creditors. After Pedro II's majority in 1840, funds pro-vided by the legislature redeemed the estate, and plans were set afoot to build a town there. In June 1845, Pedro II visited the estate and selected the site for a summer palace. Two months later, immigrants from the Rhineland were brought in as settlers. The new town took its name from the young emperor, being called Petrópolis.

In 1847 and in the two years following, Pedro II with his wife and children spent the summer at Petrópolis. This innovation upset the members of the court who disliked any change that threatened their established ways and interests. In 1849, the emperor agreed that the summer should be, as tradition required, spent at the *fazenda* of Santa Cruz. To Santa Cruz the imperial family went, and there disaster struck. D. Pedro, the prince imperial, came down with fever and died of convulsions on January 9, 1850. The emperor was devastated, as his letter to the courtier in charge at Santa Cruz attests:

> Senhor Macedo. Issue the necessary orders that, with all con-venience, to São Cristóvão come the offspring whom I still have and whom I prize more than life itself. . . . This has been the most fatal blow that I could receive, and certainly I would not have survived were it not that I still have a wife and two children, whom I must educate so that they can assure the happiness of the country in which they were born. That is also one of my consolations.[7]

What made the situation far worse was that D. Isabel fell sick with fever at the same time as her brother. For a number of days after his death her survival was also in question. Although she overcame

D. ISABEL IN 1851 OR 1852, with shorn hair following a typhoid attack. This daguerreotype is perhaps the first photograph of the princess.

Courtesy of the Fundação Grão Pará, Petrópolis

this crisis, her health remained uncertain. Writing to his sister, the queen of Portugal, in September 1852, Pedro II explained that he had appointed "two special physicians for Isabel" because "the little one is still not entirely robust" and "her ailments seem to be chronic in nature."[8] Keeping D. Isabel healthy was the more important because, by September 1852, four years had passed since the birth of the impe-

rial couple's last child. The reason for the absence of more children is
not clear. D. Teresa Cristina, then aged thirty, may have suffered gynecological problems that prevented conception, but the cause was
just as likely the end of sexual relations between the couple. By 1852
the empress, two and a half years older than her husband, no longer
possessed any attraction for Pedro II, who sought emotional and sexual
solace with a series of other women. Whatever the cause, the absence
of further offspring confirmed D. Isabel's status as the heir to the
imperial throne.

THE IMPERIAL PALACE AT PETRÓPOLIS

Courtesy of the Biblioteca Nacional, Rio de Janeiro

From 1852 onward, life for the imperial family revolved around
Rio and Petrópolis. During the winter and spring, they resided at São
Cristóvão, with occasional visits to the City Palace that stood in the
center of Rio City. After the southern summer began in December,
they moved up to Petrópolis and lived there until returning to Rio
late in April. In "Joys and Sorrows," an unfinished autobiography

written in her early sixties (see In Her Own Voice below), D. Isabel recalled the excitement caused by this annual journey up to Petrópolis and the attractiveness of the town in its mountain setting. The brief account of her childhood also identifies the people who meant most to her in the early stages of her life.

In Her Own Voice

Born in the palace of São Cristóvão at Rio de Janeiro, on July 29, 1846, I spent my childhood and youth with my younger sister in company with my much-loved parents. I hardly ever left Rio during the winter or Petrópolis during the summer. The palace of São Cristóvão is situated in the suburbs of Rio on a slight rise, in the middle of a large and beautiful park. During my childhood the park was notable above all for its shady alleys of mango, tamarind and other trees; its alleys made of bamboo of which the tops crossed so high up as to form a true cathedral vault. Underneath it, as a child, I ran with my sister and my young companions. . . . From São Cristóvão we moved in the summer to Petrópolis. Embarking at the Navy Arsenal, in my father's steam launch, we sailed for an hour through green and picturesque islands to Mauá, leaving behind us the Sugar Loaf and the fortress of Santa Cruz on its mountain top guarding the entry to Rio bay. And in front of us we had the beautiful mountains named the Serra dos Orgãos due to their peaks resembling organ pipes. At Mauá we boarded the railroad and two hours later we found ourselves at Petrópolis, our summer residence, a delicious residence: flowering gardens, canals that crisscrossed the town, pretty houses, wooded hills, and mountains in the distance, some of granite, whose flanks the setting sun turned purple. . . .

Dona Rosa de Sant'Anna Lopes, later Baroness of Sant'Anna, had been named as Lady-in-waiting to my little person from the day of my birth. The Countess of Barral and Mademoiselle Templier arrived, later on, to supervise my education. To all three of them my affectionate and grateful appreciation.[9]

When appointed to be lady-in-waiting in charge of the princess on her birth in July 1846, D. Rosa de Santa Ana Lopes was aged forty-one and unmarried. She established close, affectionate, and enduring ties with the princess, who in her letters always referred to her as "m[inh]ᵃ Rosa," "my Rosa."[10] The term captures the nature of the relationship. Despite the age difference, D. Rosa never served as a guide or role model. She was an upper-class Portuguese lady with a very narrow range of interests of the most traditional sort. Writing in 1853 about his daughters' upbringing, Pedro II commented that "the Ladies in charge of their respective chambers, even though very attentive (to their honor it must be said), do not possess the degree of education that is required even in ordinary society."[11] A courtier born and bred, D. Rosa invariably treated her charge with deference and indulgence, feeding in D. Isabel that sense of separateness and self-interest so common among royalty. However warm and intimate the relationship between the two, it was always, as the word "my" implies, one of servant and superior.

If her lady-in-waiting played no significant role in forming D. Isabel's character, the opposite was the case with her parents. In her draft autobiography, written in French, D. Isabel stated that she "spent my childhood and youth with my younger sister *autour de* my much loved parents." *Autour de*, literally translated, means "around," invoking an image of the two girls circling like planets around Pedro II and D. Teresa Cristina. This image was apt. The imperial court and household (*côrte e casa imperial*) was a closed society with no purpose other than to serve the monarch and his wife. The couple's favor counted for everything. Their authority could not be disputed. Their displeasure meant disaster. D. Teresa Cristina's unfailing kindness and good nature and Pedro II's forbearance and willingness to overlook faults did not disguise the reality of the power they held. The close proximity in which courtiers, servants, and underservants lived with the imperial couple did not imply equality or familiarity. The two stood above and apart from everyone else.

The atmosphere at court reinforced the natural tendency of the two young princesses to place their parents on a pedestal. This attitude was not the product of fear or compulsion. When D. Isabel

recalled her parents as being " much loved," she was being both honest and accurate. The two sisters circled a sun that provided warmth
and comfort. The empress lived for her family and found fulfillment
in making her spouse and her daughters happy. The emperor, a man
remarkable for his self-control, was at his most affectionate and most
outgoing with children, above all with his daughters, "whom I love
deeply," as he wrote in his diary at the end of 1861. Ten years earlier
he had written to his wife, "Give a kiss to each of the little ones and
tell them that I could not find dolls with wax faces, but I will bring
others."[12] On D. Isabel's birthday in 1852, her father constructed for
his daughters on the grounds of São Cristóvão a special garden, with
stone seats decorated with china and shells.

For all his kindnesses and concern for his daughters, Pedro II cannot be termed an indulgent parent, and he never allowed challenges
to his authority within the home. In so doing, he conformed to the
gender attitudes prevailing across the Western world. France was then
generally accepted as the center of Western civilization, supreme in
the arts and sciences. In common with most upper-class Brazilians,
the emperor accepted France as the model the young nation should
follow in both public and private life. Contemporary French culture
endorsed the concept of separate spheres. "Man's destiny was to work
and to participate in public affairs: woman's place was to organize the
household and to raise children," a historian of women in nineteenth-
century France has recently observed. As Pedro II noted in his 1862
diary, he upheld "the principle that the husband is the one who should
rule in the house."[13]

French "etiquette manuals agreed that young bourgeois girls were
to receive a sheltered upbringing. . . . They could never go out unaccompanied, either by a maid or, on more formal visits, by their mothers, or an approved substitute. They were to be deliberately kept in
ignorance of the world outside the home and treated as decorative
ornaments who might on occasions help their mothers in running
the household."[14] This passage exactly describes the sheltered existence Pedro II imposed on his two daughters.

The princesses did not live in total seclusion, as the following
news item in a Rio de Janeiro newspaper during Easter Week of 1854,
when they were aged seven and six, respectively, shows. "T[heir].

H[ighnesses]. have expressed a desire to see, for the first time, the procession of the Burial of Our Lord. Since they cannot stay up very late, the Third Order of St. Francisco de Paula has decided that the procession will start promptly at 7 o'clock, so that it passes in front of the [City] Palace at 8 o'clock, thus satisfying a wish that the Order views as a command." Such appearances by the sisters were, however, unusual. They lived very much out of the public eye, the large grounds surrounding the palaces of São Cristóvão and Petrópolis keeping them in spatial isolation. The court personnel who served the princesses formed a separate and closed world, very conscious of its superior status, protective of its perquisites and privileges, and recruited from families with a tradition of serving at court. The staff included courtiers of aristocratic lineage such as D. Manuel de Assis Mascarenhas, naturalized foreigners such as Dr. José Francisco Sigaud, and household slaves. A letter that D. Isabel wrote at the age of eighteen to her father identified the slaves who were her personal attendants: "Martha (my little Black maid), Anna de Souza (her mother); Francisco Cordeiro (my Black room servant), Maria d'Austria (his wife); Minervina (washerwoman); Conceição, Florinda, and Maria d'Alleluia (starchers); José Luiz (the Black who played for our dance lessons and who still plays on the days when we have entertainment); Antonio Sant'Ana (the Black who was my servant for some time)."[15]

Even in the closed world of the court, the facts of life sometimes intruded. In 1824, the instructions issued by Pedro I on the upbringing of his daughters, D. Isabel's aunts, had laid down that they must not "play with the young boys, and take especial care that the girls do not see them naked." In 1834, the guardian of the young Pedro II and his two sisters, then aged twelve and ten, complained that "between the hours of eleven in the morning and four in the afternoon black men, in a state of total nudity, swim in the sea in front of the [City] Palace, which is harmful for H. M. and his August sisters to see." In 1846, a few months before D. Isabel's birth, Thomas Ewbank and some friends made a short tour of São Cristóvão palace. On leaving, "we passed an oblong pond or lake," where "two negro women were knee deep in it washing, and within five feet of them two black men, perfectly nude, engaged in the same operation."[16] To ordinary Brazilians, public nudity (mainly male) was sufficiently familiar as to provoke no more than casual comment. For the ruling minority, clothing was material proof of culture and civilization. Nudity was barbarous and male nudity was abhorrent, offending the delicate feelings of females, deemed to be "spiritual" and morally superior beings. In reality, of course, the taboo sprang not from female susceptibilities but from males' perception of the penis as the supreme embodiment of power, an attribute that women lacked. Only after she married could a female see the male organ in the privacy of the bedroom and then as part of the sexual act by which her husband imposed his domination on her.

Pedro II certainly believed that strict seclusion was the best way to guard his daughters from inappropriate experiences, but this very isolation kept them ignorant of how most Brazilians really lived and circumscribed their ability to shape their own identities. Isolation made it difficult for them to question the norms, values, and habits their father instilled. If D. Teresa Cristina had any objections to this treatment of her daughters, she did not express them, nor did she do anything to sabotage or subvert her husband's plans. When decisions had to be made, her reaction was to refer the matter to the emperor. She always told D. Isabel and D. Leopoldina to ask their father.

Although the princesses rarely ventured outside the palace, they were allowed playmates of their own age, the daughters of court officials and of intellectuals in the emperor's circle. The court group included Maria Ribeiro de Avelar and Maria Amanda de Paranaguá. The former's mother, Mariana Velho da Silva, had been, in Pedro II's own words, "participant in my sisters' recreations during their adolescence."[17] Amandinha, as the second was always known, was the daughter of João Lustosa da Cunha Paranaguá, a rising politician whose family held extensive lands in Piauí province. His very visible African ancestry had not prevented his marriage to a woman of Portuguese descent. Amandinha was in appearance a light *morena*, although her social position and her intimacy with the princesses made everyone perceive her as white. Among the intellectuals' children was Adelaide Taunay, the daughter of Félix Emile Taunay, a French-born painter who had taught the young Pedro II both drawing and French. Adelaide, along with Mariquinhas, as Maria was often called, and Amandinha were to be lifelong friends of D. Isabel.

If Pedro II kept his daughters secluded from the larger world and restricted their circle of acquaintances to those of whom he approved, he did take care to ensure that his offspring did not grow up in a state of cultural ignorance. From May 1, 1854, onward, D. Isabel and her sister were taught to read and write by a male instructor who, republican in his political beliefs, addressed them as "Little Ladies" (*Doninhas*) rather than the expected "Highnesses" (*Altezas*). Francisco Crispiniano Valdetaro's lack of deference was balanced by his effectiveness as a teacher. The first dated letter of D. Isabel to her mother, at the age of eight and a half, was written in a large hand with some difficulty.

> Mummy, I send you this mottled pansy. My sister and I miss you very much.
>
> December 28, 1854
> Isabel Cristina.

Five weeks later, in the first surviving letter to her father, D. Isabel's handwriting had become small and neat (more legible, in fact, than it would ever be again).

> Petrópolis, February 9, 1855
>
> My dear Father,
>
> I hope that you arrived safely and that the weather there has been what you desired. I did my lessons very well, though I have still to read with my teacher this evening.
> Farewell Father and accept an embrace from and give your blessing to Your most loving daughter,
>
> Isabel Cristina.[18]

Both these letters were produced under direction and copied from a first draft. Nonetheless, they and their successors do provide precious evidence about the nature of D. Isabel's relationship with her parents, in particular about how she viewed her mother and father. It was, significantly, to the latter that she offered her assurances that she had done her lessons "very well."

At first D. Isabel treated her parents as a single entity, often sending them letters identical in content. In a letter of October 1859 sent to her father, she even at one point wrote "Mummy," which she then crossed out and replaced with "Daddy."[19] At this stage of her childhood, D. Isabel found communicating with her mother the easier task, in part because her letters focused on the doings of daily life and on offering and receiving gifts as proof of affection. The relationship was one of support and mutuality, of a type that at that period predominated among women. With her father, D. Isabel's relationship was more complex and so more demanding. Her letters included references both to the outside world (that lay beyond the imperial palaces) and to the realm of abstract thought (reading in particular). For D. Isabel, Pedro II was the gatekeeper to both of these worlds and also, quite literally, her instructor about them. In neither world did her mother play any part. How D. Isabel handled her parents' different roles in her life is apparent from the letter she addressed to both of them on March 3, 1857: "Daddy, tell me whether the barometer went up or down at S. Cristóvão and what the gauge reading is. Don't forget to buy me the book that I asked you for, and if you can bring a barometer, even if only a dial barometer, I will be better able to understand your lesson. Mummy, please buy the naked dolls that I can dress by my own sewing."[20]

Her parents' different roles do not appear to have struck D. Isabel. She was not introspective as a child. It was the visible externals, such as the bamboo alley in São Cristóvão, which resembled a cathedral vault, that caught her imagination and that she recalled in old age. She was very much inclined to accept the world as it was. As she commented in 1876, "I am never prone to view things entirely in black. It may be a good or bad habit, but it is nevertheless a fortunate one for me, and it will always be part of me."[21]

The princess's tendency to take a cheerful view of life and her lack of introspection were related to another trait in D. Isabel's personality apparent in the letters to her parents. By the late 1850s her handwriting has become so slapdash as often to verge on illegibility and at times so faint as to be very difficult to read. Her letters suggest that D. Isabel did not naturally possess much patience or notable powers of endurance. She moved from one interest to another as each in turn caught her fancy. She was never afraid to speak her mind, and she held strong views. However, when she encountered something she did not like, she found it difficult to focus and organize her resistance so as to make her view prevail. She tended to flare up and then to submit or to lose interest.

The traditions of the Portuguese court required that the heir to the throne be at the age of seven placed in the care of an *aio* (supervisor) who was responsible for the heir's upbringing and education. Following D. Isabel's seventh birthday in July 1853, the emperor at first contemplated taking on that role for his heir and her sister. However, as he commented late in that year, "the time that I have free after my other obligations does not permit me to do so, and, in addition, I am not the most qualified to handle ladies, above all those of this household who, when not on their turn of service, live in the most complete idleness."[22] Pedro II had to find a suitable female to serve as his daughters' *aia*.

Conventional wisdom in nineteenth-century Europe decreed that the handling of girls' education belonged to women, and, as Pedro II's remarks make clear, he had no desire to challenge this convention. The etiquette manuals of post-Revolutionary France exalted the role of the "mother-teacher" and of "maternal education." Mothers had the duty first to teach all their children moral and religious precepts and next to instruct them in the basics of reading, writing, and counting. In addition to teaching their daughters how to become good housewives, mothers supervised the academic education that their daughters received from private tutors brought into the home. Girls were restricted, in a historian's telling phrase, to "dabbling in the fine arts and preparing for a life of domesticity."[23] Pedro II did not for several reasons entrust the education of D. Isabel and D. Leopoldina to his wife. Placing D. Teresa Cristina in charge of this task would have deprived him of his monopoly of power within the imperial family. She did not, in his opinion, possess the capacity, above all the intelligence, that the task required.

As Pedro II appreciated, the type of education traditionally given to girls would not prepare his daughters for their future roles as heirs to the throne. "As to their education I will only say that the character of both the princesses ought to be shaped as suits Ladies who, it may be, will have to direct the constitutional government of an Empire such as that of Brazil," the emperor noted in 1857. "The education should not differ from that given to men, combined with that suited to the other sex, but in a manner that does not detract from the first."[24]

The emperor's problem, a considerable one, was to find a woman capable both of supervising his daughters' upbringing and of presiding over this hybrid system of education. Such a woman did not, in his view, exist in Brazil. Pedro II turned first to his widowed stepmother, D. Amélia, then living in Lisbon, requesting her to assume the post. A mother was the only woman whom a man could defer to and retain his honor. If D. Amélia would not accept his offer (and she resolutely refused to do so), then Pedro II wanted her to find for him a suitable female in Europe. The candidate should be "German, Roman Catholic, and devout, a widow and without children." She should know "the most commonly spoken languages." She should possess "a soft character and fine manners," and be "perfectly versed in the various pursuits with which ladies fill their vacant hours." The emperor was looking for an educated woman who conformed to what convention then demanded a female should be, thereby offering no challenge to his authority. The actual imparting of knowledge she would leave to Pedro II and to other men. "As to education I don't ask for much because my daughters will have male instructors."[25]

Search as D. Amélia might among the widows of Germany and Austria, she was able to find no one suited to the task. Eventually, the emperor turned to his sister, D. Francisca. In 1843, D. Francisca had married François d'Orléans, prince of Joinville, the seventh child of King Louis Philippe of France. The overthrow of Louis Philippe in 1848 had driven the Orléans family into exile in England, and into voluntary exile went a number of people closely identified with the fallen dynasty. This group included the countess of Barral and her husband. Luísa Margarida Portugal de Barros was Brazilian by birth and ancestry. Her parents had taken her to Europe where her father, the viscount of Pedra Branca, served at Paris as the first envoy of the Empire of Brazil. Raised in France and fluent in Portuguese, French, and English, in 1837 she had married a French nobleman, Jean Joseph Horace Eugène de Barral, count of Barral. In the 1840s she had served as lady-in-waiting to the newlywed princess of Joinville. After

THE COUNTESS OF BARRAL

Courtesy of the Museu Nacional Histórico, Rio de Janeiro

the overthrow of the Orléans dynasty, the Barrals withdrew to England. Summoned by the viscount of Pedra Branca, the countess's father, the couple moved to Brazil to live on his sugar plantations in the province of Bahia. It was the countess of Barral whom D. Francisca warmly recommended to her brother for the post of *aia*.

Life on a plantation, caring for an aging parent, cannot have been very attractive to someone accustomed to the delights of Paris and London. The birth in 1854 of a child, the first after many years of marriage, was a consolation that filled the countess of Barral's time. The invitation to serve as the princesses' *aia*, made in early 1856 by the imperial *mordomo* (steward of the household), came at an opportune moment. Her father had just died, and the couple was undecided as to their future course. The countess did not immediately accept the invitation but with great skill negotiated what would nowadays be termed an excellent employment package. She was given the rank of *dama* (lady-in-waiting) to the empress, a handsome salary, a residence, and a carriage. She was assured of independent authority over her charges and the assistance of a governess, approved by her, who would do most of the actual work of supervision.

The Barral family arrived in Rio at the end of August 1856, and the countess took up her duties a week later, on September 9. D. Isabel was ten years and one month old and her sister, D. Leopoldina, a year younger. What did the two girls see? Their new *aia* was small, with dark hair and olive skin. Forty years old, she was attractive without being beautiful, and above all she dressed and behaved with style and self-assurance. She exuded a sophistication and a savoir-faire conspicuously absent at the imperial court. What the countess wrote about the Archduke Maximilian of Austria when he visited Petrópolis in 1860 was really a self-portrait: "He has an elegant turnout and good manners, he talks a great deal and makes great use of these drawing room-type conversations."[26] The countess's letters give ample proof of her ability to charm and to flatter. They pulsate with sparkling prose that entertains the reader without in any way committing or compromising the writer.

The countess of Barral's style and her pleasing ways masked a powerful intelligence and a strong will. She was adept at ingratiating herself with the influential, at charming anyone who might prove useful, and at being gracious but firm with the unimportant. Possessed of an acute sense of what was feasible, she took good care not to offend the conventions and, above all, not to overstep limits allowed to women. When she became *aia*, she systematically set about gaining the affections of her charges, charming the emperor (whom she had first met during a short visit to Brazil in 1847) and rendering harmless all potential opponents within the court.

These goals the countess of Barral achieved swiftly and with a minimum of open contention. The one person who did suffer from her success was the empress. The two women were quite similar in physical size and coloring, but there the resemblance ended. The countess was elegant and sophisticated. The empress was neither. The countess was well educated and skilled in how to please. The empress was neither. The countess was self-confident and resourceful. The empress was neither. In sum, the countess possessed all the qualities that made a woman attractive to Pedro II. From the moment of her arrival in Rio the countess of Barral entranced him. She did not encourage but neither did she repel the emperor's attentions. She knew exactly how to handle him. With consummate skill she kept him attracted to her while not permitting to him any act that would compromise her reputation as a wife, mother, and good Catholic.

The countess of Barral's ties to the emperor gave her an unchallengeable position at court. Pedro II even issued an order, through the *mordomo,* that read: "H[is]. M[ajesty]. the emperor trusts that the lady and the maid of H[er]. I[mperial]. H[ighness].'s chamber will not continue to hinder by their acts and words the influence that the Countess of Barral ought to have over T[heir]. H[ighnesses].'s education that the emperor has entrusted to her, so that the said August Lord will not find himself obliged to take some extreme measure."[27] For Pedro II these were very strong words indeed. The countess's access to the emperor made the politicians anxious to cultivate her goodwill, so that she would say nothing that might prejudice them in Pedro II's mind. In return they paid favorable attention to the desires she expressed about the making of minor appointments and granting of small favors, the petty change of patronage, critical to the exercise of power. She took care not to ask for too much or to be insistent. Without ever ceasing to be discreet and ladylike, she made the best use of the opportunities available to a woman in her social position.

The countess always treated D. Teresa Cristina with fulsome deference and elaborate courtesy. "Your Majesty wanted to give me great happiness and perfectly achieved that end by writing me a short letter that, having read, I put to my lips and my heart," ran a letter written in October 1859. "Thousands and thousands of thanks, Madam; it is a treasure that after my death will pass on to my son."[28] Effusions such as these cost nothing, nor did they alter the reality that by her simple presence at court and in the imperial family the countess had made D. Teresa Cristina's position more marginal than ever. The empress actively disliked the countess, but, realizing that any expression of resentment or open recrimination would improve nothing, she disguised her feelings as best she could. She put up with the countess's constant company and tolerated her influence over her daughters and husband.

D. LEOPOLDINA AND D. ISABEL AS YOUNG CHILDREN

Courtesy of the Museu Nacional Histórico, Rio de Janeiro

How far D. Isabel and her sister became conscious during their late childhood and adolescence of their father's infatuation for and their mother's dislike of the countess of Barral we do not know. Since their father often sat in on the lessons that the countess gave, they were most likely to have noticed Pedro II's feelings. Probably, at first, the changes to their daily routine wrought by the countess's arrival and the color she brought to their singularly dull lives absorbed all their attention. The countess came not just with a husband but with a son, two and a half years old, whom the princesses came to treat very much as the younger brother they never had. Early in June 1857 there arrived Mlle. Victorine Templier, recommended by Queen Marie Amélie, the widow of Louis Philippe, to act under the countess's authority as governess (*institutrice*) to the princesses. She was unmarried, plain in looks, unpretentious in manner, and devoted to her task. D. Isabel became deeply attached to her. The two girls began to spend almost all their time in the classroom.

From the start the countess of Barral acted towards the princesses rather as though she was a benevolent aunt with whom they could have fun and exchange confidences. D. Isabel she called her *camadarinha* (little comrade) and D. Leopoldina her "bosom friend" (the English term being used). Of course, the countess knew how to maintain her authority. The whip was always there to be cracked, and from time to time she did so. "Believe me that I suffered a great deal today mortifying you so much," she wrote to D. Isabel on June 29, 1863, "but I never perhaps gave you a greater proof of love. A sad proof of love Y[our]. H[ighness]. will say! and in truth it cost me a great deal to give up the role of your comrade in order to assume the strictness of a governess, but what other remedy if YY. HH. are unwilling to reform your ways by any other means."[29]

Although the *aia* sought to avoid any appearance of partiality in her treatment of the two princesses, her letters betray her preference for the elder sister. D. Leopoldina "is getting plumper, with a pretty complexion, and since she can't read this letter, I can say, without making her conceited, that she is becoming very pretty," the countess wrote in November 1859. By comparison, "Princess Isabel is very plump, and her constant goodness and angelic innocence increasingly enshrine her in my heart." Of the two sisters, D. Isabel seems to have possessed a stronger personality and greater intelligence. D. Leopoldina suffered all the disadvantages of being the younger sibling. A certain tension existed between the two that caused intermittent bickering. In October 1859, when her parents were paying a visit to the northeastern provinces of Brazil, D. Isabel informed D. Teresa Cristina, "We have not quarreled, at least almost not at all, merely in passing. You should not be astonished, Mummy!" Three months later,

D. Leopoldina's unhappiness at her parents' continued absence flared up into open resentment. "I am not happy with Her Highness Princess Leopoldina's behavior," the countess of Barral reported. "She has treated everyone badly, especially poor Mlle. Templier who, without the least cause, has become what she terms her aversion."[30] The governess was probably a convenient substitute for the actual object of D. Leopoldina's dislike. It is not clear that the countess of Barral ever commanded the younger princess's real affections. Certainly, after her marriage, D. Leopoldina increasingly avoided intimacy with her.

In contrast to her sister, D. Isabel formed enduring bonds with both her *aia* and her governess. Through letters and visits she remained in constant contact with them until their deaths in 1891 and 1883, respectively. As D. Isabel approached adolescence, the relationship with the *aia* gave her more satisfaction and stimulation than did her ties with her mother, close and loving as they were. The empress's range of interests was too pedestrian and her approach to life too passive to satisfy her elder daughter. A great part of the empress's time was spent in knitting and crocheting. Further, she played no role whatever in the classroom where her children spent most of their time. In the classroom the dominant personalities were the countess and Pedro II.

For D. Isabel, her father continued to be the gatekeeper to the world of knowledge and to life outside the palace. The countess of Barral did and said nothing to lessen D. Isabel's perception of him. The *aia* believed in and taught her pupil traditional gender attitudes. "God gave to men their share of work and another one to women. Let each remain in that sphere, unless it is Joan of Arc inspired by God."[31] However intimate the countess's relationship with Pedro II became, it never transgressed these precepts. The countess might dispute and banter with the emperor, but she never challenged his male preeminence. By both precept and example, D. Isabel was taught to regard women as ancillary to and dependent on men. Males alone could command and take action.

By the end of the 1850s the formidable program of instruction that Pedro II had drawn up for his daughters kept them busy in the classroom for nine and a half hours a day, six days a week. The range of academic subjects they studied included Latin, French, English,

D. ISABEL AND D. LEOPOLDINA IN LATE CHILDHOOD

Courtesy of the Fundação Grão Pará, Petrópolis

and German languages, Portuguese, French, and English history, Portuguese and French literature, geography and geology, astronomy, chemistry, physics, and geometry and arithmetic. To these subjects were added drawing, piano, and dance. By 1863, when the princesses respectively became seventeen and sixteen, their lessons also included Italian, history of philosophy, political economy, and Greek.

The countess of Barral and Mme. Templier did teach some subjects, mainly French, literature, and history, but all the other instructors were men, several of them having taught the emperor in his own youth. Pedro II took as active a part in the instruction as his duties as ruler permitted. At the end of 1861 he characterized "my principal enjoyments" as "learning, reading, and the education of my daughters whom I love dearly." At the start he taught his daughters geometry and astronomy, and he even wrote a treatise on the second subject for them. "It was perfect in its exactness and information for the period in which I composed it," he boasted in old age.[32] In the early 1860s, both at Petrópolis and at São Cristóvão palace, he found time to give his daughters lessons in Latin and to read to them from Luís de Camões's *As Lusiadas* and João de Barros's *Décadas da Asia*, two classic works in verse and prose that celebrated the epic deeds of the Portuguese as they established a maritime empire in India and the rest of Asia.

Pedro II certainly intended his program of studies to prepare his daughters for their future roles, but it is difficult not to conclude that it mainly catered to his own enjoyment and self-instruction. The education he had received during the 1830s had been far from adequate, and he loved to study. The program he created was, in other words, entirely suitable for a knowledgeable adult in his thirties but not appropriate for anyone, male or female, moving from childhood into adolescence. Two exchanges, dating from late 1863 or 1864, with question and reply written in each case on the same sheet, suggest that D. Isabel often could not handle the stream of information cascading upon her, especially since she was not by nature much attracted to abstract ideas.

> What should we read in place of political economy?
> *Read physics or chemistry.*
>
> Daddykins, are you still a bit upset with me?
> *No, young lady, and accept this embrace, expecting that you will do a good lesson with me tomorrow. Fuel is already arriving for the fire.*[33]

To be successful the princess's course of instruction would have had to make the knowledge contained in books comprehensible in terms of her own personal experience. An effective way of preparing

D. Isabel for her role as Brazil's ruler would have been to give her from an early age personal experience of the tasks she would face and to relate it to what she learned in the classroom. Pedro II did not adopt any such course. In the early 1860s, when the princesses were no longer children, their father continued to keep them secluded within the palace. The spare time they did enjoy from studying was devoted to pursuits deemed suitable for women. A letter sent to D. Teresa Cristina when D. Isabel was thirteen points up the gap existing between the classroom and her ordinary life. "Mummy, I forgot to tell you something. Recently, I had such a desire, Mummy, to sew at night that I could not stop doing so. On another occasion I was going to sew, but the Countess did not want me to do so because Mummy had forbidden it. I hope that Mummy will forgive me."[34] The princess's transgression, far from being an unauthorized foray into the world of knowledge, involved an occupation that was, according to the assumptions of the time, exclusively feminine. The classroom instruction given to D. Isabel may not have differed, to quote Pedro II's instructions, "from that given to men," but in all other respects her upbringing was entirely traditional. The unintended consequence was that D. Isabel learned to view knowledge as essentially a male preserve, as something to which she was an outsider.

Pedro II's personal involvement in his daughters' education made D. Isabel equate the world of learning with her father. "How greatly I thank you for having taught me, for having given me teachers," she wrote to him at the start of her first visit to Europe, "so that I now understand the greater part of the things I see, even though I am ignorant about so much."[35] He had, by an act of generosity, admitted her to the male realm of knowledge. Having been taught by experience not to compete with or challenge her father, the princess was inhibited from embarking, as she grew older, on any independent foray into the world of learning. Such a foray might have brought her to question traditional roles or inspired her to chart her own course as heir to the throne.

During D. Isabel's childhood, the upbringing and the education that her father chose for her brought no great problems. But time did not stand still. As she grew up, she experienced physical and psychological changes. The arrival of adolescence was symbolized by a public ceremony held on her fourteenth birthday. On July 29, 1860, a procession of six state coaches escorted by numerous palace officials and two squadrons of cavalry set out from São Cristóvão palace. In the last coach rode D. Isabel. When the procession reached the Senate building in the middle of Rio City, a commission of senators and deputies greeted her and conducted her into the Senate chamber. There, as Article 116 of the constitution required, she took an oath at the hands of the Senate president. She swore to "maintain the Apostolic Roman Catholic Religion, to observe the political constitution of the Brazilian nation, and to be obedient to the laws and the emperor."[36]

The onset of menarche that marks the start of adolescence was not considered in upper-class families a fit subject for mention, much less for discussion. Girls were not prepared for this physical change, and its sexual meaning was not explained to them. D. Isabel was no exception. Her ignorance about her body is evident from a letter she wrote in August 1865 to her husband. "I have had this month less of my period, I no longer have it today. Tell me, is it possible that I won't have my period next month if you don't come back? I don't know about that, darling, and I don't dare ask anyone but you."[37]

The physiological changes that occur at adolescence—menstruation, breast formation, growth of body hair—are often accompanied by and indeed contribute to mood swings, psychological unhappiness, and aggressiveness. Adolescents seek to establish their own identity, to assert their personality, and to claim an autonomous space, often by means of behavior that adults view as antisocial. D. Isabel clearly went through this phase. Whereas in April 1860 her weekly grade sheet recorded four bad conduct marks, in March 1862, when she was fifteen, she incurred fourteen such marks. An undated letter to her parents, probably written about 1860, begins: "I ask a thousand pardons of you for all the faults I have committed against you. Today I spent an hour in the confessional."[38] Among the faults she confessed were probably rude, insolent speech, slovenly dress and appearance, untidiness and tardiness, and petty acts of disobedience.

This lack of care and concern may have been a contributing factor to an accident for which D. Isabel was the cause in the middle of 1862, around the time of her sixteenth birthday. Digging with a spade

D. ISABEL IN HER ADOLESCENT YEARS

Courtesy of the Fundação Grão Pará, Petrópolis

in her garden at São Cristóvão, the princess did not notice Amandinha de Paranaguá standing behind her and hit her in the right eye. Despite treatment by a specialist, she suffered what was called "a small defect in her sight," in fact, a general loss of vision in that eye. The accident, although it did not affect the friendship between the two girls, must have intensified worries about D. Isabel's behavior. Certainly, the incident did not make D. Isabel mend her ways. A year later, the countess of Barral took the unprecedented step of writing her charge a formal letter of reproof. "Realize, my dear Princess, that Y[our]. H[ighness]. is shortly going to be 17 and that you should not lose a single day in order to remedy what we all have, due more or less to excessive love and indulgence, permitted until now!"[39]

Handling adolescent offspring is never easy for parents, who find no guaranteed method of avoiding problems. Unwillingness to acknowledge that offspring are no longer children and refusal to treat them as incipient adults virtually invite trouble and retaliation. D. Teresa Cristina fell into the first error and Pedro II into the second. The empress's devotion to her children meant that she could not grant them the personal autonomy they desired. Any problem experienced by D. Isabel aroused in her mother an intrusive and smothering concern expressed in "an avalanche of unceasing questions that annoy me and which annoy me all the more when I try to make a polite reply."[40] The result was rudeness on D. Isabel's side and unhappiness on her mother's.

The reasons for the emperor's refusal to treat his daughters as incipient adults are more complex. When he was only fourteen and a half, Pedro II had been declared of age and installed as head of the government with full powers. His behavior from that moment onward had perforce been that of an adult. This experience might have been expected to give him some sympathy and understanding for his daughters' hunger for an adult style of life. The opposite was the case. He allowed almost nothing to change. The princesses' social life remained restricted to the palace. In October 1864, when the sisters were respectively eighteen and seventeen, a visitor from Europe reported in amazement: "Can you believe that these unfortunate princesses have never been to any ball or to any theater and they are burning to go there?" The most that their father would concede was their participation in amateur theatrical productions at São Cristóvão to an invited audience that he, not his daughters, selected. Amandinha de Paranaguá recalled in old age: "In 1862 and 1863, we put on productions on the little stage of the Palace." When asked about the plays, she replied that she remembered "many things of that period. Offhand I recall a piece *Who laughs last laughs best* and *Le Plaideur* by Racine . . . and others. Princess Isabel was one of the cast." These diversions were the exception. The young women continued to spend their days in the classroom. "Family dinner takes place at 5 o'clock, eaten at a prodigious rate," a visitor from Europe reported. "Next, if the weather is fine, they go for a walk in the *chacara*, a sort of garden, virtually wild with alleys of mango trees and giant bamboo. Then they go in to drink tea. The princesses play the piano, look at photographs, or play word games, and everything ends at 9 1/2."[41]

In addition to denying D. Isabel any independent social life, Pedro II kept her totally excluded from all contact with public affairs. This exclusion was the more odd because, by Article 121 of the constitution, the princess came of age at eighteen, on July 29, 1864. From that day onward, her father's death would make her empress, playing the key role in government affairs. Pedro II himself had received no exposure to state affairs prior to his premature majority in July 1840. His apprenticeship was a hard one. His first months as ruler had been largely taken up by visiting government offices and other public institutions. As D. Isabel approached the age of eighteen, her father might have begun to prepare her for her future role, but not so. He showed her no state papers. He did not discuss politics with her. He did not take her with him on his constant visits to government offices. He did not include her in the *despacho*, his weekly meetings with the cabinet ministers, nor did he allow her to attend the public audiences that took place twice a week. D. Isabel was *princesa imperial*, the title given to the heir to the throne, but by his treatment of her Pedro II deprived the honor of any meaning.

Since the emperor unquestionably loved his elder daughter and since he was a master of realpolitik, his treatment of D. Isabel seems contradictory and indeed self-defeating. The explanation lies in part in the emperor's own psychology. He had to have total control of his world, both political and familial. By teaching D. Isabel the arts of rule, Pedro II would have created a center of power both at home and in government that was autonomous and thereby capable of competing with him and even of replacing him. This perceived threat, probably never consciously stated or even understood, was one cause for the emperor's exclusion of his heir from public affairs.

Significant as this factor may have been in motivating Pedro II, his gender attitudes probably played a larger role in shaping his conduct. With the notable exception of extensive classroom instruction, the upbringing Pedro II bestowed on his daughters was that given since the colonial period to women of the ruling class. D. Isabel and D. Leopoldina were under his authority and constituted his property. They were kept secluded because their physical integrity symbolized their family's honor and attested to their father's power. Pedro II's attitude toward females was not, it must be emphasized, misogynistic. He sought out the companionship of attractive, intelligent, and cultured women. He enjoyed being with his elder daughter because they could converse freely on his favorite subjects. She stood up for what she believed and was not afraid to contest her father's views. He found her company stimulating. Pedro II's relationship with females never went beyond being a private diversion or entertainment. In respect to public affairs he could not conceive of women, his daughters included, playing any part in governance. Nature did not intend them for such a role. In consequence, although he valued D. Isabel as his daughter, he simply could not accept or perceive her in cold reality as his successor or regard her as a viable ruler.

Just as important, Pedro II believed, as did most men of his day, that a single woman could not manage life's problems on her own, even if she possessed the powers and authority of an empress. The emperor would not have dissented from the dictum of Jules Michelet, the leading French historian of this period: "The woman who has neither home nor protection dies." In September 1863, ten months before D. Isabel reached her majority, when she could rule by herself, her father launched a search for suitable husbands. "I would very much like for my daughters to marry when Isabel becomes 18 or shortly thereafter."[42]

3

BRIDE, 1864–65

Courtesy of the Museu Nacional Histórico, Rio de Janeiro

Marriage was, during the nineteenth century, the destiny of most women born into the middle and upper classes of the Western world. A woman's lot in life was to give support, comfort, and loyalty to her husband and to bear and bring up his children. Mothers raised their daughters not just to expect but to welcome their fate. The lack of alternatives in life, the prospect of escaping from dutiful dependence as a daughter, and the allure of male sexuality were powerful inducements to accept their destiny. Marriage gave a woman status in the eyes of society and a certain influence. We now see romantic love—"the capacity for spontaneity and empathy in an erotic relationship"—as the indispensable preliminary to marriage.[1] This view did not exist in D. Isabel's day, certainly not among her class. At best, young women could select the most personable from among a few approved suitors. At worst, they had no choice at all. Marriage was essentially a property transaction arranged by parents who possessed, some French etiquette manuals asserted, a better understanding of their offspring's needs than did the children themselves.

In the making of marriage the children of royalty, both male and female, were at the greatest disadvantage. The pool of suitable spouses was very small, and matches were often arranged with a view to creating family ties or achieving political advantage. A letter that Queen Victoria of Great Britain wrote to her daughter in April 1858 shows how such betrothals—in this case between the crown prince of Saxony and the queen's cousin, Princess Maria of Portugal—were orchestrated. On his journey south the crown prince visited the queen at Windsor Castle. "Prince George of S. [Saxony] left at a little after 8 yesterday morning for Southampton and sailed at 2 for Lisbon, where I really hope that he may be successful, as I think in every way it would be desirable. It relates our family to the royal Saxon line—she is clever—unbigoted—amiable, strong and healthy and may do a great deal of good—in every way. He is a nice young man, only excessively absent[-minded], like his father, but he has the most beautiful talent for music that is his passion."[2] Princess Maria, also first cousin to D. Isabel, duly agreed to wed her wool-gathering suitor.

Royal marriages were often planned—plotted might be the better word—years in advance, before the individuals involved had reached puberty. Late in 1855, when D. Isabel and her sister were aged nine and eight, Pedro II speculated with his brother-in-law, King Fernando of Portugal, about making a match between their families. The topic came up again in 1857, but discussions never became serious because press speculation about such a match aroused intense opposition in Brazil. A husband controlled and directed his wife, it was then believed. For D. Isabel to marry a Portuguese prince would be tantamount, in the public's mind, to a recolonizing of Brazil. Conversely, D. Isabel could not marry a Brazilian, since the country contained no man of suitable lineage. Even if he had existed, such a match was not acceptable because it would have allowed her husband's relatives to batten on the government, monopolizing posts and pensions. Husbands had to be found among the European royal families of the Catholic faith.

Marrying one of their sons to the future empress of Brazil or to her sister possessed a certain appeal for these royal families. Brazil was, however, a distant country and its monarchy an exception among the republics of the New World. The bridegroom would have to reside in Brazil and to renounce his rights of succession to the throne his family occupied. The first article of Brazil's Constitution forbade "any form of union or federation inconsistent with its independence." These disadvantages were not sufficient to discourage interest. Archduke Maximilian of Habsburg, the younger brother of Emperor Francis Joseph of Austria, visited Rio de Janeiro and other parts of Brazil early in 1860. The archduke, who was already married, came up to Petrópolis, where the princesses were living during their parents' absence on a tour to the northeast, and he met three times with his cousins. As the countess of Barral reported, "some say that he has come to *look over* our princesses for his brother the Archduke Louis Joseph Anthony Victor, who is eighteen, and others for his brother-in-law the count of Flanders, who is twenty-three, and that put me on guard." The countess did all she could to enhance her charges' attractiveness, selecting for their first encounter dresses "of rose-colored gauze that matched the freshness of their faces." The princesses behaved charmingly. They played the piano for their cousin, danced with him, and presented gifts. The archduke approved of what he saw, reporting back to his brother, Emperor Francis Joseph, that the two "would assure the felicity of any European prince."[3]

D. Isabel and her sister enjoyed their cousin's visit, as well they might, since it gave them a rare taste of the adult world. Maximilian was also a man. "He is very friendly, handsome, tall, and resembles Daddy a little I think," D. Isabel informed her mother. Aged thirteen and a half, the princess was already interested in the opposite sex. Her upbringing meant that she daydreamed about attractive men only in the context of marriage. Being already wed, Maximilian was not available, but there existed plenty of other male cousins in her age group about whom D. Isabel could dream. Recent improvements in photography, including the taking of studio portraits and printing of multiple copies from a negative, meant that the princess could obtain images of these cousins. For a time she slept with the picture of one of them under her pillow. Her interest rapidly fixed itself on the tall, blond, rather willowy figure of her first cousin, Pierre, duke of Penthièvre, son of her aunt D. Francisca and the prince of Joinville. With her usual high spirits, D. Isabel informed her father late in 1860 that she would wed only Pedro, as he was called in Brazil, "and no one else!" Three years later, her preference for her cousin, by then serving in the U.S. Navy, still held. "Isabel has repeatedly told me that she does not wish to marry anyone save your son Pedro," the emperor told Joinville in September 1863, "but I only answer her that she will marry whom I choose, to which she agrees since she is a very good daughter."[4]

Pedro II's remark went to the very heart of the existing dynamic of gender relations. A key element in that system was a father's ability, when his daughters reached adolescence, to retain control of their bodies and thereby deny them the ability to lead autonomous lives. Any challenge to this prerogative aroused in men, for a variety of reasons, deep fears and strong resentments. For women to choose partners on the basis of sexual attraction made nonsense of the prevailing belief that the greater inherent purity and morality of women compared to men was due to females' supposed lack of a strong sexual drive. Freedom of girls to choose husbands contradicted the assumption, which underlay the Code Napoléon of 1804, that "man alone was the true social individual and that women were only 'relative creatures,' to be defined by their relationship to men—fathers, husbands or other male relations."[5] Freedom to choose would end the father's

D. ISABEL, ABOUT THE AGE OF EIGHTEEN, in a studio portrait possibly taken to be
sent to Europe

Courtesy of the Fundação Grão Pará, Petrópolis

absolute authority within the family, and it would also deprive him of
control of an important form of property, his daughters' bodies, as
well as undermine in their minds his sexual superiority.

In Brazil women, particularly upper-class women, were often
married in early adolescence to considerably older men. In consequence, the ideal female was for many males someone in the first
glow of her new sexuality and still displaying a childlike innocence.

Widowers sometimes married women no older than their daughters by their first wife. Pedro II's wife was very much alive, but by the early 1860s she had long ceased to give him sexual and emotional satisfaction. It was his daughters and their *aia*, the countess of Barral, who provided him with the female company he most desired. The three of them constituted, as he himself admitted, "the tripod of my keenest affections."[6] It is not surprising that he resented his elder daughter's showing interest in other men. D. Isabel would marry only when and whom he chose.

Since Article 20 of the constitution laid down that "the marriage of the princess who is heir presumptive will be made as the emperor pleases," Pedro II was acting strictly in accord with his rights. In his letter of September 21, 1863, to the prince of Joinville, which stated his desire that D. Isabel and D. Leopoldina marry when the former "becomes 18 or shortly thereafter," Pedro II identified the husbands he wanted. "I would prefer as husband for Isabel your son Pedro [duke of Penthièvre] and for Leopoldina the count of Flanders," the second son of King Leopold I of the Belgians. "You know as well as I do what sort of qualities they ought to have, above all Isabel's husband, and therefore I will only add that Isabel it seems is going to be willful, and her sister the opposite." If the preferred bridegrooms were not willing or available, then Joinville was to suggest other candidates. "The husband should be Catholic, liberal in views, and not be Portuguese, Spanish, or Italian, and preferably not Austrian."[7]

Pedro II did emphasize to Joinville that he would not force D. Isabel and D. Leopoldina to accept husbands regardless of their feelings. "No commitments will be made without my daughters being first consulted and consenting. To which end I shall have to use the information that you will supply, and you will send me non-flattering photographs of the intended and indeed other pictures that will give a good idea of their appearance."[8] This insistence was motivated less by a respect for his daughters' autonomy than by his own bitter experience. When D. Teresa Cristina arrived at Rio in September 1843, he found that she in no way resembled the alluring woman portrayed in the painting sent to him. It took a whole night to persuade him that he could not send D. Teresa Cristina back to her family and that he must go through with the marriage. That experience he wanted to spare his daughters.

To the emperor's long letter, Joinville replied on November 6, 1863, accepting the commission but also observing "there is nothing more difficult than marrying off a young princess, as Queen Victoria not long ago remarked to me." The duke of Penthièvre, who was totally deaf, socially maladroit, and not at all interested in women, refused point blank to consider the match with D. Isabel. The count of Flanders similarly proved unwilling to marry D. Leopoldina. In their place Joinville proposed another two of his relatives. "Think about my nephew August [of Saxe-Coburg-Gotha, son of his sister Clementine]. There are lots of advantages and guarantees on his side. He for your oldest and one of the sons of Nemours [Joinville's brother] for your youngest. That would be for me the most ideal arrangement. I am sending you some photographs that will give you an idea of the individuals." In February 1864, Joinville reiterated his suggestion. "I am sending you the most recent photograph that I can find of the count d'Eu, eldest son of my brother Nemours. If you could put your hand on him for one of your daughters, it would be perfection. He is tall, strong, attractive, good, gentle, very friendly, very educated, loving study and, in addition, he already has a certain military fame. 21 years old. He is a bit hard of hearing, but not enough to be a defect." Joinville added, almost defensively: "August of Saxe-Coburg is younger [aged 18]. I believe him to be good and intelligent. He has been well brought up but he doesn't have the count d'Eu's talent for study. He is good-looking and well built. He is very lively and will be perhaps a bit flighty. I believe that his service in the Austrian navy will do him good."9

The duke of Penthièvre's preemptory refusal to marry his cousin D. Isabel caused her father "intense disgust." "I profoundly regret that your son will not be my son-in-law." Pedro II gave a cautious welcome to Joinville's suggestion of his two nephews as possible husbands. On the basis of the information and the pictures supplied him, he expressed a preference for the count d'Eu to marry his elder daughter. The two young men and their parents proved amenable to the idea of marriage, but all insisted that, before committing themselves,

the two cousins must first travel to Brazil and see the princesses. Then
a difficulty reared its head. In Joinville's words, "the thought of securing a new throne has turned the heads of the entire Coburg tribe and
they have leaned on him [August] to make him accept the offer" of
D. Isabel's hand.[10] The emperor, however, refused to agree to this
demand. Only after the cousins arrived in Rio de Janeiro could they
choose which sister each preferred.

In May 1864 the emperor's speech opening the legislative session
announced "with pleasure that I am arranging the marriage of the
Princesses . . . , which I hope will take place in the present year." No
information was vouchsafed about the identity of the proposed husbands. A law providing D. Isabel and her sister with dowries and
incomes was introduced and rapidly enacted. Meanwhile, August's
parents continued to pitch their demands very high, insisting that
Gousty, as their son was known, marry the future empress and requir-
ing changes in the draft marriage contract. At the last moment they
did consent that Gousty should go with Gaston d'Orléans, count d'Eu,
on the August steamship to Rio, where a final decision would be made.
The lack of a cable line to Brazil meant that Gousty's parents could
not control this final round in the negotiations that much resembled
a modern real estate deal. In fact, the two matches were nothing less
than a complex transfer of property. As King Leopold I of the Belgians, uncle to both the young men, reportedly remarked, "we have
sent you good merchandise."[11]

As for D. Isabel and D. Leopoldina, whose bodies and lives were
being haggled over, they were kept in entire ignorance of the negotiations. As their father informed Joinville in April 1864, "My daughters
know only what is in the Speech from the Throne, and their minds
are entirely unsuspecting." D. Isabel and her sister did not learn the
identity of the men their father had selected for them until three weeks
before they first saw their intendeds. Not until the middle of August,
when the steamship carrying the two cousins was in the mid-Atlantic,
did Pedro II finally communicate the suitors' imminent arrival "to
my daughters, to whom I also gave the good information received
about the two young men, not forgetting however the deafness of the
count d'Eu in order to obviate any surprise."[12]

On September 2, 1864, the day of their arrival, the two cousins were brought to the palace for a short visit with the princesses and their parents. The next day, a much longer encounter took place, including a dinner and meetings in D. Teresa Cristina's drawing room and her study. The letter that the count d'Eu wrote to his sister shortly after his arrival, describing his first impressions, is a very male document in its self-centeredness. It is, however, honest according to its lights, and it does provide a frank description of what D. Isabel and her sister looked like. "The princesses are ugly, but the second *decidedly* less attractive than the other, smaller, more stocky, and in sum less sympathetic. Such was my first impression, obviously before learning what the emperor's intentions were in respect to them. As to their character, they did not reveal anything because during the first two interviews they only answered, as was natural, in monosyllables."[13]

On September 4, Pedro II informed the French general who accompanied the young men to Brazil as their adviser that he had, in accord with his long-settled intention, chosen the count d'Eu to be D. Isabel's husband. The count did not reject this proposal. The next day the emperor told his elder daughter that Gaston d'Orléans preferred her to her sister as his bride.

Twelve months later, D. Isabel wrote a series of letters to the count d'Eu, then absent from Rio, in which she, consulting her 1864 diary, recalled "every little thing that happened last year at this time."

> SEPTEMBER 2: Today is the happy anniversary of your happy arrival at Rio.
> SEPTEMBER 3: Anniversary of our first dinner and the conversation in Mummy's study. . . . It was during this day that I definitively began to prefer you to Gousty, that I began to feel a great and tender love for you.
> SEPTEMBER 5: My darling, it was a year ago today that I wept from joy when Daddy said that you preferred me.[14]

Unlike D. Isabel in retrospect, romantic love did not enter into the count d'Eu's calculations. The emperor's proposal "at first greatly upset me," he told his sister, "but I believe less and less that it is my duty to reject this important position that God has placed in my path." He was marrying to advance his family's interests, not out of personal

GASTON D'ORLÉANS, COUNT D'EU, IN HIS SPANISH UNIFORM

Courtesy of the Fundação Grão Pará, Petrópolis

desire. However, he enjoyed social activities with D. Isabel, which warmed him to the idea of wedding her.

Let us return to D. Isabel's chronology:

> SEPTEMBER 5: It was also a year ago this afternoon that we laid out the croquet pitch in the garden.

SEPTEMBER 7: It was a year ago today that I found you so attractive in your [Spanish] uniform with its red facings, that we played "Hunt the slipper," and we enjoyed ourselves so much in the City Palace.

SEPTEMBER 8: A year ago today we visited Tijuca in that torrent of rain, and we wore red plumes in our hats.

SEPTEMBER 11: My darling, it was a year ago today that we went to Piraí! A year ago you gave me that precious pin that I always wear.[15]

If D. Isabel and Gaston d'Orléans found growing pleasure in each other's company, the same was true of August of Saxe-Coburg-Gotha and D. Leopoldina. August's parents had given him specific instructions to marry only the heir to the throne. Gousty himself, as he told Gaston d'Orléans, "never had the least desire to do so, that he willingly renounced it," or so the count d'Eu informed his father.[16] D. Leopoldina was in character as unlike Gousty's domineering mother, Princess Clementine d'Orléans, as a person could be. The young men were thus content with the wives Pedro II offered them. However, the two of them held off giving their formal consent to the marriages until September 18 so that August could assert that he had not been easy to persuade. The delay also allowed some last-minute haggling over the fine print in the marriage contracts. The princesses were simple bystanders to the decisions that settled their fates.

D. Isabel recalled the day of her engagement with intense emotion. "Today a year ago at this very hour, I had the happiness to be proposed to by you," she reminded Gaston d'Orléans on September 18, 1865. "How we trembled, but how content we were as well."[17] The view of the engagement that the count d'Eu gave to his sister was a good deal more down to earth.

Two days ago, on September 18, I made up my mind to accept the hand of the Princess Imperial. I believe her more capable than her younger sister is of assuring my domestic happiness; the country in which she must reside has not displeased me; and I have found the possibility of making everything bearable by making trips to Europe, no limit being put on the number and duration of these. So don't be too upset because within four months from now I will bring to Claremont a new sister who will love you dearly, and we will have very good times together.

However, so that you will not be shocked when you see my Isabel, I warn you that her face is not in any way pretty; above all she has a characteristic that I could not fail to notice. It is that she completely lacks eyebrows. But her turnout and her figure are attractive.[18]

THE ENGAGED COUPLES: D. Isabel, the count d'Eu, D. Leopoldina, and August of Saxe-Coburg-Gotha with Pedro II and D. Teresa Cristina

Courtesy of the Arquivo Histórico do Museu Imperial, Petrópolis

The princess was now caught up in the excitement of being engaged to a desirable young man and of starting a new life in his company. The delight of being the central figure at the ceremony and the proximity of the wedding day, just four weeks away, left no room in D. Isabel's mind for speculation or for second thoughts. She did not think only of herself. She wrote to her father requesting that in honor of her marriage he grant freedom to ten palace slaves, eight of whom had been her personal servants. The other two were a mother and a wife.

On October 15 the great day came. After the bride and groom had heard Mass at São Cristóvão Palace, a convoy of ten carriages took the imperial family and court officials to the Imperial Chapel in the heart of Rio City. The baroque church with its lavish gilt carvings was packed to bursting by a throng of courtiers, nobility, and politicians. As had been the case at the time of D. Isabel's birth, so now the congregation at her marriage was predominantly male. Under an elaborate canopy sat the emperor, empress, and D. Leopoldina. Bride and groom were each supported by two sponsors. The young couple knelt before the high altar, and there the archbishop of Bahia, assisted by a phalanx of priests, joined them in a union that could not be dissolved and that only death would end. D. Isabel was no longer just a daughter. She was also a bride.

That same day D. Isabel and her new spouse went up from Rio City to Petrópolis, where they were to spend a two-week honeymoon in the house belonging to the father of Maria Ribeiro de Avelar, the princess's childhood companion. The journey took its usual course— by steam launch across Guanabara Bay, train to the foot of the mountains, and finally a slow climb by carriage up the escarpment. She had traveled the route hundreds of times before, and at every stage of the journey she received the accustomed treatment and deference due to the heir to the throne. Yet on this occasion everything was different. "On the way, if Gaston had not been with me, the boat and everything would have seemed to me desolate."[19] She was not in the company of her parents or her sister but alone with a young man. She had met him for the first time six weeks before, and their meetings since then had been so limited and so controlled that she possessed no real knowledge of his character and habits. She had no experience whatsoever of intimacy with men of her own age. She lacked all sexual experience, and her knowledge on the subject was restricted to some discreet explanations, almost certainly provided by the countess of Barral. Yet now she was traveling with the young man as his bride. That night and every night thereafter that he so chose, she was under the duty to submit her body to his sexual gratification. Her own pleasure and her own needs were irrelevant. She was obliged to serve her husband, to put his interests first, and to produce the children who were the principal justification for both marriage and for sexual relations.

The prospects for the young couple when they reached Petrópolis in the early evening were fraught with the potential for unhappiness and even disaster. They were both tired by the day's events, psychologically on edge, and troubled by the expectations about the coming night. The telegrams of good wishes and inquiry that Pedro II dispatched to Petrópolis reminded the young couple that they existed under the constant surveillance of D. Isabel's parents. In fact, that very evening, D. Isabel sat down "in my study" and, as a dutiful daughter, sent her father a short note telling him that she was "very happy" and how much she missed him.[20]

What happened that night we know from a letter D. Isabel sent to Gaston on her first wedding anniversary. "I shall certainly sleep more tonight than I did a year ago, but what a difference!!! I was agitated, yes, but I was so content and so happy!!! That good little house of the Avelars!!!" The next day, October 16, she recalled: "It was this morning a year ago today that you gave me a kiss on getting up. How pleasant that was for me!!!" D. Isabel did not just survive her sexual initiation. She reveled in the physical side of marriage, as Gaston indirectly informed her father on October 17. "I have the joy of telling you that Isabel feels perfectly well."[21] The satisfaction was mutual. "I am sure," Gaston wrote to his sister about D. Isabel, "that you will love her greatly when you meet her and that you will have great pleasure in her company. Because she is truly very good and sweet and she makes me extremely happy. We are living here in a very pretty cottage set in the midst of mountains covered with the most beautiful vegetation and almost always covered in mists."[22]

Writing a week later to his nephew King Luís I of Portugal, Pedro II described the wedding, adding that the young couple "consider themselves to be entirely happy and I conclude that they will always be so since they possess excellent qualities and very similar tastes." The emperor showed much shrewdness in this assessment. The couple's honeymoon at Petrópolis ignited what can only be termed a lifelong and passionate devotion. Nothing in the princess's upbringing and education had taught her to equate marriage with romantic love. The emperor, seconded by the countess of Barral, had certainly encouraged his daughter to view count d'Eu as a Prince Charming, not as a piece of merchandise. That D. Isabel, once wed, fell head over heels in love was not at all strange. What is remarkable was the ease and speed with which she learned to deck her marriage with the concepts and language of romantic love. She persuaded herself that theirs had been from the start a true union of hearts in which she had exercised choice. On the first anniversary of their wedding, she wrote to Gaston: "Oh, my darling, I will never regret having accepted you as mine and even having chosen you, because prior to your selecting me I had already had a mind for you, I loved you so much."[23] Over forty years later, in her autobiographical memoir, D. Isabel recalled: "On September 22 1864 the count d'Eu and the duke of Saxe arrived in Rio. My father had arranged this journey with our marriages in mind. The count d'Eu was intended for my sister and the duke of Saxe for me. God and our hearts decided otherwise, and on October 15, 1864, I had the happiness to marry the count d'Eu."[24]

Ensconced in Petrópolis for their honeymoon, the couple may have fallen in love, but D. Isabel did not thereby escape her assigned role of dutiful subordination. During the first weeks of the marriage, Gaston gained much satisfaction in acting as mentor to his bride. "We read a great deal of Portuguese, French, and German," he informed his sister. He could have added "English" to the list, since he introduced D. Isabel to Sir Walter Scott's *Ivanhoe*, perhaps the most popular romantic novel of the period. "I do indeed appreciate that Gaston does not avoid serious reading," Pedro II reassured his daughter three weeks after the wedding. He then made crystal clear how he viewed the young couple's relationship to him. He told his daughter, probably in all sincerity, "I am every day more pleased at having abdicated my power as father to him and at having in its place the love of yet one more child."[25]

Since her upbringing had deliberately denied her both autonomy and responsibility, D. Isabel understandably found it difficult to behave as the world expected a married woman should. She had been wed but one week when the countess of Barral gave her a firm lecture on the subject of proper appearance and grooming: " 'I change my clothes when I am very sweaty or very dirty,' Y[our]. H[ighness]. writes to me. What, have you forgotten my teachings in so short a time? If a wife is to continue to please her husband she must always unite physical accomplishments to those of the heart and mind. She ought always to be well dressed and above all very clean. God spare me that Y. H. should ever take more care over your appearance for outsiders than for your husband and that you should become slovenly in your person."[26]

Following their two-week honeymoon the newlyweds returned to Rio for the balls and festivities honoring the marriage. At this point, as she had often done before her wedding, D. Isabel asked the countess of Barral to carry out some commissions for her. This request earned a double rebuke. Pedro II, consulted by the countess, instructed her, he informed his daughter, that "it was better that someone in your household should undertake your commissions." The countess of Barral unleashed a new lecture: "Y[our]. I[imperial]. H[ighness]. should today get used to thinking for yourself and to consulting solely your Husband even in the smallest questions, because the smallest things rapidly become the largest; and a wife should not wish to act independently even in thought, if that thought does not agree with her Husband's."[27] No wonder that one of the princess's former teachers, visiting the young couple at Petrópolis early in November, noted that while "D. Isabel received me with a smile on her lips as an old acquaintance," she was "a bit perturbed due to her new position."[28]

If the princess found her public behavior as a married woman difficult to manage, she was at first similarly uncertain about how to handle her double role as spouse and daughter. Not until after her honeymoon did she cease to end her letters to her parents with the words "your daughter very much from the heart," replacing them with "your daughter and friend very much from the heart."[29] In a letter sent to Pedro II three weeks after her marriage, she found it necessary to reassure him that her burgeoning love for Gaston and her duties as his bride did not mean that she cared less for her father: "I am truly very happy; Gaston is always very kind and considerate towards me; I am also constant in trying to please him and I believe that I have not carried out my task at all badly. Accordingly, I feel very happy, but Daddy you must also appreciate that this does not stop me from missing you and looking forward to Saturday [when they would next meet]."[30]

The decisive moment when D. Isabel finally reconciled the roles of spouse and daughter came in the middle of December, at the time her sister D. Leopoldina at last married August of Saxe-Coburg-Gotha. Attending that ceremony in her quality of a married woman triggered the change in self-perception. Also contributing was the fact that her father finally began to treat her as an adult. Two days after her sister's wedding, Pedro II took D. Isabel and her husband on a tour of inspection, showing her "everything that needs to be seen, so that she can have an idea about the whole lot, fortresses, ships, military camps, public departments, everything, in fact." Following these visits, the young couple went up to Petrópolis. From there, she wrote a letter to her father that is significant in two ways. Her handwriting is markedly clearer and more self-assured than before, and it contains far fewer errors in grammar and spelling. A postscript to this letter reads: "No doubt S. Cristóvão will now seem very boring for you, but no doubt as well your feeling of sadness is linked to the pleasure of seeing us happy and content."[31] As the word "us" reveals, D. Isabel now viewed herself as part of a binary. Previously, she had signed her letters to her parents "Isabel Cristina" or "IC." Now and ever afterward she signed all her correspondence, no matter the recipient, with "Isabel, Countess d'Eu."

This new maturity and self-confidence were not matched by a similar expansion in the princess's horizons. Her upbringing had neither given D. Isabel an understanding for nor awakened any interest in public affairs. The reading course that the count d'Eu set for his bride was intended to remedy at least the first omission. It would include, he informed Pedro II, works on "the contemporary history of her country and others that will provide her with good and bad examples of the way to perform in her future position." He added: "Today we started a little English book that contains very clear and precise ideas about the constitution of that notable country."[32] These readings were supplemented by the emperor's giving his daughter, as already noted, tours of government offices in Rio City. A sudden political and military crisis involving Uruguay, Brazil, and Paraguay should have aroused in her, if anything could, an interest in public affairs.

Buenos Aires, the capital of Argentina, lies on the western bank of the Rio de la Plata estuary. The lands lying on the opposite bank, the Banda Oriental, had been claimed during the colonial period by both Spain and Portugal. After independence, Brazil and Argentina had fought to control the territory. In 1827, under British mediation, both countries renounced their claims, and the territory became the independent state of Uruguay with its capital at Montevideo. The northern third of the new republic was mainly peopled by settlers from Brazil's southernmost province, Rio Grande do Sul. The temptation for Brazil to meddle in the internal affairs of Uruguay was very great, particularly since the settlers and their descendants constantly complained to Rio de Janeiro about oppressive treatment by the Uruguayan authorities. For a time, Uruguay was shielded from Brazilian intervention by the support of Argentina. In 1864, the Argentine and Uruguayan governments were at odds, allowing Brazil a free hand. In September, Brazil, using the sufferings of its citizens as justification, sent its forces into Uruguay. By December the Brazilian army and navy had taken Montevideo and laid siege to the city of Paysandu.

The Brazilian government had, however, failed to take into consideration what would be the reaction of the republic of Paraguay, a landlocked state lying north of the Rio de la Plata and bordering on both Argentina and Brazil, under its young president Francisco Solano López. Ambitious to play a major role in the region's affairs and determined to uphold the existing government in Montevideo, López issued an ultimatum to Brazil in August, warning it not to attack Uruguay. Rio de Janeiro paid no attention to this warning. As soon as he learned of the Brazilian invasion, López sent his own troops to attack Mato Grosso, the Brazilian province bordering on Paraguay.

D. Isabel's response to these dramatic events can be gauged from the postscript to a letter sent her father on December 20: "The developments in the south are very interesting." In another letter, written three days later, her comments were somewhat more extensive. What aroused her interest in the crisis in Uruguay was the impact it might have on the lives of her personal acquaintances. She did not view the crisis more broadly as a problem involving high public policy and the country's destiny. It was not that she lacked patriotism. "Love of one's country is a very beautiful quality," she remarked to Gaston, "and I would be ashamed not to possess it, especially for my country that has always treated us so well."[33] Politics as such lay beyond her purview, notwithstanding that her appointed destiny was to guide her country's political destinies. Several reasons explain her outlook.

First and foremost, D. Isabel's attitude reflected the prevailing body of opinion. Women had no place in politics, both traditionalist and progressive thinkers agreed, because they lacked all the attributes— intelligence, knowledge, strength, attentiveness, dedication, and self- denial—that the exercise of power required. Only men possessed these attributes, which belonged to the sphere of action. The qualities as- cribed to women (assumed to be members of the middle or upper class) were quite different—modesty, purity, devotion, self-denial, and caring. These virtues, indispensable for domestic felicity, flourished only in the private sphere and would not survive in the rough-and- tumble of public life. Men were therefore doing a favor to women by preventing their participation in politics. These beliefs were hegemonic in the Western world in the midnineteenth century. Nothing caused D. Isabel to question them. Her situation as a young woman did not resemble that of Queen Victoria who, aged just eighteen when her uncle King William IV died, ascended the throne and had no choice but to take a public role and to participate in politics.

The princess was entirely willing to leave public affairs and poli- tics in the hands of her father and her husband. She was more than content to let Gaston, who had a talent for analysis, explain political developments to her. Public affairs, along with the world of knowl- edge, she perceived as belonging by right to Pedro II and to Gaston. She entered into them only at their invitation and on the terms they laid down. Moreover, public affairs were, as her familiarity with her father's daily schedule made her well aware, an exhausting, stressful, and time-consuming business. Unlike Pedro II, D. Isabel did not con- sider the performance of "duty" to be at once virtuous and fulfilling. She preferred her life to be pleasant and comfortable. "The air is deli- cious here, what a difference from the city," she wrote to D. Teresa Cristina from Petrópolis in the middle of summer. "While Mummy is dying of heat with the windows open, we are enjoying a very pleasant temperature with the windows closed." To D. Isabel, domesticity and social relations were pleasures indeed, and she devoted her time to them. "Tomorrow we are going to dine at 6 o'clock at the house of the duke and duchess of Saxe," she told her father. "I hope to have a good dinner; however, I have already been informed that, in respect to the dessert course they offer, the *doces* (sweets) are not outstanding."[34] What intensified her passion for domesticity was the prospect of acquiring her own home, which the couple's marriage contract required be purchased for them. A suitable mansion set in extensive grounds was found in the Laranjeiras district, then an outlying suburb of Rio City.

D. Isabel's introduction to public life and her forays into domesticity were cut short less than three months after her wedding. On January 8, 1865, the young couple sailed from Rio de Janeiro for Europe on an extended honeymoon. During the next six months they visited Portugal, England, Belgium, Germany, Austria, and Spain. As a dutiful daughter, she sent back to Pedro II and D. Teresa Cristina long and revealing accounts of everything she saw and did during this journey, which was a great success.

D. Isabel already had a good idea of what to expect of Europe. Her identity as a woman had been mainly formed by her *aia*. Both had been born in Brazil, but the countess of Barral was in essence European in style, deportment, and outlook, and her pupil resembled her. D. Isabel therefore experienced no cultural shock when she arrived in Europe. Nothing occurred that might have ignited in her a desire for independent action or aroused resentment against her lot. The way of life she encountered, as she visited with her husband's family and his other relatives in England and on the Continent, was already familiar. The longer she experienced it, the more she enjoyed it. It was a pleasant and comfortable existence for all concerned, whether male or female. No one had to earn a living. No one worried about keeping within a budget. The external world was organized for the individual's benefit and convenience. Homes were spacious and staffed with endless numbers of servants. The days were filled with activity and entertainment. Fine clothes, massive jewelry, and elaborate coiffures meant that much time was spent on one's wardrobe and at the dressing table.

Walking, riding, paying social visits, staging amateur theatricals, reading aloud, painting, and playing the piano occupied the hours between meals, and in the evening there were balls, opera and plays, concerts, and dinner parties. Those of an intellectual bent read the latest books and reviews, attended lectures, and participated in *conversaziones* (intellectual evening parties). Those interested in good works acted as patrons of hospitals, orphanages, and other charities, organized fund-raising fêtes and parties, and visited the deserving sick and poor. Any possibility of boredom was banished by frequent travel to stay with relatives and friends, to visit the innumerable spas and watering places of Europe ostensibly for health reasons, and to spend the winter in Italy or southern France. The life cycle brought births, baptisms, engagements, marriages, anniversaries, sicknesses, and death that provided the occasion for ceaseless correspondence and gossip.

This aristocratic way of life enchanted D. Isabel, aged eighteen and a half and still accustomed to the schoolroom and the austere existence of São Cristóvão. Neither her appearance nor her behavior marked her as an outsider. She gained general approval wherever she went. The prince of Joinville, upon meeting his niece on her arrival in England in February 1865, commented that "she is not pretty, but she is good, simple, and *ladylike* as the English say. She converses very well and she does not make a show of the education she has received."[35] Queen Victoria shared Joinville's opinion. "Nemours arrived at 2 with Marguerite & Gaston with his Brazilian Bride Isabelle, who is the future Empress of Brazil. She is very quiet, simple, & unaffected, & seems very good & kind. We remained a little while with them after luncheon, then they left."[36]

The letters the princess wrote home give much information on her activities, which in England included not only lunch at Windsor Castle but also balls and receptions given by the Orléans family and by the future King Edward VII. She took painting lessons from the teacher of Marguerite d'Orléans, her new sister-in-law, and made numerous visits to art galleries, museums, universities, and even factories. Traveling across the European continent, she dined in Brussels with the Belgian royal family and in Vienna met Emperor Francis Joseph and the other members of the Habsburg family. One activity

D. Isabel, taken in Bayswater, London, about March 1865

Courtesy of the Fundação Grão Pará, Petrópolis

THE COUNT D'EU, TAKEN IN BAYSWATER, LONDON, ABOUT MARCH 1865

Courtesy of the Fundação Grão Pará, Petrópolis

she did not participate in was discussed in a letter of April 1864. "Yesterday evening I received your letter that you sent by the *Bearn*. I am very pleased to know that you Mummy have the expectation of soon becoming a grandmother; for the present I have no such plans."[37] In contrast to her sister Leopoldina, she very definitely was not pregnant.

The attraction that an upper-class way of life possessed for D. Isabel was enhanced by the fact that she equated it with a warm and close relationship with her relatives in Europe. In Brazil her family consisted only of her parents and her sister, with the countess of Barral as a surrogate mother. In Europe resided her father's two surviving sisters and her mother's four surviving siblings. "Aunt Tuscany came to see us in Prague with her husband and daughter and we went to see them in Brandeis the next day," D. Isabel wrote on May 2, 1865. "Aunt reminds me very much of you Mummy, her features and her expression are very much like yours."[38] To these aunts and uncles, the princess could add her husband's relatives, including his father, four uncles, and one aunt, Gousty's mother. Since most of these aunts and uncles, her own and her husband's, had produced children, D. Isabel met numerous first cousins of her own age.

The language used by D. Isabel in these family relationships and in her wider social relations during her months in Europe was French. She had learned the language in the schoolroom, her courtship had been conducted in it, and she and Gaston used French in private conversation and in the letters they exchanged. During the months in Europe she became more skilled and more at ease in both speaking and writing French. Because a language expresses in its vocabulary and indeed in its very structure a distinctive set of cultural values and concept of existence, use of a particular language influences the user's outlook and sense of identity. Bilingual individuals often display two distinct persona or identities. Switching from one language to another changes the way in which such individuals both think and act. So it was with D. Isabel. In December 1864, she had begun to sign her letters "Isabel Condessa d'Eu." Her enjoyment of the aristocratic way of life, the warmth of her new family ties, and her immersion in French combined to build up D. Isabel's self-confidence and satisfaction in her other identity as "Comtesse d'Eu."

D. Isabel's acquisition of this bilingual and bicultural identity did not detract from or undermine her primary sense of identity as her father's daughter and heir that was expressed in Portuguese. All her letters from Europe to her parents are written in that language. She continued fiercely loyal to her native land as a physical entity, noting in a postscript to a letter of May 2, 1865, to her father, "I still have not seen anything approaching Brazil in respect to nature."[39]

If D. Isabel's months in Europe intensified her love for her homeland, her experiences did not give her opportunities to perceive herself as the next ruler of Brazil. During her visit she had no occasion to represent her country in her capacity as princess imperial. The state of relations between Brazil and Great Britain, where the princess spent the first weeks of her visit, contributed to the absence of official duties. High-handed action by the British early in 1863, seizing Brazilian shipping outside Rio harbor, caused Pedro II to break off diplomatic relations. Accordingly, the British government provided no official welcome to the princess when she landed at Southampton. Queen Victoria invited her to lunch not as the heir to the Brazilian throne but as the bride of the count d'Eu, whose mother, Victoire of Saxe-Coburg-Gotha, had been the queen's favorite first cousin. Since the Orléans family, to which Gaston belonged, had been deposed and banished from France, European governments preferred not to offer state receptions to the princess and her husband. The monarchs who did invite the young couple to their courts received them unofficially as relatives, not as princess imperial and consort. D. Isabel did not much enjoy the etiquette she encountered at these courts. Following her stay in the Austrian capital in May 1865, she commented, "Vienna is a beautiful city, but God spare me from having to live there permanently, given the immense number of archdukes and archduchesses &c., whom one has to endure from morning to night; there are dinners on dinners, visits on visits."[40] She valued an aristocratic existence with its pleasures and informalities more than life at court with its drudgeries and ceremonies. Her time abroad encouraged D. Isabel to be countess d'Eu rather than princess imperial of Brazil.

The months in Europe had the opposite influence on Gaston d'Orléans. They increased his belief in his own abilities and importance and reinforced his desire to play a role in governing Brazil. Like

King William III of England, he could not stomach the prospect of serving for the rest of his days as his wife's "gentleman usher," always walking two or three paces behind her. As heir to the throne, D. Isabel had a legitimate place in public affairs. The count d'Eu believed that by marrying him the princess had in effect transferred that place to him. In his letters to Pedro II, which rarely contain more than passing mentions of his wife, the count d'Eu's principal concern was to assert his rights. He tried to keep the emperor abreast of current events in Europe, and he was swift to comment and offer advice on developments in Brazil. Distance made the count d'Eu bold. He sought to demonstrate to Pedro II that he must be treated as an equal, as a power in his own right, as someone who carried weight in the conduct of affairs. He simply ignored the thrust of Pedro II's letters, which made clear that D. Isabel was his prime object of concern and that Gaston had no role beyond being her husband. A contest of wills was in the making.

The crisis confronting Brazil in the Rio de la Plata at the time of the couple's departure escalated into a full-scale war just before their return to Rio de Janeiro on July 16, 1865. Following the invasion of Mato Grosso province at the end of 1864, a second Paraguayan force entered Argentine territory in April 1865, violating that country's neutrality. In June, these troops invaded the province of Rio Grande do Sul. Pedro II perceived Paraguay's actions as a violation of the nation's and his own honor, a violation that only total victory could expunge. Taking his son-in-law August with him, the emperor embarked for Rio Grande do Sul on July 10. He left behind a letter inviting the count d'Eu, as soon as he arrived, to join him at the war front. This command, for it was nothing less, Gaston obeyed with alacrity. He had already seen action, fighting in Morocco as a Spanish artillery officer, and he was anxious to increase his military reputation. He sought a man's role. As to D. Isabel, she celebrated her nineteenth birthday on July 29, three days before Gaston's departure. At that same age in 1844 her father had already been Brazil's ruler for four and a half years. If D. Isabel had been a man, she might have been named regent of Brazil during her father's absence at the war front or even have joined the fighting herself. At the very least, she would have played an autonomous role, participating in the task of governing. She would have obtained invaluable training for her future duties as ruler. As a man, she would certainly have been allowed to live in the couple's new home in the Laranjeiras district. But she was a woman, not a man. Her exalted status availed nothing against her gender, as the letter she sent to Pedro II on July 31 attests: "My Gaston is going to leave tomorrow; Daddy can well imagine how much this separation is going to cost me. I don't need to ask you to take care of my good, excellent and dearest Gaston. . . . My sister has spent these days with me. Tomorrow we are going to dine at S. Cristóvão. Gaston will leave at 10 o'clock and I will remain there."[41]

During their husbands' absence the two sisters were compelled to live under their mother's charge secluded from the world. That was not all. On the day Gaston left, D. Isabel received from him a long list of directions on how she should behave during his absence.

> Try to remember, as much as possible, where all your belongings are and to that end always put them back in place.
> *Never* leave *the grounds* [of the palace] without them [the baron and baroness of Lajes, the couple's attendants].
> *Never receive a man* save in the company of another woman.
> Don't slouch: stand straight on both feet. When seated, don't show them. Don't make grimaces and think about Banting [dieting].
> Take care of your physical appearance.
> Be gentle, be deferential to your mother. In my absence, it is your first duty. It is your duty to God, duty to yourself, duty to me, duty to mankind.
> Every evening and at Mass, pray for Brazil, for me, and for your father.
> Read all this over several times.[42]

This piece of sublime male pomposity makes it hard to realize that, had Pedro II met his death on the war front, D. Isabel would have ascended the throne, wielding the sweeping powers that the constitution entrusted to the monarch.

D. Isabel acquiesced in her lot. If residing with her mother was what her father and her husband decreed, she would not resist. "My longing for you is already great, my darling," she wrote to Gaston a few hours after he left. "I have read your paper and I will try to do what you want." The next day she reported: "I slept well with your

D. Isabel with her mother and sister in August 1865

Courtesy of the Biblioteca Nacional, Rio de Janeiro

picture and your paper under my pillow." Her succeeding letters show
how resolutely she strove to fulfill his wishes, despite her secluded and
dull existence. "I can't say that the passing days don't resemble each
other, because there is very little variety in my life at São Cristóvão,"
she wrote to him on August 11, adding, "I love to do tasks for you, I
love so much to be useful to you in any way." She struggled to lose
weight, by following the first popular diet system. "Banting is going
well enough. Today I courageously resisted an appetizing black bean
stew." "Banting has in truth not been closely followed," D. Isabel

confessed late in September. "I will try to keep to it more rigorously. But at São Cristóvão it is really difficult to follow it with great rigor. There are a great many filling foods." D. Isabel also tried to apply herself to the program of cultural self-improvement that Gaston's instructions required. "I discovered today that since you left I have read 181 pages of pious works, 687 of French ones, 1392 of Portuguese ones," she reported on October 9, "that I have translated 10 and a half of English, 10 of Italian, and 14 of German, that I copied 137 pages from Daddy's book of psalms. I don't think that's too bad." These activities did nothing to lessen the utter tedium of D. Isabel's life. Within the palace the only event worth reporting was the engagement of Martha, her personal maid who had been freed from slavery in honor of the princess's wedding. "Today I gave 100$000 [$51.00] to my little Black girl [*ma petite négresse*] who is going to get married. She can buy her trousseau with that." Twelve weeks after the count d'Eu's departure, D. Isabel was forced to confess: "I have nothing new to tell you. My days creep by and are much the same."[43]

As the days became weeks and the weeks months, and her husband still did not return, D. Isabel's longing for Gaston came to dominate her thoughts and her letters. "Every day I have earnestly prayed to the Good Lord for you, for Daddy, and for Brazil," she explained, rather than "for Brazil, for me, and for your father," as Gaston had recommended. She wrote to him twice a day, seeking thereby to assuage the ache of his absence. "A week has passed since you left and it seems to me longer than the six months that we spent in travelling." "My body is at São Cristóvão but my thoughts are often very far from here." "I can find no other consolation than writing to you, my darling, and the thought of you has made me cry at this moment," she lamented, adding: "You are so good, so good, you love me so much, every day I appreciate that the more." Some weeks later, she wrote, "it is two months since you left and it seems to me like a century. This evening, I cried from loneliness for you, my darling, this evening when with Mummy."[44]

Much of D. Isabel's loneliness sprang from sexual frustration. "My bed here is much smaller than that at Laranjeiras, but it seems to me much more empty!!!" she wrote on the day following Gaston's departure. In the princess's letters, the use of three exclamation marks always signaled that she felt an emotion more powerful than she was capable of conveying in words. Erotic desire suffused the letters' references to the first anniversaries of the couple's meeting and courtship. So desperate was she for physical contact that, recounting Gaston's marriage proposal, she even pulled out a tuft of hair that she enclosed in a letter (see In Her Own Voice below). A folded sheet of paper still holds that twist of light brown hair, as fresh and as lustrous as on the day the princess sent it to her husband. By October her letters give open vent to her sexual desire. "Today I no longer have my period. I am sure that you are also impatient to see me pregnant. I so much want to be Mother of your child, to have a child by you whom I love so much, whom I love above all else, my love!!! What *saudades* [heartache] I have for you." Five days later, she wrote, "How I burn, my darling, to see you again, I love you so much, my friend, my little darling, how pleased I will be to find myself in your arms always so good to me!!! When will I be able to sleep on your dear little shoulder!!! I hope that it will be soon!!!"[45]

In Her Own Voice

September 18, 1865, São Cristóvão, 8 o'clock in the evening

My darling, my beloved Gaston,

It was a year ago today at this hour that I had the happiness of being proposed to by you, in the same drawing room that I left only an instant ago to write to you. I can't let this blessed day of today go by without writing something at this hour, a little separate letter. I have already shed tears looking at the spot where we were last year on this very day at the same hour. How we trembled, but also how content we were. O darling, I will never repent of having chosen you originally in my heart and later of having accepted you with all my heart, accepted you as my husband. I love you tenderly, my darling; every day I love you more. How I would like to see you here, my darling! What consoles me somewhat, as it does you, is thinking of how you are thinking of me, of how you also love me tenderly. I am sending you as a memento of today a little tuft of my hair that I have torn out at this moment. Oh my love, my darling, my beloved, my everything, never doubt the love felt for you by your little beloved wife who adores you.

Isabel

My *saudades* (longings) are very strong, above all on days like this.[46]

The correspondence the couple exchanged was one-sided, as the opening of one of Gaston's letters makes clear. "My darling, I received on the 5th your good letters up to August 12, and you can imagine the happiness with which I devoured them," he wrote on September 11 from "the camp outside of Uruguaiana." "I would very much like to reply point by point to everything that you tell me in them, but the perpetual motion in which Daddy makes us live every day does not allow me to do so."[47] After his arrival in Rio Grande do Sul province, the count d'Eu found himself facing a world far harder and more demanding than he had ever known. His dreams of playing a leading role in the fighting and of having a voice in the direction of affairs were brought to naught. Two male egos clashed during the long weeks in Rio Grande do Sul. Unwilling by inclination and experience to share power and resentful of any type of coercion or control, Pedro II had no intention of giving Gaston an autonomous military command. Young for his twenty-three years, the count d'Eu was highstrung, easily offended, and just as easily discouraged. The emperor, then entering middle age, was totally self-controlled, slow to take offense, and a master of politics. He had no difficulty in blocking his son-in-law's requests.

The reasons the emperor gave for his refusals were so plausible that no open breach or appearance of a quarrel resulted, but the relationship between the two thence forward took on a certain tension and distrust. Following the surrender of the Paraguayan force besieged in Uruguaiana, a victory witnessed by the emperor and his sons-in-law, the count d'Eu abandoned all hope of participating in the planned invasion of Paraguay. "I shall have to confine myself to Laranjeiras and plunge myself into books," he told his father.[48] The confrontations with his father-in-law, the thwarting of his desires, and the stresses

of the campaign laid Gaston low with a stomach ailment late in October. The treatment given by an elderly French doctor selected by
the emperor made his malady worse, or so he complained to D. Isabel.
He could eat only chicken soup.

Pedro II, who was never ill and who flourished under stress, showed
scant sympathy for his son-in-law, laconically reporting home: "There
is no news other than Gaston's sickness from which he is almost entirely recovered. He is not traveling with me to Porto Alegre so that he
can rest. There is no cause for worry." The emperor's departure did
indeed speed Gaston's recovery. "I was very comfortable at Pelotas,
being spared the interminable visits to schools and *repartições* [gov-
ernment offices] that Daddy so greatly enjoys."[49] His approaching
reunion with his spouse after three months' absence also raised Gaston's
spirits. On November 9, 1865, the imperial party landed in Rio City.
There the princess was waiting. The long separation was over, and
that night D. Isabel found herself, as she had dreamed, once again in
her Gaston's arms. She could now devote herself heart and soul to
being his wife.

4

WIFE, 1865–1872

Courtesy of the Fundação Grão Pará, Petrópolis

"The Paço Isabel [Isabel Palace], our residence in Rio after our marriage, situated on the edge of the town, quite far from São Cristóvão, is a pretty mansion standing in the middle of a large garden at the base of a quite high hill," D. Isabel recalled in old age. "Its wooded and winding paths, awhirl with masses of butterflies, some with huge wings of an iridescent blue, led us up to a splendid view over the bay, the Sugar Loaf, and the bay's other islands and mountains." D. Isabel and her husband had briefly occupied the mansion in July 1865 before he left for Rio Grande do Sul, and thereafter it represented for the princess her contentment at being a wife. "I wasn't able to contain my tears," she told Gaston after visiting the Paço Isabel shortly after his departure, "on seeing the house where we have spent happy days together." "I have no pleasure going there without you, my friend," she confessed two months later; "it is so sad; everything there reminds me of you and that makes me so sad!!!"[1] After the count d'Eu's return from the far south in November 1865, the young couple settled into their home, on which they soon put their own stamp. The gardens they filled with exotic plants and trees. Down the newly opened Rua Paisandu, running from the palace to Botafogo Bay, they planted a double row of royal palms, which survive to this day. They decorated and furnished the mansion's interior in the heavy style and taste so favored at the time. For the next twenty-four years, the Paço Isabel was their residence in Rio City and the main setting in which the princess carried out her duties as wife.

During the nineteenth century, a married woman from the middle or upper class had five principal obligations. First and foremost was to serve her husband, giving him unstinting support, affection, loyalty, and protection. She had, second, to run the household, making his private life comfortable. Her third duty was to be a mediator and facilitator within the family network, conciliating all four parents and other relatives senior to her. She had, fourth, to build up a circle of friends and acquaintances and to undertake social activities that would both proclaim her husband's status and create a web of rewarding friendships. The last and not the least important of a wife's five duties was to give birth to and bring up her husband's children.

The extent and complexity of these obligations and the heavy burdens they imposed may seem to us exploitative and intolerable, and in fact they were at times unbearable. Some wives, overwhelmed physically or mentally, took refuge in invalidism, never leaving their beds for months or years on end. Whether D. Isabel at the start of her married life ever paused to consider what was demanded of her we do not know, but given that she was, in her own words, "never prone to view things entirely in black," she probably did not. She accepted the responsibilities laid on her. She told her father-in-law early in 1867 that she regretted any situation in which she "could not do everything for him [Gaston] that would be in my power."[2] That she was the heir to the throne did not, for D. Isabel, alter or diminish her wifely obligations. During the first years of marriage, the princess's determination to be a model spouse shaped her life.

THE PAÇO ISABEL, LARANJEIRAS, RIO DE JANEIRO CITY

Courtesy of the Biblioteca Nacional, Rio de Janeiro

When the princess took up residence in the Paço Isabel, she was much better equipped to perform her duties as a wife than she had been at the time of her marriage the year before. During the months spent with her own and Gaston's relatives in Europe, she gained an understanding of the role played by wives in the aristocratic way of life that she took as her model, and her travels gave her greater poise and polish. Her three months' confinement in São Cristóvão, during which she gallantly tried to carry out Gaston's instructions, taught her self-discipline and increased her powers of perseverance and self-confidence. Although still young in years—not yet twenty—and lacking in experience, she had matured considerably since October 1864.

D. Isabel gave every satisfaction in carrying out the first of her tasks as wife, lavishing unstinting support, affection, loyalty, and protection on Gaston. Her adoration for her spouse certainly facilitated her task. When sending her father-in-law a photograph of Gaston in the uniform of a Voluntário da Pátria (National Volunteer), she remarked "in my opinion he is cute [charmant] in this uniform," adding in a flash of candid introspection, "it is true that for me he is always cute." The count d'Eu had only praise for his wife. "Here we lead a very pleasant life," he wrote to an acquaintance in Europe in August 1866, "and every day I thank God the more for everything I have found in my marriage." The warm companionship D. Isabel gave her spouse accounted for much of her success as a wife. No less important was the support and sympathy she provided during his illnesses, usually bronchial in nature, which he tended to suffer at moments of stress. "Gaston has for these last few days been very poorly," she told his father in February 1867, "the day before yesterday he spent the greater part of the day in bed, but thank God, today he is better. He had such a bad sore throat he could hardly speak."[3] In her role as a ministering angel she served not so much as his wife as a replacement for his mother, who had died when he was thirteen and a half.

The princess sought to fulfill, as best she could, her second duty, that of providing her husband with a comfortable home life. The management of the Paço Isabel was in the hands of a steward and a myriad of servants, and the count d'Eu seems to have involved himself in household matters. The princess took some time to work herself into her role as housewife, if a comment made by her husband in July 1867 can be trusted. "Isabel, who is becoming a good household organizer in conjunction with Borges's daughter, is absorbed in preparing trays of candies and ices for Monday night."[4] Any imperfections Gaston readily forgave his wife, since D. Isabel threw herself willingly into carrying out a wide range of domestic tasks. In the kitchen she made foods such as peach preserves and cakes. Her needle and paintbrushes she used to create artwork, some of which decorated the house.

INTERIOR SCENES OF THE PAÇO ISABEL

Courtesy of the Biblioteca Nacional, Rio de Janeiro

In the garden of the Paço Isabel the princess cultivated a large orchid collection. The first mention of these plants comes in a letter to her father of January 21, 1868. "I am making a collection of orchids and I confess to you that some of them I stole from the garden." Two weeks later, she added: "I am making some progress with the album of orchids; almost every day I have painted one, two or three." By the end of April she had collected a total of ninety-three specimens. In September 1869 she reported to Gaston, "our orchids at Laranjeiras [Paço Isabel] are at this moment producing the most flowers and are of the prettiest sort."[5]

In handling her third role, as mediator and facilitator within the family network, the princess showed herself to be assured and quite adept. Her letters to her father-in-law, the duke of Nemours, reveal a relationship that was friendly and respectful on both sides. D. Isabel also kept up close ties with her many aunts and uncles in Europe. With D. Leopoldina and Gousty, who lived in Rio City, relations were cordial but not close. It was her own parents who caused D. Isabel the most difficulty. Early in December 1865, after his return to Rio City from the war front, Pedro II complained to the countess of

Barral, "My life is not what it used to be; I am reminded of that every day, but my daughters are happy."[6] In fact, the emperor still looked to his daughters to provide him with the interest and stimulation he could not find in his wife's company. Similarly, the empress, who lived her life for and through others and found contentment in family relations, desired constant contact with D. Isabel and her sister.

Brought up to be a dutiful daughter and with close emotional ties to her father, D. Isabel strove to fulfill her parents' expectations. The princess was "obliged to see T[heir]. M[ajesties]. every two days," the count d'Eu informed his father in December 1867. "Isabel never goes 48 hours without jolting over the town's pavements, which at times leave a great deal to be desired."[7] Her new standing as spouse and housewife greatly aided D. Isabel in maintaining a comfortable relationship with her mother. The two women sent each other endless gifts ranging from foodstuffs to dress materials. They ran errands and made purchases for each other. By 1868 the relationship had developed a familiar routine not demanding, at least in D. Isabel's view, much thought or concern.

For a variety of reasons, the princess could not adopt such a carefree approach in her relationship with Pedro II. By the conventions of the time, a daughter's duties to her father did not cease when she married. She was required to please him, not the other way around. Pedro II expected his wishes to be obeyed, even when they related to minor concerns and were not expressed as orders. Early in 1867, he co-opted his daughter and her husband for the task of correcting and proofreading—"a bore of the first order," Gaston grumbled—the French-language catalog, "very badly done in every respect," for the Brazilian exhibit at the forthcoming Paris Exposition. At this time, with the war against Paraguay not going well, the emperor was concentrating his time and energies on securing victory. He still wanted to meet with his daughters, but at times and in ways convenient to him. Arranging mutually satisfactory dates for dining together and for joint visits to the theater called for tact on D. Isabel's part. "If Daddy would like to go today to the Lyric Theater to see Melrose Abbey, the cathedral at Paris, and other pretty sights, he would be doing us a great pleasure," she wrote in November 1867; "I await a reply which I believe will be favorable." She sometimes used her mother to prepare the way. "Could we come to dine at São Cristóvão on Thursday? Since Daddy will be conducting business with the ministers in the morning, we suppose it would be best for us to come to dinner, spending the afternoon there."[8]

The factor creating the most difficulty for D. Isabel in her relationship with Pedro II from 1865 onward was a growing tension between her husband and her father. On the surface, relations between the two were correct, even cordial. Underneath, emotions seethed. The cause was quite simple. The count d'Eu wanted to return to the front line, and the emperor was determined that he should not. Pedro II never declared his reasons for this refusal. They probably included an unwillingness to let Gaston d'Orléans out of his sight, concern about the possible risks (above all, death in combat) if the young man were allowed to join the Brazilian forces, and a basic dislike of granting anyone autonomy of action. Two weeks after their arrival from the south on November 9, 1865, Pedro II appointed his son-in-law to be commander in chief of the artillery and president of the Commission for Improving the Army. Despite the glorious titles, neither post involved real responsibilities, being desk jobs that intensified the count d'Eu's resentment. Starting in July 1866, he made repeated public requests to be released from his posts and to be sent to fight in Paraguay. Each time Pedro II deftly blocked the request without appearing to be involved, using the cabinet ministers and the Council of State (ever compliant to the emperor's desires) to deny his son-in-law's petitions. In time, the count's discontent became public knowledge, so much so that political elements, radical Liberal in views and in opposition, began to court him, seeking both to create and exploit an open breach between him and Pedro II.

A public quarrel did almost erupt in December 1867, at the start of the southern summer. The emperor decided, so that he could deal with any sudden emergency in the war against Paraguay, to remain in Rio City, regardless of its stifling heat, rather than to move up to Petrópolis. The empress had no choice but to keep him company. "My daughter Isabel and her husband left on Saturday [December 21] to spend the hot season in Petrópolis," Pedro II informed the countess of Barral. "I am left here almost alone."[9] The count d'Eu, writing to his father, justified the change in residence for health and other reasons. However plausible the explanation, the move could be seen, and was so interpreted by the radical Liberals, as an act of protest, a declaration of independence by the heir to the throne and her husband.

The mounting tension between D. Isabel's husband and father, who both commanded her love, rendered her existence difficult enough. An open split between the two would make it intolerable and would signify her failure to carry out her duties as a wife. She had been able thus far to behave as if no tension existed and so avoid referring to the subject. Contemporary perceptions of women, held to be by nature innocent and unworldly, facilitated this course. In January 1868, the distribution in the streets of Rio of printed flyers, to the effect that the count d'Eu was about to withdraw to Europe in protest against the government's mistreatment of him, made it impossible for her to stand aside or be silent any longer. She wrote to her father from Petrópolis on January 24.

> I write to you truly very vexed by everything that I hear. Today I received a stupid bulletin. Daddy is the one who can give us comfort. Tell us what we ought to do, should we return to Rio? We are ready to do so if that is of any use, even though the reason for our stay here is not just recreation but our health and so that Gaston may rest a little. We can't do a single thing, I truly believe, without attracting more or less ridiculous and disagreeable remarks! Thank God we have always lived in the greatest harmony with our good Daddykins, and this is a great boon for us! Evil tongues don't leave people quiet! Believe me that I am very upset, but in the midst of it all I continue to give thanks to God for not inflicting on me a real torment. I expect your reply tomorrow.[10]

The princess's expressions of outrage about the rumors and their untruth could be taken at face value. They could also be interpreted as a reproach to both men for behavior that had given the ill-natured an opportunity to stir up trouble and as a warning to the two to mend their ways. Whether or no the princess's outburst was calculated, her letter was certainly effective. Gaston backed off, sending Pedro II a conciliatory letter that offered their immediate return to Rio City if so desired. The emperor wisely made light of the whole incident and, whatever his real feelings may have been, sent soothing replies to his daughter and son-in-law. Thereafter, although the two men's relationship remained fraught, they both sought to avoid any act that might exacerbate the situation. In this specific case, D. Isabel achieved a notable success in promoting a façade of unity and harmony in her family, her third duty as a wife.

The fourth task required of D. Isabel was the organizing of an active social life that added luster and influence to her husband. During her time in Europe, the princess had participated in the balls and receptions that lay at the heart of the upper-class life she so much enjoyed. As early as October 15, 1865, when still absent in the far south, Gaston d'Orléans suggested "giving a ball to celebrate our happy return and the victory of Uruguaiana, if that suits you. I believe the best day would be December 1."[11] The count fell sick immediately after writing this letter, and no such ball took place. In fact, no formal social event, either party or ball, seems to have been held in the Paço Isabel until early in 1867.

The reasons for this delay are clear. The couple were at first absorbed in a second honeymoon, putting their new home in order and, to use D. Isabel's own words, "amusing ourselves or studying together!!! and enjoying the happiness that we find in each other's company."[12] In a letter sent to Europe in August 1866, the count d'Eu confirmed his wife's view of their life.

> Since social life is both little developed and little developable in these parts, our existence is entirely private. I go out only for as long as it takes to carry out my military duties. At home, if I have any work to prepare, she [D. Isabel] acts as my secretary and at the same time corrects any errors that I may still make in Portuguese. Next we read a lot or rather mostly aloud, alternately French and Portuguese books, ranging from the serious to . . . novels (for we have to instruct the young [D. Isabel]). . . . Music and painting always occupy certain hours of the day.[13]

Gaston d'Orléans's remark about the lack of social life was fully justified as it applied to the imperial family. Pedro II had not offered a state ball since 1852. No parties of any sort were given at São Cristóvão palace. Formal entertainment at the Paço Isabel would challenge this practice, and this fact, combined with the princess's inexperience in managing the household, probably delayed the young couple's embarking on a social life. In January 1867 they began to be "at home," to use the social phrase of the period, to callers for two hours on Monday evenings. Occasionally, they also gave large evening parties on Mondays with supper, an orchestra, and dancing, to which they invited eighty to 100 guests. These parties sometimes featured programs of music, with guests singing the vocal parts of Mozart's *Don Giovanni* and of Gounod's *Faust*. Appearing at these parties were prominent politicians, foreign diplomats, and leading intellectuals, who conversed with the count d'Eu.

Social practice of the period meant that D. Isabel talked mainly to the female guests, mostly wives and daughters of the men present. Her closest friends continued to be those from her childhood, such as Amandinha de Paranaguá and Adelaide Taunay. The princess greatly enjoyed interacting with other women by means of social and cultural activities in small groups and informal settings. Her sheltered upbringing and the constraints under which most upper-class women still lived in Brazil meant that during the first years of her marriage, D. Isabel took no leading role in the social affairs of the national capital. Her social life was very much within the home.

The fifth and final duty demanded of a wife was to give her husband a large number of children. Since the continuance of the imperial dynasty depended upon Pedro II's two daughters producing offspring, preferably several sons, their marriages were warmly welcomed. Within four months of her wedding day, D. Leopoldina was pregnant. Although she suffered a miscarriage at the start of May 1866, she had conceived again by the middle of June and gave birth to a son, christened Pedro Augusto, on March 19, 1866. A year later she was once more pregnant, her second son Augusto being born on December 6, 1867. Two more sons were to follow in May 1869 and September 1870. The Brazilian public could not have asked for more.

D. Isabel did not become pregnant prior to the count d'Eu's departure for the far south. Early in October 1865, she wrote to him, "I am sure that you are also impatient to see me pregnant. I so much want to be Mother of your child."[14] He returned early in November.

Amandinha de Paranaguá

Courtesy of the Biblioteca Nacional, Rio de Janeiro

The months rolled by, the second anniversary of her marriage (October 15, 1866) came and went, and the princess still gave no sign of being pregnant. In the opinion of the time, failure to conceive was a wife's fault, her failure to be truly female. The husband could not be responsible. Since men embodied power, they could not by definition be impotent. By the middle of 1867, D. Isabel's continued lack of children was giving cause for considerable concern. The countess of Barral wrote from Paris, mixing confession, advice, and exhortation.

> I suffered for many years from a condition and it was only when this had gone that I produced my child. But you, my love! who are so well made, if by chance you are suffering from something, don't hide it, consult, have yourself examined by that horrible Torres Homen [a court physician], and submit to any treatment in order to have a child who would be so cute, with such attractive parents.
>
> Your husband only came into the world two years after his parents' marriage and later had three siblings. God, let me not lose hope, but don't be imprudent, don't take long walks, and don't risk riding on horseback.[15]

Since D. Isabel very much wanted to produce children, she certainly submitted herself to examination. She perhaps already had done so at the time the countess of Barral wrote to her. The court physicians were, however, all men, and their treatment of women's bodies was based on antiquated practices. It is not surprising that the remedies they prescribed bore no fruit. No baby arrived.

If D. Isabel had not possessed an ability to take things at their best, her sister's fecundity in contrast to her own apparent sterility might have induced moods of depression or fits of jealousy. In January 1868, noting that his wife liked to play with her nephew Pedro Augusto, the count d'Eu commented with some wonder to his father, "It is very fortunate that she is so entirely exempt from a sentiment of envy."[16] The couple's desire for children caused them in September 1868 to spend four months drinking the waters at three different spas in the province of Minas Gerais. The minerals in such waters could cure, so nineteenth-century physicians asserted, almost any ailment

D. Isabel with her sister, mother, and sister's sons, july 1869

Courtesy of the Arquivo Histórico do Museu Imperial, Petrópolis

including sterility, but neither the "efficacious waters" (*aguas virtuosas*) of Campanha, nor those of Lambarí, nor those of Caxambu changed the princess's condition. She did not conceive.

During her stay in Minas Gerais, D. Isabel, now twenty-two years old, celebrated the fourth anniversary of her wedding. Her letters reveal where her social interests lay. "What we lack is music; there is no piano in the house," she complained to her mother, asking her to "carry out my commissions as you did when I was at Petrópolis." She

wanted to be sent "not a concertina . . . but another kind of instru-
ment of the same type, also portable. . . . In French I think the instru-
ment is called harmonica or accordion." A postscript requested a set
of bagpipes as well and sheet music for both instruments. A month
later she included in her letter to D. Teresa Cristina a glove, "not as a
challenge [to a duel] but to ask you to send me 4 or 6 pairs of the
same quality as soon as you can. Where is my accordion?" When it
finally arrived, she wrote: "Many thanks for the pretty and fine accordion you sent me. Only it is a little heavy, but perhaps practice will
make it easier to play."[17]

Public affairs did not command D. Isabel's interest. When her
letters do mention them the cause was almost always personal experience. A comment on the "many poor people here" was motivated by
the problems she faced when giving alms. "If I give them [the poor]
paper money, they often don't know its value," so she asked her mother
to send her 200$000 [$68] in a variety of silver coins. On another
occasion, "When will the vote be free?" D. Isabel asked her father
after watching "from our dining room window" the municipal elections at Campanha, in which the police threatened to throw opposition voters in jail if they dared to vote. Her recommendation in favor
of a judge who served for seven years in "the most miserable" districts
was motivated by personal acquaintance. "He is someone of great
kindness" who, on encountering in Campanha a sick man, "took him
to his house, gave him his bed, and slept on the floor." "God grant
that he be heard" in his petition for a better post.[18]

D. Pedro II's failure to answer his daughter's letters caused her
to send him on October 10, 1868, a missive that reveals both how
she perceived their relationship and why he found her company
stimulating.

> Most ungrateful Sir,
>
> How many mails have gone by without your honoring me with a note, in
> spite of the promise you gave me that you would write to me a lot? Please
> forgive [this from] your ill-bred little chatterbox, because she has to carry
> out her job from afar, not being able at present to do so in person. *Ridendo
> castigo mores* [Through laughter I correct behavior], and I want to see if I
> can thus make my Daddykins write more to me.[19]

D. Isabel does not seem to have paused, when writing her bantering rebuke, to consider what might have caused her father not to write. Although the princess knew exactly where Pedro II was likely to be at any particular hour of the day and what his round of duties entailed, she displayed small interest in the business of governing that occupied him. Since the end of 1864, the emperor had devoted his time and energies to securing Paraguay's defeat. He let nothing stand in the way of this goal. At the end of July 1868 his desire for total victory in the war caused him to dismiss the sitting cabinet, despite its majority in the legislature, and call the opposition party to office. He granted the new Conservative ministry dissolution of the Chamber of Deputies. The rigged elections that followed, which D. Isabel observed in Campanha, resulted in the Conservatives "winning" every seat.

At no moment since the war began had the conflict merited more than passing references in the princess's correspondence. It was almost a topic to be avoided. A letter sent to her father in August 1866 remarked: "La guerre du Paraguay va toujours son train?, malheureusement [Is the war with Paraguay taking its usual course? Unfortunately so]."[20] D. Isabel almost never used French in her letters to her father, who insisted that the countess of Barral write to him only in Portuguese. Employing French in this letter served as a means of distancing herself from an unwelcome topic. In February 1867, she revealed to her father-in-law her feelings on the subject.

> Nothing of real importance from the war front. I hope that this unhappy affair will end, for every reason. I live in perpetual fear that something will occur that will oblige Gaston to go to the South. If you knew my state of mind when this subject comes up for discussion, you would feel pity for me. I am sure that the Good Lord will always protect Gaston and that Grandmother [the deceased Queen Marie Amélie] will keep watch over him. Nonetheless, one can never be sure about what will occur, and how grieved I would be if the least thing happened to him, above all if he is far away from me, when I could not do everything for him that would be in my power.[21]

The link in D. Isabel's mind between her husband and the war is also evident in a letter sent her mother from Campanha on September 20, 1868. "The news from Paraguay is very good, thank God, and gives promise of a rapid end to the war. The day before yesterday Uruguaiana fell 3 years ago and 4 we were engaged! How time passes."[22] During December, as the princess and her husband traveled back to Rio City, the news continued to be very good. The Brazilian forces smashed the Paraguayan army in three major battles that opened the way to Asunción, the enemy's capital, which was occupied on January 5, 1869. One task remained. President Francisco Solano López, whom Pedro II insisted must be exiled from Paraguay, had not been captured or killed in the battles. He had retreated into the eastern hinterland of Paraguay, where he set about reforming his forces.

The marquis of Caxias, the commander in chief of the Brazilian forces, then aged sixty-five and in uncertain health, was in no mood to undertake, as the count d'Eu phrased it, "the abominable task of chasing López God knows where."[23] Refused permission to resign his command, the general simply left his post and returned to Rio, where he arrived on February 15. Pedro II, after an initial refusal to meet with Caxias, controlled his feelings. The two men were reconciled, and the insubordination was forgiven. Having done his duty, the emperor turned to finding a new commander in chief. Quite literally, the only high-ranking officer with sufficient prestige and known ability for the post was his own son-in-law, the count d'Eu, to whom he had previously refused permission to fight in the war. Pedro II did not balk at sacrificing both pride and consistency in order to get his way.

On February 20 the emperor wrote to the count d'Eu, then in Petrópolis with D. Isabel, offering him the post of commander in chief and asking him to travel down at once to Rio City. The count, who came down the next day, refused to be hurried or bullied into agreeing to the proposal. He insisted that, prior to his making a decision, his father-in-law must obtain approval from both the Council of State and the cabinet ministers who had previously advised against his going to the war front. Neither Pedro II's letter containing the offer nor the count's discussions with the emperor (according to the account he sent to his father) made any reference to D. Isabel. Both men acted as though she had no standing or voice in the question.

D. Isabel, February 1869, wearing "my silk dress with white and gray stripes"

Courtesy of the Fundação Grão Pará, Petrópolis

Women were bystanders in respect to public affairs and the exercise of power.

A long letter D. Isabel sent her mother on February 16 contained a single, brief reference to current events. "Having learned from your telegram of Caxias's arrival, I wrote a little letter to the Baroness [of Suruí, Caxias's sister] to get news of him. I ask you to send it to her." The princess must have realized what the consequences of Caxias's return would be and, on the evening that Gaston received the emperor's proposal, she wrote to both her parents, venting her feelings. "If Daddy knew my state of affliction you would take pity on me!" "Mummy, now I understand why pleasant weather, a clear sky, a pretty sunbeam can at times make you sad. Thinking of this now and then, I recall the happiness of which they wish to rob me and I become very sad."[24]

When Gaston returned to Petrópolis in the afternoon of February 22, D. Isabel learned her fate. Subject to approval by both the Council of State and the cabinet minister stationed in Asunción, Gaston would agree to become the new commander in chief. Her first reaction was to weep, but her despair moved her to abandon the passivity that gender conventions imposed on women. She wrote a long letter to her father (see In Her Own Voice below). In it she tried to employ the tight chain of argument, logical organization, and abstract thought that characterized the scientific, literary, and political tomes (authored by men) that she had read in the classroom and at Gaston's direction. But she found herself in difficulties. Her way of life, including her duties as wife, had kept her from acquiring the experience and skill needed to use this type of discourse, and, crucially, she did not have the knowledge to back up and to give force to her arguments. She could suggest no one but Caxias as a suitable substitute for Gaston. She fell back, as the text shows, upon the form of discourse familiar to her with its multiple approaches, reiterated arguments, appeal to feelings, and personal involvement. Her resolve and fierceness faded as she wrote. The very act of expressing her sentiments on paper purged them and made submission seem more tolerable. Her innate unwillingness to offend her father, much less break with him, robbed her threat—following Gaston to Asunción—of any credibility.

In Her Own Voice

Petrópolis, February 22, 1869

My dear Father,

Gaston arrived three hours ago with the news that Daddy has expressed a most ardent wish that he should go to the war. How can it be that Daddy, who respects the constitution so much, wants to impose your will on the ministers or that they are so weak in character that they switch from saying white one day to black the next? Can they have unanimously and simultaneously changed their opinion, as Daddy has!!? Why don't they invite [General] Caxias to go back? He is already better and the doctors prescribe for him the climate of Montevideo. How can it be that Gaston must, on your say-so, depart immediately for the war front, simply because there are rumors of mutinies among the soldiers from Rio Grande do Sul? And it's Daddy who immediately believes all this, when you so often refuse to believe what you hear! Does Daddy not remember that at the Tijuca waterfalls three years ago you told me that passion is blind?

May your passion about the war not make you blind! Besides, Daddy wants to kill my Gaston. [Luís da Cunha] Feijó [the couple's physician] strongly advises him against too much exposure to sun, and no rain or damp; and how can he avoid these if he is in the midst of a war? Caxias cannot remain in his post due to his dizzy spells that are curable, and besides he can command while in Montevideo, which suits him, so why should it be my Gaston who would pick up, while there, a chest ailment that is rarely curable? The loss of my Gaston would be much more harmful to Brazil than that of Caxias. And now there is a cholera outbreak in Montevideo.

What Daddy should know is that, if Gaston goes to Asunción, I will follow him there with my Rosa [lady-in-waiting], who truly shares my sorrows. I will go to the ends of the earth with my Gaston.

Daddy can perhaps understand what I am suffering and so will forgive any discourtesy on my part; burn this letter but keep well in mind what I have told you about Gaston's health. I have to unburden myself and I can't do so merely by crying.

I continue to hope to God that Gaston will not go! Perhaps the war may end before the reply from [José Maria da Silva] Paranhos [cabinet minister resident in Asunción] arrives, or other things may intervene.

My God! My God!

I truly don't know how this sudden request came about, when all that is now needed is someone to play the role of a slave catcher pursuing [Francisco Solano] López. Any one else is good enough to assume command at Asunción (Daddy himself told me that it was not the job for Caxias, that of personally pursuing López). The soldiers from Rio Grande do Sul make up only a small part of the army.

Good bye, Daddy, forgive

Your most loving daughter

Isabel Countess d'Eu

I don't believe that Daddy will be angry with me for writing this, so I do so.[25]

The rebellion to which the letter gave expression was a brief one, an unavailing protest against the prevailing view of gender relations, so graphically stated in an English poem of the period: "But men must work, and women must weep."[26] D. Isabel was not happy about her surrender and continued to hope for an unexpected turn of events, but she now resigned herself to a woman's lot of being a mere spectator. She did not lose her Gaston so quickly as she feared. He was not named commander in chief until March 22 and did not sail from Rio for another week. The day before, he wrote to his wife:

Laranjeiras, 29/3/69

My darling, I am leaving you once again at São Cristóvão as I did nearly four years ago.

Reread the instructions I gave you on that occasion. In general they should still be followed.

Look at what I said on the subject of Rosa: don't permit her to share a bed with you.[27]

There followed other advice slightly less preachy in tone and restrictive in content than its predecessor. She was, for example, allowed to open and read all his letters, save those from his father.

Nothing could have made more evident the lack of independence held by even married women than D. Isabel's being, aged almost twenty-three, again required to leave her home at Laranjeiras and reside with her parents. Because her Gaston had decreed the move, she seems to have made no effort to resist it. Her husband's absence alone concerned her, as her first letter to him shows: "My dearly beloved of my heart. Where are you at this moment? The day has seemed so long without you. When will I see you again, my little darling? After you left, I stayed with Mummy and Leopoldina and we went to pray in the chapel, then each went about her separate tasks. Later we were in my room arranging things."[28]

The princess resumed the life that she had followed nearly four years before. There were some differences. Her father's presence made her existence much less cloistered. She paid visits to her house in Laranjeiras and to her sister D. Leopoldina and her family until they left for Europe early in August. She went to concerts and the theater with her parents. Much time was spent on crocheting, writing to relatives in Europe, copying Gaston's letters to send on, and listening to her father read aloud books and newspapers. "There can never be enough of these [news items] for me when they are about you," she told Gaston early in October.[29]

D. Isabel's daily round at São Cristóvão was controlled by what her parents, above all her father, were doing. "There is Daddy calling so that he can finish his reading. Good-bye for now!" Another time: "Daddy won't stop talking Italian with me both in the evening and at midday. I am a bit fed up. You know how he carries on when he sets his heart on something." He frequently gave her materials to read. "I've finished the novel by [Count Arthur de] Gobineau. I have read *As Minas de Prata* [by José de Alencar]. Now, having cleared the backlog of reading that Daddy gave me a long while ago, I will try to push ahead with the book by [the count of] Paris."[30]

The princess automatically turned to Pedro II for advice on any matter, however minor, that involved her intrusion into the public sphere. She wrote to Gaston, "I have just wept hot tears, thinking that it might displease you if I attend the *cortejo*," the formal ceremony held on September 7, the anniversary of Brazil's independence. "I have consulted Daddy and having explained everything to him, he told me that I would do best to attend, that he would assume entire responsibility." In respect to questions of private conduct, she was not nearly so dependent. The French envoy, count Gobineau, following a public scuffle with a professor at the Rio medical school, challenged the Brazilian to a duel. The latter refused the challenge. Reporting the incident to the count d'Eu, D. Isabel commented: "In my view he replied as a Christian should do, but according to the false precepts of this wicked and proud world (Daddy and Gousty expressed this view) there ought to have been a duel. This discussion took place over the table at Leopoldina's. I was not afraid to declare my fixed and firm opinion on the subject of duels."[31]

The letters sent by the princess to her husband during his absence reveal a growing interest in and understanding of public affairs. "Today I finished the book by [the count of] Paris, and I'm sure that will satisfy you as well. This book is very interesting. I had no idea about Trade Unions and now I am really informed about them." A systematic reading of the newspapers made her knowledgeable about current events, particularly the conflict in Paraguay, and since she did not lack intelligence, her understanding grew. "I read all the articles about you appearing in the *Diário Oficial* and the *Jornal do Comércio*."[32] The count d'Eu's plan of campaign was to encircle and crush the remaining Paraguayan forces, capturing President López in the process. Three victories in August 1869 did indeed smash the foe, but López and a handful of troops escaped into the northern fastness of Paraguay. The conflict became an affair of reconnaissances, with flying columns in pursuit of a swiftly moving enemy. At this crucial moment, the Brazilian army's supply system broke down, leaving many of the troops on short rations, even starving.

The count d'Eu was nervous by disposition, and stress made him fall ill, as D. Isabel well understood. "You know how upset these moments of altercation make you," she warned him on February 21, 1869. "Take lots of precautions, I beg you, my darling pet." "Gaston has taken with him a personal physician," she informed her father-in-law at the start of April, "who is said to be very clever." As commander in chief the count d'Eu performed admirably during his first weeks in Paraguay, but strain soon began to tell on him. In June, informing his wife that her letters showed her to be unnecessarily vexed by small problems, he remarked, "Just compare your troubles there with mine."[33] At the end of October, with López still uncaptured, his own troops starving, and no end to the war in sight, the count's self-confidence collapsed. He became irritable, moody, and disheartened. He desired only to escape a torment to which he saw no end, and he wrote to the government demanding that the war be declared over and that the bulk of the troops, led by him, be brought home.

This request D. Isabel did her best to further. A cabinet minister, visiting São Cristóvão to transact business with the emperor, asked D. Teresa Cristina if she were going to Petrópolis. "Mummy told him that it depended on the war. 'Que guerra! A guerra está acabada!' [What war! The war is over!] I retorted: 'Se a guerra está acabada mandem a licença.' [If the war is over, you should send the permission to return.] He went upstairs and so it was that this evening Daddy showed me his letter to you."[34] Pedro II refused to sanction his son-in-law's leaving Paraguay until López was captured or killed. Fortunately, the end came much more quickly than anyone had anticipated. On March 1, 1870, the president of Paraguay was surprised in his camp and conveniently killed. The rapid success, made against all of the count d'Eu's expectations, served to undermine what remained of his self-confidence and to intensify his sense of insufficiency. On the day he received the news, he wrote to his father-in-law:

March 4, 1870

Dear Father,

I imagine that, thanks to Paranhos, the glorious dispatches will reach you more quickly than these letters.

At this moment of such great and so unexpected emotion I cannot fail to think of Y. M. and to kiss your hand, asking you to forgive me for my lapses in faith and other childish acts.

Your loving and submissive son

Gaston[35]

In writing these words, the count d'Eu reached a turning point in his life. Henceforth, he ceased to compete with his father-in-law or to perceive of himself as a power in his own right. The news and the letters he wrote reached D. Isabel at São Cristóvão late on March 17. "What joy, what happiness! Your great little letter of March 4! Oh! My darling! The war finished entirely, completely and so well! The most sincere and happy congratulations from my Rosa. . . . You can't imagine Daddy's joy as well! And he was so satisfied with your great little letter to him! which is so gracious."[36] Pedro II would at once arrange for his immediate return, she assured her husband.

On April 29, 1870, the count d'Eu entered Rio de Janeiro in triumph. He was restored to his wife, who could once again live in her own house. The thirteen months' separation and Gaston's experiences had not lessened the couple's mutual devotion and closeness, but it did alter the dynamics of their relationship. Writing to his wife from Paraguay in the middle of March, Gaston d'Orléans commented on "this constant diarrhea I have here has made me extremely emaciated and weak; my phlegm had increased due, I believe, to the excessive heat." His health problems became chronic. As late as February 1873 he was taking quinine for what he thought might be malaria attacks, "picked up I don't know where."[37] Probably during his time in Paraguay, he did become infected by one or more tropical diseases that the physicians could not diagnose, much less cure. But there was a larger dimension to his health problems that the princess well understood: "Gaston is better today, but still is not well and is very bronchial. He wrote to Feijó [their physician] today about his complaints, but I would be very pleased if Feijó could come and spend a day here in order to examine him carefully and drive these ideas of sickness from his head. I am sure that he does suffer; but the imagination can do much and even make illnesses intensify."[38] Replying to his father's request for information about his recent experiences, Gaston acknowledged and identified the psychological tensions underlying his ill health. "As for my writing about Paraguay I am totally incapable of doing this henceforward for some time. The Paraguayan war has provided me with some good memories; but it has wiped me out intellectually and has created an invincible repugnance for any prolonged business or work."[39]

D. Isabel and the count d'Eu, 1870, on his return from Paraguay

Courtesy of the Fundação Grão Pará, Petrópolis

   The count d'Eu was, no less than his wife, a product of the prevailing system of gender relations. He had been brought up to believe in and to fulfill a model of manliness: real men don't cry, don't shirk responsibility, and don't falter under stress. In Paraguay prior to the death of López, the count d'Eu had conspicuously failed to meet these expectations, a failure evident to the emperor, the generals, and the leading politicians, who all embodied power and exemplified manliness. His visible failure bred in Gaston d'Orléans a feeling of guilt, a sense of inadequacy, and a fear of responsibility. Recurring sickness and increasing deafness both reflected and served as a release from these tensions. Sickness also justified his avoiding contact with the outside world and not shouldering responsibilities. "Given my character, the only life that suits my health is a life of complete tranquility and isolation," he told his former tutor.[40]

In March 1870, writing to his wife about his state of health and her desire to visit Europe again, the count d'Eu observed, "it appears to me that I would recover more completely in a quiet corner of Brazil, such as Novo Friburgo or Baependi, than amidst the bustle of Europe." Nonetheless, if D. Isabel wanted to go to Europe, he would consent to the plan. This letter indicates a shift in the dynamics of their relationship. Previously, Gaston viewed his wife essentially as an extension of himself. He made the decisions, and he controlled whatever she did. In July 1869, for example, he had written to her from Paraguay: "I am happy to learn that you have finished reading Mme de Motteville; you ought also to be satisfied that by persevering you have obtained this result. Now, my dear pet, I am allowing you to read what will entertain you. I only ask you to consult your father before starting on a book so that you won't read undesirable novels or anything that might stuff your head with trivialities."[41] The count did not immediately abandon this patronizing conduct, to which D. Isabel did not object, it being a wife's duty to obey. But as time passed he came to depend more and more on her to share in the making of decisions and to support him in his moments of self-doubt. Although prevailing restrictions on women meant that she could not take his place in dealings with the outside world, the princess did shield and protect him as much as she could from external pressures, and she provided the comfort that made interaction with the outside world more tolerable for him. In 1877, Gaston, writing to congratulate his former tutor who had just made a late marriage, described what D. Isabel meant to him:

You know my preference for being alone, a preference that borders on misanthropy. But I can assure you from experience that life shared with a person whose interests are so identified with our own as to make necessary no shadow of concealment one from the other is the best support, the most valuable resource for surviving moments of discouragement. And these moments of discouragement, which your physical sufferings make inevitable, are thanks to my peculiar and little enviable character even more frequent in my case.[42]

In 1870, this psychological dependence on D. Isabel was not yet complete, but it existed and explains why he agreed, despite his own preferences, to visit Europe. Early in July, Pedro II informed them that he intended to make in the following year a long-intended and repeatedly postponed journey to Europe. During his absence his elder daughter would serve as regent. If she and Gaston were to make their trip, they would have to leave almost at once, returning by the end of April 1871. "You know that we have less than a month that we can be together," she wrote to her mother on July 26. "I am very pleased about the trip to Europe, but it does have its sad side, which is leaving you and Daddy all by yourselves. If only we could take you with us!" The sole cause for concern was the sudden outbreak of the war between France and Prussia but, as D. Isabel commented, "what matters for us personally is that in England itself we shall be entirely secure."[43] By the time they reached London, late in September, the French had suffered crushing defeats, and Paris lay under siege. Among the refugees from that city was the countess of Barral, staying with the princess of Joinville, D. Isabel's aunt.

Writing to the countess almost twenty years later, the count d'Eu fondly recalled the last months of 1870, spent in his father's home near Hampton Court. "I have never since felt so much calm, namely, since the time at Bushy [Park] where we had you as a neighbor at Twickenham." At the start of January 1871, he wrote to Pedro II, pleading for more time. "Over half of our leave has already elapsed without our realizing it, and it would be sad for us to see it end without being able to make use of the better weather in order to take the waters. These observations are specially relevant should Y. M. decide to delay your visit," either because of the need for him to stay in

Brazil to oversee the enactment of a program of reforms or because of the continuing state of war in France. "If the departure of Y. M. has to be delayed, I beg you to give us an extension, as many months as you choose, to the leave you gave us."[44]

At the end of January, D. Isabel and her husband left London for a visit to Italy, traveling by way of Vienna where she intended to see D. Leopoldina, who had recently given birth to her fourth child, another son. En route, the princess received news that her sister had contracted typhoid fever. At first kept out of the sickroom, she was allowed to see her sister when all hope of recovery was lost. D. Leopoldina died on February 7, 1871, twenty-three and a half years old. Her sister accompanied the body to Coburg for the burial. "My good Leopoldina whom I loved so much and who loved me so much," the princess lamented to her father-in-law, "my only sister, the trusty companion of all my childhood and my youth!" "Faith is indeed the only consolation for such a loss! Leopoldina was so good that she is in Heaven!" "After these sad events I could not go on with our intended trip to Italy," she continued. "I passionately desire to be back again at that dear Bushy. I have spent such wonderful days there!"[45]

To D. Isabel's credit she did not think only of herself at this moment. She realized that her mother would be devastated by the loss. Three of her four children were now dead. "By the last Liverpool line mail boat Gaston wrote to you, I could do no more than weep and to pray. Remember my dear Mummy that you still have a daughter, and for the love of God don't fall sick on me! The horrible misfortune I have experienced, the worst that I have had up to now, is more than enough. Poor August! I feel so sorry for him! And the four little boys!"[46] A sudden and unexpected death of a family member is always upsetting, especially if the family is small and close-knit. For the princess, who had no offspring of her own, the loss of her sister created an emotional void that she tried to fill by greater closeness to and dependence upon her parents.

Pedro II shared his daughter's fear that D. Teresa Cristina might fall sick and die of grief. He had already affirmed his intention of going to Europe in May 1871. On learning of D. Leopoldina's death, he wrote: "I am persisting with the journey; above all for the sake of your mother who fortunately I have been able to cheer up largely through the idea of this journey."[47] D. Isabel and her husband had therefore to forsake the delights of Europe and return to Brazil. They arrived at Rio de Janeiro on May 1. D. Isabel found herself at the heart of a new and unfamiliar world in which she now occupied a central and testing role. It was her father who had placed her there.

The emperor was indifferent to the trappings and perquisites that go with power, but for power itself he cared everything. His habitual caution and lack of ostentation disguised how tightly he controlled public affairs and how adamant he was in refusing to share power. These same qualities also disguised his tenacity of purpose, of which D. Isabel was fully aware. As she commented to her husband, "You know how he carries on when he sets his heart on something." During the second half of the 1860s, Pedro II worked towards two goals, as a political observer commented: "It was notorious that the emperor particularly supported two ideas: the extermination of López in Paraguay and the liberty of slaves in Brazil."[48] The first goal accomplished in March 1870, Pedro II turned at once to achieving the second. The abolition of slavery in the United States following the defeat of the South in the Civil War had left Brazil, along with Spain's colonies in the Caribbean, as the only areas in the New World countenancing slavery. In March 1871, the emperor named a new cabinet, led by the viscount of Rio Branco and committed to a broad program of reforms, including the gradual extinction of slavery.

This program would be presented in the Speech from the Throne when the new legislative session opened at the start of May. But Pedro II would be in Europe, not in Brazil, when the debates began on the government's bill on slavery. By thus removing himself, he undercut the bill's opponents. They could not denounce the emperor for inhibiting by his presence an open debate on the cabinet's bill. Instead, he left the country in the hands of an inexperienced young woman. "I view with dread the emperor's journey," one leading politician wrote to another. "Should I be anxious? Reassure me." In the words of a political commentator, "it was then reported and generally believed that the emperor's intention was not to return to Brazil if the chambers failed to pass the law."[49]

Having previously kept his daughter excluded from public affairs, Pedro II now found both her and her inexperience a useful tactical

Courtesy of the Arquivo Histórico do Museu Imperial, Petrópolis

weapon. It was the viscount of Rio Branco, head of the cabinet, who would effectively be in control during the emperor's absence, but Pedro II appreciated that D. Isabel had to be given some guidance on her role as regent. On May 3, the same day that he delivered the Speech from the Throne, the emperor gave D. Isabel a long memorandum. It began: "My daughter, an intelligent sense of duty is our best guide; however, the councils of your Father will be of assistance to you."[50] There followed detailed advice on how to govern Brazil. The cabinet presented a bill granting Pedro II permission to leave the country and declaring D. Isabel regent with full powers. This law was enacted on May 15. Five days later, D. Isabel took the oath as regent, and on May 25 her parents and a large entourage left for Europe.

D. Isabel's total lack of experience and her ignorance of politics do not seem to have caused the emperor any concern. The reason for his equanimity is evident from a passage in his memorandum of advice of May. "So that my daughter's role in public affairs will not give the ministry the least cause for suspicion, it is indispensable that my son-in-law, otherwise the natural adviser of my daughter, behaves in a way that gives no hint that he influences, even by his councils, my daughter's opinions."[51] In other words, the count d'Eu, utilizing the innate ability to command and to take action that distinguished men from women (or so it was believed), would enable D. Isabel to carry out her duties as regent. He would have to remain discreetly behind the scenes so as to avoid giving possible offense, the more so since he was not a Brazilian and therefore suspect. In fact, at the formal ceremony in which D. Isabel took the oath of office as regent, her husband was denied permission to walk at her side. Rather than being relegated to the role of spectator, Gaston d'Eu preferred not to attend.

Prior to becoming regent, D. Isabel had no incentive to concern herself with public affairs, as the postscript of a letter written in August 1866 shows. "Mummy, please tell Daddy that they have asked me to remind him of the petitions that I gave him on March 14 and 19. Do me this favor; I often forget the messages they give me to pass on."[52] Now, at the age of almost twenty-five, the princess found herself transacting the nation's business with the cabinet ministers, seven men ranging in age from thirty-five to sixty-two, all college or university graduates and most of them experienced in public affairs. She had power over some 11 million people scattered over half a continent.

On June 3, D. Isabel held her first *despacho* with the cabinet. Her reaction to the experience is graphically revealed in a letter sent to her father the next day (see In Her Own Voice below), a letter that attests to her innate good sense and her powers of observation. The scene in the "little corner room" is brought vividly to life, and the dynamics of the meeting are intelligently presented. What was to her novel and unusual was a scene utterly familiar to her father, who had been meeting the ministers in *despacho* for over thirty years.

D. Isabel struggled with the gender contradictions her new role entailed. She was "in a curious way a kind of emperor without changing my skin." A collapse of the ministry would give her *calças pardas*, a catchphrase best translated as "caught in a predicament" but literally meaning "in stained trousers." Since no respectable woman at that time wore trousers, D. Isabel used instead "soiled dress." D. Isabel's letter indicates that she could manage affairs quite deftly, as her handling of the proposed resignation of her former teacher indicates, but it also shows that she had no thought of distinguishing her style of government from that of her father. Her reply to the delegations from the two chambers was, indeed, "laconic like yours." In fact, Gaston d'Orléans asked the viscount of Rio Branco what form D. Isabel's reply should take, and the latter recommended that used by the emperor. The princess consented, in part because men knew best, but in part because she desired, above all else, to keep "the shack . . . standing" until she handed it back to her father on his return ten months later.

In Her Own Voice

Laranjeiras, June 4, 1871

Dear Father,

Yesterday I had my first *despacho*. But let me remark first that when Daddy left it seemed to me such a strange thing to see myself in a curious way a kind of emperor without changing my skin, without having a beard, and without having *a very large belly*. Forgive me, that's naughty. Speaking of bellies let me tell you that Daddy beats out Valponto whom I have seen several times since you left. But let's talk about the *despacho,* held in the City Palace in the little corner room. 5 ministers were there when I arrived. Missing were [Francisco de Negreiros] Saiao [Lobato] who came later and the minister of Marine who never came. When I entered the room, I was absolutely appalled; 5 enormous portfolios, some of them stuffed full in a monstrous fashion, were awaiting me. Fortunately everything turned out to be easier than I judged at first glance. Happily a great part of the papers were letters to the Sultan, the Emperor of Austria, etc., etc.— and I don't know if there wasn't one to the Emperor of China, because only the addresses show whom they are for—for me to sign, as well as an infinity of Baronies, Viscounties, etc. The first to which I put my best scrawl with malice aforethought was one making the baron of Prados a viscount. I also signed the retirement of Pereira Jorge. Luckily my purse held good goose quill pens of every color, similar to those that Daddy took, which greatly aided my task. There were also some resignations to sign to which I did not object, since the reasons given seemed good and I don't know the individuals. Let those who know more assume responsibility. On one case alone did I make a comment. It involved [Padre José de] Santa Maria [do Amaral]'s requesting his resignation due to sickness from the post of inspector of public education. I asked the minister if Daddy had been informed of this; he told me no. I thereupon concluded that I, who had been his pupil and who hold him in high regard, ought not to accept his resignation immediately on the minister's first proposing it but instead on the minister's recommending it again after discussing with me why he should not retain the job. [Domingos José Nogueira] Jaguaribe seemed almost as much a novice as I, since the others did not hesitate at times to tell him what he ought to do.

Daddy will have seen in the newspapers the debates on the vote of thanks [to the Speech from the Throne], which in the end was passed in the form the government wanted. The kettle came near to being tipped over and I would have had, I can't say, "soiled trousers" but a soiled dress from the gravy thus spilled, which I would have had to clean up and which would not have been at all pleasant. There seems to have been too much touchiness between the ministers. Anyway, the shack remains, for now, standing, and I very much hope to hand it over before it falls down. Tomorrow I am going to the City Palace to receive the delegations on the subject [the "Vote of Thanks"] from the Senate and Chamber of Deputies. To them I will give a response, laconic like yours, in these terms. "I acknowledge with thanks, in the emperor's name, the sentiments that you present on behalf of the

Senate (or of the Chamber of Deputies) and the cooperation that each promises to give the government." And that's it; and so farewell until tomorrow morning when I will close my letter. You will have already grasped that my face is not swollen, nor has it prevented me from writing so much to you. Good-bye!

Forgive me, forgive me a thousand times. I have a splitting headache. I have only looked where the Southern Cross should be and the sky is full of clouds.

Your most loving daughter

Isabel Countess d'Eu[53]

One month into her regency, D. Isabel made clear to the duke of Nemours, her father-in-law, that she intended to leave the everyday business of government well alone. "As to the affairs of government I was very afraid that they would torment me more than they have. As long as no change in ministry, dissolution, or adjournment of the chambers occurs, everything keeps to the routine. Accordingly, I am obliged to leave the house only one day a week, in order to receive petitions, to hear what some people have to tell me, or to meet with the ministers. But I would be in difficulties if I did not have beside me my good Gaston who helps me so much and gives me such good advice."[54] This last comment was not written to satisfy the duke of Nemours's paternal pride. At the start of September, complaining to Pedro II that she had received no letter from him by the latest mail boat, D. Isabel remarked that she would be justified were she to tell him that "the high affairs of state" left her no time for writing. "To tell you that would, however, be a most terrible lie since, having above all Gaston to do the greater part of the chores, I have more than enough time to sleep as much or more than previously, to take walks, and even to read novels."[55]

D. Isabel's attitude toward her appointed role of regent did not stem from want of knowledge or lack of intelligence, both of which are evident in her letters to her father. Nor did she lack guile or determination. One of the monarch's prerogatives was that of bestowing titles of nobility—baron, viscount, count, marquis, duke—on anyone deemed worthy. "I confess that I found a way to grant Feijó [her physician] the title of baron, and the minister of the Empire [Interior] gave me an opening by remarking that he deserved something in return for the way he acted during the student question. I delayed his nomination to the 14th [of March, the empress's birthday] on which day he will be made baron of Santa Isabel."[56] With these rare exceptions, D. Isabel did not seek while regent to establish a separate and autonomous identity or to create a direct relationship with the Brazilian people. There existed in her mind no likelihood of her father, then aged forty-five and in very good health, dying in the near future. She could expect to spend another quarter century or more in private life. Any attempt by the princess to take the initiative while she was regent would have required stepping outside her assigned roles and into the public arena, inviting comment and criticism. Such a step would have involved a profound change in her relationship with both her husband and her father.

The government's bill for the gradual extinction of slavery gave freedom to all children of slave women born from the date of the bill's enactment. D. Isabel never faltered in her public commitment to the measure, and her support helped to secure its passage. However, she took no active role in the struggle to force the bill through the Chamber of Deputies in the face of unrelenting opposition. To her father she even expressed doubts about the wisdom of enacting the bill that year, "since so little time remains before the session closes and given the agitated state of mind visible in the planters who have declared their opinion." D. Isabel signed the law on September 27, 1871. Informed by the princess of the fact, the countess of Barral aptly commented, "Papa never showed himself more your friend than in giving you the opportunity to sign this act or law." Her signature "provided you with the occasion during your regency to link your name to this great event, and it is a glory that he renounced in your favor. Long live the parents who are not egoists and the children who are thankful and appreciative."[57] These remarks effectively checked any tendency that D. Isabel may have had to overemphasize her role in the passage of the Law of Free Birth, as the measure was known.

The final months of D. Isabel's regency ran smoothly, troubled only by student protests in the law and medical schools. She had become accustomed but not reconciled to her work. "Tomorrow I have a *despacho* and a public audience. When finally free of these tasks I will give thanks to God. At times they are enough to put one in a rage, but happily they don't last long, and I only unburden myself in private."[58] The last letter she wrote to her father before his return to Brazil contained, quite exceptionally, a reasoned critique of his style of governing, indicating that the princess did understand the workings of power.

> What troubles me most is the *poder pessoal* (personal power), of which they accuse my good Daddykins, and which I judge must arise from the stubbornness they attribute to you. I will put my cards on the table. The fault is not yours, at least not yours alone. Daddy has intelligence, has a will (tenacity or stubbornness if you wish), and the means to make it work. Our ministers in general are less firm, tenacious, or stubborn, and therefore the weaker gives way. What to do? Don't judge yourself to be so infallible, show more confidence in them, don't intervene so much in matters that are entirely within their mandate (and I will have more of your time), and if some day you can no longer give them your confidence or you see that public opinion (the real one) is against them, into the street with them![59]

Her father's other fault as ruler, D. Isabel pointed out, was that, while unwilling to reward and advance his personal friends who had rendered good service, he was quick to reward and advance those who publicly opposed him: "The best way for them to act is to speak against Sr. D. Pedro 2° in order to obtain from him everything (due not to any fear that he feels but to his excessive scrupulousness)." Concerned that she had overstepped her filial role, she closed her letter: "These are the councils or political testament of your chatterbox with whom you can discuss all these points when you are here. Forgive me for so much boldness, but it is for your good and the good of everyone."

Whether or no Pedro II ever talked with his daughter about her observations, we do not know. Probably he did not refer to them or passed them by with a noncommittal comment. D. Isabel's suggestions certainly did not produce any change in his behavior. On returning to Rio on March 30, 1872, he reassumed the reins of government as though he had never been away. He did not consult his daughter about anything that had occurred during his time in Europe. He did not, any more than he had done previously, admit her to the governance of Brazil. Early in May 1872 the opponents of the Law of Free Birth succeeded in defeating the government in power by a single vote in the Chamber of Deputies. The viscount of Rio Branco requested a dissolution from the emperor. Pedro II called a meeting of the Council of State to seek its advice on the request. Both D. Isabel and the count d'Eu were members of the council, but neither was notified of the meeting. The emperor did not need or want their advice. D. Isabel found herself and her husband once again relegated to private life.

For the couple the change was not resented. The count d'Eu had found handling the business of government on his wife's behalf so stressful that the result was a renewed bout of ill health. D. Isabel had other things on her mind. It now seemed possible, even probable that she was at last about to fulfill her fifth role as wife, giving birth to her husband's children.

5

MOTHER, 1872–1881

D. ISABEL WITH HER FIRST SON, PEDRO, BORN IN OCTOBER 1875

Courtesy of the Fundação Grão Pará, Petrópolis

A woman's destiny in the Western world of the nineteenth century was to bear and to raise children. The qualities that made women inferior to men were, prevailing opinion held, precisely those that fitted her to be a mother. A woman's worst fate was to be an "old maid," *uma solteirona*, unmarried and not a mother. Motherhood did not depend on formal marriage. In Brazil, many women bore children within what may be termed consensual unions, at times short, sometimes long lasting. Whether a woman became a mother within or outside wedlock, one thing was likely. She would bear many children. For a woman to give birth ten, twelve, or even fourteen times was not uncommon.

Several factors explain this high rate of female fertility. Death claimed many children at birth or in their first years. At all levels of society, children, from an early age, were a resource. For the poor their labor would contribute more to the family economy than their maintenance cost. In the middle and upper classes, children constituted an essential tool for the advancement of family fortunes. Among royalty, a large family, especially sons, assured the succession to the throne. The need of men to demonstrate their virility by fathering a large family also played its part, as the diary entry made by a leading politician indicates: "*My* child Paulino was born Friday, April 21, 1834, at 11 and a half in the morning, in Tapacorá."[1] Large families were not necessarily deliberate. The relationship between conception and the menstrual cycle was not understood, either in official medicine or in popular lore. Women might well enter marriage without understanding the connection between sexual intercourse and pregnancy. (The author's own great-grandmother, born in 1848, did not grasp the connection until after she had given birth to one or two of her eleven children.) Methods of contraception were undeveloped, although not necessarily ineffective.

Childbearing was nothing less than dangerous, even deadly, at every stage from early pregnancy to postpartum. During late pregnancy, toxemia would cause a miscarriage and could also kill the mother or cause total blindness. Miscarriage and childbirth could cause hemorrhaging that unchecked would bring death. A stillbirth could easily kill the mother. Postpartum infections, above all puerperal fever, were the more likely and the more deadly due to the absolute lack of antisepsis (sterile cleanliness). These dangers were enhanced by the incompetence of official medicine, all too evident in the sphere of obstetrics. Popular medicine, based as it was on experience and tradition, was almost certainly less harmful, but even a midwife's accumulated knowledge could not prevent infection and death.

In fulfilling her destiny as the producer of new life, a woman faced during the nineteenth century the very real possibility of being the cause of her own death. The responses to this dilemma, for such it was, were diverse. Some women accepted the possibility of death as part of their fate and a consequence of their duty. Other women took to their beds and used sickness—real, psychosomatic, or feigned—to avoid sexual intercourse and so pregnancy. If their husbands sought sexual solace elsewhere, that was an unlovely but condoned facet of maleness. Some women took such precautions as they could (not necessarily with their husband's consent or knowledge) to prevent pregnancies. Many women sought psychological reassurance, consolation, and distraction in religion. This tendency was sanctioned by dominant opinion that regarded religion as integral to women's role as guardians and perpetuators of the established order. Religion enabled women better to exemplify purity, morality, and obedience.

D. Isabel very much belonged to the world of married women. She defined herself in terms of motherhood. "I so much want to be Mother of your child, to have a child by you whom I love so much, whom I love above all else, my love!!!"[2] Despite the couple's best efforts, medical advice, and prayers and vows to God, the princess did not become pregnant during the first five years of her marriage. Evidence in her letters on her gynecological condition does not indicate any specific problem that would of itself have prevented conception. The couple's second visit to Europe offered, as their aunt D. Francisca pointed out to Pedro II, the opportunity for "Isabel to consult a good *specialist* doctor."[3] The princess probably did so, because in the middle of May 1871, shortly after her return to Brazil, her menstrual period was considerably overdue. The advice and treatment, if any, she received in Europe would have given grounds for optimism about her condition. Her parents, then on the eve of their departure, drew up what were termed a "short" and a "long" program for their time in Europe. If their daughter were indeed pregnant, then Pedro II and

D. Teresa Cristina would return by the end of 1871 in time for the birth. If not, then they would keep to their original plans.

As the weeks passed without the return of her period, D. Isabel became increasingly exasperated. On June 21, she wrote to her mother: "About our business, there is nothing positive; it's unbearable!! Feijó [her personal physician] continues, however, to say that there is more probability of its being *yes* than no. *We will see!*" She had to wait for some weeks. On August 5, Gaston wrote to Pedro II: "Unfortunately we have to inform you definitely that on our side there is no longer any reason for the short program. This is for us a huge disappointment."[4] The end of D. Isabel's possible pregnancy meant more than a personal disappointment for the couple. The prospect that she would never have offspring meant that the throne would after her death pass to one of her nephews, the sons of D. Leopoldina. When the emperor returned to Rio de Janeiro at the end of March 1872, he brought back with him his two eldest grandsons, Pedro Augusto and Augusto. They were to be raised by their grandparents in Brazil, so as to prepare them for their role as heirs to their aunt.

However necessary this step may have been to secure the dynasty's future, the presence of her nephews was a standing rebuke to D. Isabel for her failure to fulfill her mission to be a mother. The reproach was not long justified. In the second part of 1872 her menstrual period was once more overdue, and this time there was no question that she was pregnant. However, the good news was more than balanced by concerns about her physical state. In addition to dizzy spells, avulsion to eating, and sickness, she began to discharge blood and to display other worrying obstetrical symptoms. In October 1872, she suffered a pronounced miscarriage.

It is difficult to overestimate the psychological impact on D. Isabel of this miscarriage. Her sister's death from typhoid fever in February 1871 had distressed her deeply. Her family's history of pregnancy and childbirth gave little or no cause for confidence. Her paternal grandmother, Empress Leopoldina, died in 1826 after miscarrying her eighth child. Her aunt, Queen Maria II of Portugal, died in 1854 from physical exhaustion during the delivery of her eleventh child. Gaston d'Orléans's mother, the duchess of Nemours, died following the birth of her fifth child, a daughter who did not survive. Another of D. Isabel's aunts, D. Francisca, princess of Joinville, experienced two miscarriages in succession that put her life in danger. In January 1867, the count d'Eu had reported that "Isabel is very distraught by the death of one of her childhood friends, who died in childbirth nine months after her marriage."[5] Her own sister miscarried during her first pregnancy. The princess would not renounce her hopes of motherhood but, at the end of 1872, she had every reason to fear what pregnancy might bring.

D. Isabel sought strength and comfort in the Christian faith. During the nineteenth century, men continued to control the institutional structures of the churches, both Protestant and Catholic, but new types of religious devotion emerged. Both in format and in the message conveyed they catered to women and their concerns. In the Catholic Church, the cult of the Virgin Mary, whose Immaculate Conception (birth without taint of sin) was declared a dogma in 1854, appealed strongly to women as did adoration of the "Sacred Heart of Jesus," declared a universal feast of the Church in 1856. These new forms of devotion gave married women in particular both validation—the Virgin Mary being the universal, all-loving, and all-powerful mother—and reassurance, "the heart of Christ" being "the symbol of the total love of His person."[6] God, being love, ordered the course of the individual's life for the best. Trust in His mercy and beneficence made all trials bearable.

Religion had been an integral part of D. Isabel's upbringing; its practice and its precepts she accepted without question. Both her mother and the countess of Barral were pious Catholics. So was her husband, who advised her in October 1865, when she consulted him on a religious matter, "there can never be an excess of devotional practice, especially for women who don't have as many serious pursuits in this world as men do." In 1868, when staying at Caxambu spa, the princess made a vow to erect a church there dedicated to St. Elizabeth of Hungary (known as Santa Isabel de Hungria in Portuguese), in the hope that God would give her a child. This natural piety became much more intense following her presence at D. Leopoldina's deathbed in February 1871. "Faith is indeed the only consolation for such a loss!" the princess observed.[7] The Catholic Church now became for her a bulwark of support, a consolation in times of sorrow, and an assurance of God's beneficence.

D. Isabel became increasingly willing to defend the Church and its teachings against all comers, no matter how exalted. During his trip to Europe in 1871 and 1872, Pedro II made visits both to the pope in the Vatican and to the king of Italy in Florence. Since the king had recently seized the city of Rome from the pope, D. Isabel chastised her father for the latter visit. "Couldn't you have taken a rest or, if your legs wouldn't stop moving, couldn't you have gone to see the sights?" Two letters later she rebuked him on a different subject: "I am going to start with a reprimand. Not even a short line for me, yet you find time to visit George Sand, a woman of much talent, it is true, but also so immoral! . . . However much you try to preserve your incognito, everyone always knows who D. Pedro d'Alcântara is, and shouldn't he be above all else a good Catholic and keep away from everything that is immoral?"[8]

George Sand (the pen name of Aurore Dupin) was a pioneer feminist. Married to an abusive husband, she had left him and moved with her two children to Paris, where she made her living by journalism and writing. To enable her to move freely in literary and bohemian circles, she often adopted male dress. She had numerous love affairs, notably with Frédéric Chopin and Alfred de Musset but also one with an actress. In politics, she was a republican and a radical. She was everything that D. Isabel had been brought up to know that a woman should not be. The princess probably did not expect to influence what her father did, and, moreover, at the end of the letter chastising him for visiting the king of Italy, she apologized, as was her habit, for speaking her mind. But speak her mind she did.

D. Isabel was determined to make a third visit to Europe in search of medical advice following her regency in 1871 and 1872. "You will understand that it can't be immediately upon my parents' return following such a long absence," she told the duke of Nemours. Her miscarriage in October 1872 made the princess all the more anxious to depart. Shortly after the miscarriage and perhaps as a result of it, the count d'Eu suffered another bout of ill health that was, as D. Isabel grasped, basically psychosomatic: "I am sure that he does suffer; but the imagination can do much and even make illnesses intensify."[9] The couple finally left for Europe on April 19, 1873.

They spent their first weeks in Paris. In June 1872, the French National Assembly not only revoked the banishment of the Orléans family but also restored to it the properties confiscated by Napoléon III. Gaston's father and uncles had returned to live in France, which meant that the couple were kept extremely occupied. "But what compares to life in Paris?" D. Isabel enthused to her father in May. "I haven't had a moment even to scratch myself." Five days later Gaston, living in his native land for the first time in twenty-five years, told Pedro II: "Paris is very pretty, does not resemble any other city, and I am very content to have seen it."[10] More important, in Paris the princess consulted a specialist, who advised her to seek treatment at Bagnères-de-Luchon in the French Pyrenees, a spa with forty-eight sulfur-laden springs.

The couple first visited the Universal Exposition in Vienna, spending time at Badgastein spa in Austria (for Gaston's health) and arriving at Luchon early in August. There they stayed for some two months, accompanied for much of the time by the countess of Barral. In October, after leaving Luchon, D. Isabel made a pilgrimage to Lourdes. In a grotto there in 1858, Bernadette Soubirous had several times seen the Virgin Mary, who told her: "I am the Immaculate Conception." The grotto with its springs soon became the site of miraculous cures. It attracted pilgrims, particularly after the railroad reached the town. By the early 1870s the grotto was attracting group pilgrimages involving thousands of people. D. Isabel, seeking a child, was among them. She sent D. Teresa Cristina "the rosary that I bought for you Mummy at Lourdes and which was blessed and touched on the rock and 9 medals of Our Lady that have also been blessed and placed on the rock."[11]

Whether the cause was her pilgrimage, the waters of Luchon, or medical skill, D. Isabel was rewarded. Writing from Venice on November 29, 1873, the count d'Eu reported that his wife "frequently complains of dizziness, avulsion to food, and sickness, but nothing can be said for certain until after December 1." On her father's birthday, December 2, D. Isabel wrote him a letter of best wishes, to which she added a postscript: "Daddy mine, pray earnestly for your little

Courtesy of the Arquivo Histórico do Museu Imperial, Petrópolis

daughter and your little grandchild, because I am now almost certain of the fact." She now behaved with the greatest caution. Only at the end of December did the couple move to Paris, where D. Isabel was examined by a leading obstetrician. "I believe that we can consider Isabel's condition as certain," Gaston reported on January 19. "Dr. [Jean Marie] Depaul who examined her at her request some days ago has declared that all the indications are that she is three months pregnant. She is well but is in a state of constant disquiet and anxiety, principally due to the sea voyage that she rightfully fears."[12]

The question of a sea voyage became urgent because Article 2 of the couple's marriage contract required that their first child be born in Brazil. Early in March, D. Isabel wrote to her father: "With great willingness and pleasure on our part you would be the first person to hold in your arms our dear little child! But the idea that I might run the risk of losing him and even of making his health suffer has kept us here. In a few days we expect to have a medical consultation on the subject, and the result will be sent to you, Daddy mine, to decide on." A few days later, as the medical report was being dispatched to Rio de Janeiro, she gave voice to her fears again:

> Daddy mine, consider well all the risks and dangers that mother and child will run if they embark on the voyage before the birth of our child. In view of this, I believe that you will not hesitate in letting us leave here only in July [after the birth]. Our greatest desire would be for the birth to take place there if we did not run the risk of losing what amounts at this moment to our complete happiness. Daddy mine, consider that you might lose not just your little grandchild but your daughter as well because I don't know how I would endure the loss of all my present hopes in the circumstances I would then face in such a weakened condition.[13]

All his daughter's pleadings and warnings did not move Pedro II, a man for whom the performance of duty came first and foremost and who assumed childbearing to be females' assigned lot. "I would regret it profoundly if my grandchild, the heir presumptive to the throne, were born outside of Brazil," he wrote on February 18, 1874.[14] He could and did point to the provisions of Article 2 of the marriage contract. The question was referred to the Council of State, which, as might be expected of a group of elderly males very much under Pedro II's influence, advised that only if there existed a virtual certainty of disaster during the period of travel should the birth occur in Europe.

D. Isabel, now almost twenty-eight years old, could not bring herself to disobey her father. The count d'Eu, while arguing against such a strict interpretation of the marriage contract, would not on this matter break with the emperor. In May, therefore, the couple embarked at Bordeaux, taking with them a French midwife. "The *Gironde* on which we are traveling touches at Corunna, Lisbon and Dakar. Suppose we have to remain behind in one of these places?! God, the Virgin Mary, and all the Saints have mercy on me!?"[15] No problems arose during the three-week voyage. On June 23, D. Isabel reached Rio de Janeiro. She took up residence at Laranjeiras and there awaited the birth.

At midnight on July 25, 1874, the princess began to feel her labor pains. Four doctors were summoned to attend her. Also present was the countess of Barral, who had come from France to be present at the birth. The next morning it was realized that the baby was in danger of asphyxiation. The physicians proved totally incapable of inducing birth. The delivery dragged on for fifty hours. By the evening of the 27th the child was dead, but the body could not be extracted from the womb and the princess's life saved until two in the morning on the 28th. As the count d'Eu sorrowfully told his former tutor, "Our little girl was at term, perfectly formed, very pretty, with a large quantity of curly blond hair extraordinarily long and thick."[16]

Throughout her daughter's "horrible sufferings," the empress wrote in her diary, "she behaved with an incredible courage." "Thank God, the princess has recovered wonderfully," her husband informed his former tutor on August 8; "she has almost no fever and is calm, although sad, but uncomplaining; religious beliefs are helping her to bear this trial." As D. Isabel noted a year later, "at least I had the great consolation of seeing our beloved little girl baptized." In retrospect, when writing her recollections, she saw her loss as a critical moment in her life. "My sister's death and the loss of my first child, during delivery, July 28, 1874, have been my only sorrows during 44 years!"[17]

His daughter's anguish and the loss of his granddaughter affected even Pedro II, usually the most controlled and stoic of men. "After the joy of my daughter's arrival, how much have I had to suffer," he wrote on August 14 to an acquaintance in France. "Happily she is almost on her feet again and everything makes me hope that she will surround me with grandchildren."[18] The emperor's reaction was typically male in both the self-centeredness of his grief and in the attitude toward women and their role. No matter how appalling her ordeal had been, everyone expected D. Isabel, as heir to the throne, to produce children. On one level, the princess accepted that she was bound to perform this duty, and she did want a child to replace the baby she had lost. However, at another and deeper level, the prospect of once again experiencing conception, pregnancy, and delivery aroused feelings that she at first tried to suppress.

This internal struggle between duty and foreboding, together with the nightmare memory of her ordeal, resulted in moods of deep depression and in strong aversions and obsessions. D. Isabel sought escape and solace through household duties, social encounters, and religious activities. The countess of Barral devoted herself to keeping the princess constantly engaged and so distracted. "I have woken up every day at 5 1/2 wishing to be there in the Princess's room when she wakes up," she wrote from Petrópolis six weeks after the stillbirth, "and finding myself so far away [from her] makes me sad." The two filled their days with such diversions as the traditional "female" tasks of making cakes and cookies and sewing clothes. So great was the countess's success that the princess remarked in October, when the former *aia* was absent: "I am so used to her good company that I can't stand another day without seeing and talking to her."[19]

To remove D. Isabel from the Paço Isabel, which constantly recalled her loss and her suffering, the count d'Eu rented a furnished house in Petrópolis. To this residence, which the countess of Barral put in order, the princess and her husband moved on September 21, 1874. A modest one-story dwelling, the house was (and still is) attractively sited within large grounds. It so pleased the princess that the count d'Eu soon purchased the property, which became known as the Palácio da Princesa (Palace of the Princess).

Petrópolis, not Rio de Janeiro, now became the real center of D. Isabel's life. She felt most at ease in the town, where she could be herself. The social life there mirrored the aristocratic society she enjoyed in Europe. Her circle of acquaintances was composed mainly of childhood friends, of families in attendance at the court, and of foreign diplomats who spent the southern summer in Petrópolis. Early in November 1874, she commented: "This afternoon we went for a walk to the Public Gardens where the diplomats were playing or watching croquet. They seemed to be enjoying themselves." The countess of Barral, whose son Dominique was then serving as an attaché in the

French mission at Rio, belonged naturally to this circle. The larger world of Brazil hardly penetrated into D. Isabel's life in Petrópolis, as a comment she made in March 1875 to her father shows: "Thank you for your letter and the Speech from the Throne. Obviously I read the letter at once but the Speech I left for later on."[20]

What did command the princess's time and attention was the Catholic faith, attending Mass, going to confession, and participating in devotions such as the Adoration of the Eucharist. "We spent the entire day today in the Church, starting by hearing Mass there," she informed Gaston d'Orléans on October 15, their tenth wedding anniversary. "We were kept fully occupied and it did me good thus working for the Good Lord." In a letter written to the empress on November 28, D. Isabel reported that "we spent the entire morning chanting Vespers," and the countess added a note: "I am very tired from having washed the church." The princess's zeal was not limited to a weekly cleaning and decorating of the church at Petrópolis. During May 1875, for example, she was fully occupied with "the Month of Mary," during which special altars in the church were each day decorated with fresh flowers, with services in honor of the Virgin. "Petrópolis is emptying rapidly," D. Isabel wrote to her father on June 1, "but its church is very small, even for its permanent population."[21] She set her mind on the construction of a new church, one built in gothic style and of a size to bring glory to God, and this goal she pursued for the rest of her life.

In the months following the loss of her first child, D. Isabel became engrossed with "ultramontane piety," characterized by a historian as "a taste for flamboyant ceremony appealing to the heart rather than to the head" and as "a feminization of piety."[22] Ultramontane piety, controversial and divisive everywhere, aroused particular hostility in Brazil, where it offended established gender conventions. Churches in Brazil were viewed as public space, all elections being held in them. For women to take charge of the churches' interior meant that they intruded into the public sphere reserved for males. Catholic priests associated with ultramontane devotions such the Sacred Heart and Adoration of the Eucharist were often foreigners, as was Pe. Nicholas Germain, the curate in charge of Petrópolis. The cassocks that these priests wore marked them out from the mass of the clergy, who dressed like other men. Their piety, asceticism, and self-denial made these priests untrustworthy, almost traitors to their sex, in the eyes of most Brazilian males. Especially objectionable were the close relations the priests maintained with the females in their congregations, particularly in their role as confessor. Brazilian men simply could not believe that priests did not use the confessional to influence and direct women, thus usurping a right that belonged to fathers and husbands. Nor could men comprehend that women might view their priests as "honorary women," as part of the female network of support and advice that made marriage and the home bearable.

This hostility toward ultramontane piety underlay what was known as A Questão Religiosa (the Religious Question), which began early in 1873. Freemasons had played a leading role in the struggle for independence, and their lodges continued to be important centers for political and social activities. Many leading politicians, including the viscount of Rio Branco, head of the cabinet in 1873, were Masons. Several popes had issued orders forbidding Catholics to be Freemasons, but the imperial government (and the Portuguese before it) never permitted the publication in Brazil of the papal bulls (orders). Even though the papacy recognized the government's right to withhold its approval, the new ultramontane bishop of Olinda, a diocese in northeastern Brazil, found it intolerable that the pope should not be obeyed in matters of faith and morals. Young and impetuous, Dom Vital plunged into action, ordering an *irmandade* (lay brotherhood) attached to a parish church in Recife City to purge itself of all Freemasons. When the *irmandade* refused to obey, in January 1873 the bishop placed the parish church under an interdict; that is, no services could be held there. When the bishop of Pará followed his colleague's example, the quarrel became a crisis. The *irmandades* appealed to the imperial government, which ordered the prelates to withdraw the interdicts. In the middle of 1873, both bishops refused. The emperor was determined to assert the government's authority and bring the two men to order. The cabinet decided to lay criminal charges, for obstructing the law, against the bishops.

D. Isabel and the count d'Eu were at this time in Europe. The princess's letters left her father in no doubt as to her views. The

D. VITAL MARIA GONÇALVES DE OLI-
VEIRA, THE ULTRAMONTANE BISHOP OF
OLINDA

*Courtesy of the Museu Nacional Histórico,
Rio de Janeiro*

bishops could have been "more prudent," she granted, but "the government also wants to meddle too much." In her opinion, "we should defend the rights of the Brazilian citizen, and those of the Constitution, but what surety is there in all this, and in sworn oaths, if we don't give our first obedience to the Church!" Her husband's comment to Pedro II was both perceptive and percipient. "By giving them [the *irmandades*] support and significance, it [the government] is, it seems to me, entering a dead end, because the ecclesiastical power must resist to the point of suffering martyrdom, given that it is guided by principles superior to human laws and concerns."[23]

What the count d'Eu foresaw came about. In February and July 1874, the two bishops were tried and convicted. The sentences of four years' imprisonment with hard labor, the emperor commuted to simple imprisonment. Condemnation and imprisonment solidified support within the Brazilian Church for the bishops, who continued defiant. The government's victory achieved nothing. The Rio Branco cabinet fell in June 1875, and its successor, which was determined to bring the Religious Question to an end, forced a compromise on the emperor. A general amnesty covering all persons and acts involved in the dispute would be issued, and thereafter the papal chargé d'affaires in Rio would lift the interdicts. The necessary decree was, with Pedro II protesting to the last, issued on September 17, 1875. The confrontation was over, without the central issue being resolved.

The Church's defiance angered and the amnesty outraged the Freemasons and their sympathizers, who included what would be now termed the "progressive" sections of Brazilian society. The grant of the amnesty was widely ascribed to D. Isabel's influence. *O Mequetrefe*, an illustrated weekly, even published a cartoon, entitled "The Amnesty," in which the princess's head in profile eclipsed the sun, marked "Liberty." This belief was so widespread as to cause Pedro II to write in angry protest to the head of the cabinet. "A reading of today's newspapers obliges me to insist on the need to declare what is the truth. My daughter in no way influenced my mind nor did she try to have influence in the matter."[24] The emperor was correct. Neither the princess nor her husband ever took any public stand in favor of the bishops. To the Freemasons and their allies, however, D. Isabel's religious practices identified her with the bishops' cause. Although the princess never involved herself in public affairs, her silence during the controversy was held against her. That she did not speak out showed where her sympathies lay. Prevailing attitudes that saw lack of rationality, incapacity for public affairs, and emotional instability as innate to women made D. Isabel an easy target for demonizing. She became the embodiment and the agent of the forces of reaction that were holding back Brazil on the path to progress.

During the year following the stillbirth of July 1874, D. Isabel's health and state of mind prevented her, even if she had so desired, from refuting these accusations. A letter that the count d'Eu wrote to his father from Petrópolis on January 27, 1875, at the start of the southern summer reveals the princess's psychological condition:

> We are saddened to find that it [the summer] has had no favorable effect on Isabel's health. On the contrary she has had a return of the minor discharge that attracted [Dr.] Depaul's attention and which he got rid of. Since she has also formed an antipathy, in my view exaggerated, for all Brazilian doctors, her wish would be to return to Europe so that she can go again to Luchon. But the emperor naturally has not the least intention of consenting to that, preoccupied as he is with his own journey [to North America and Europe]. As a result of that the idea has come up of bringing Depaul to Brazil.[25]

At the start of April 1875 the princess knew she was pregnant again. "I am well, my little darling, and I also think that our darling little one is also well. Pray greatly for her and for your big darling who embraces you with all her heart." At the end of May, D. Isabel wrote in triumph: "You will be very happy when I tell you that during the morning I felt a movement that I can only attribute to our dear little child." In a footnote she added: "They have been stronger and more marked than on any other day this time." Two weeks later, she reported: "Our dear little one has given a good stretch and the countess of Barral felt the movement clearly. God! How I would like for the month of October to have come and gone! And gone *as we wish it to!* Pray to the Good Lord and to everyone in Heaven for us!"[26]

Her new pregnancy inflicted on D. Isabel an emotional strain and an acute psychological distress, the intensity and the depth of which are evident in the letter she wrote to her husband on June 11 (see In Her Own Voice below). That she refused point blank to let her father visit her on the first anniversary of the stillbirth was a rare, virtually unique, act of rebellion against him. That she persisted in her refusal shows how intense was the strain. Her condition worsened as the weeks passed. "Not only does she weep and lament without cause, but she does not want to be spoken to or even have others talk in her presence, so that all of us in the house are reduced to silence," Gaston d'Orléans told his father on August 2. "Today, even though she is not suffering physically, she has refused to leave her room (at 1 in the afternoon) so that she can dine there all alone and so that her personal maids have no reason to enter." A short stay at São Cristóvão brought some improvement, but she continued "to lament and to say that she does not have the strength to survive the birth."[27]

In Her Own Voice

June 11, 1875, Petrópolis

My beloved,

Your journey to São Paulo puts me on edge. Two weeks away from me! Without the consolation of opening my heart to you! My two old ladies [D. Rosa de Santa Ana Lopes and the countess of Barral], whom I love with all my heart, are very good company, but when I need to be by myself, it's quite another matter. Either I have to pretend that I am going to say my prayers or going to a place that I don't dare mention in the same breath as prayers. And even then I can hear them close at hand, and God knows what they do as they try to ensure that nothing happens to me. It is very affectionate on their part, and I thank them for it, but at times it is a burden. When I am alone in my bedroom, a fear that they are about to open my door sometimes breaks in on my train of thought and so I have to start my thoughts from the beginning. It is foolish, but my meditating alone calms me down, while all these interruptions set me on edge.

Another thing, my darling: I have been told by the countess, but under a pledge of secrecy, which you won't break, that Daddy intends to spend July 26, 27, and 28 here, in order to cheer me up. Far from cheering me up, that would only disturb me. You could therefore tell him that I prefer to be alone with my sorrow on those days. Since, due to all this traveling on his part, I am afraid that his biweekly visits may be changed, I would ask him in any case not to come to Petrópolis on those days.

Returning to your trip to São Paulo, do you really want to do it?! Do what you deem best, and in any case pray for me and our little darling!

There is so much more I could say to you perhaps, but enjoy your trip to Campos; don't forget all my recommendations; and I hope that the Good Lord, the Holy Virgin, and the Saints in Heaven will aid me! and bless you!

6 1/2 I have just taken a walk in the Public Park with my two old ladies who send you lots of *saudades*. Forgive the tiresome opening to this letter but I had to unburden myself to you. I embrace you as tenderly as I love you.

Isabelle

P.S. I felt our little one move.

I am not in a state of nerves at present, thank God.

I have written to Mummy asking her not to come here on July 26, 27, and 28. You don't therefore need to say anything. Above all don't say that the countess has spoken to me.[28]

The Count d'Eu behaved with what appears to have been exemplary patience, kindness, and resolve. In June, he performed the thankless task of informing Dr. Feijó, their personal physician, that Dr. Depaul had been summoned from France, and he wrung from the emperor an acquiescence, if not a consent, to this decision. Early in September, Gaston d'Orléans must have been desperate. His wife, so he told the duke of Nemours, "has alarmed me by her state of despair, her utterly gloomy ideas, which are intermixed with insomnia and periods of obstinate silence lasting for hours."[29] At the same time, the news that Dr. Depaul was coming to Brazil to supervise the delivery unleashed a barrage of largely critical press comment. The summons wounded Brazilian physicians in their professional pride. No woman had the right, it was implied, to cast doubt on their competence, which attested to their masculinity. The fact that four leading doctors had failed in the previous year to secure D. Isabel a successful delivery of her child weighed nothing against these considerations.

Dr. Depaul's arrival on September 26 brought reassurance and so greater calm to the princess, but it revived in the press what the count d'Eu termed "the odious polemic." All the couple could do was to disregard the attacks made on them and have patience. On October 14, Gaston d'Orléans wrote hastily to Pedro II: "When Isabel was very happily supervising the making of ice cream, she felt herself wet and when she got up the waters poured to the ground. Depaul happened by chance to be present. He ordered her to lie down, and when she did so, examined her. He recommended that she did not move and then left, telling me, while in the garden, that everything was going well and that sufficient waters remained. There are no pains."[30]

Gaston d'Orléans suggested that Dr. Feijó should, as a courtesy, be summoned, though he should not speak to D. Isabel. The postscript added: "The countess [of Barral] is here!" D. Isabel tried to prevent Feijó from being called, but Dr. Depaul, in a gesture of professional and male solidarity, advised that he should be in attendance. At four o'clock that afternoon, the princess went into labor that continued for thirteen hours. "Nothing was more heart-breaking than the emotional state of the count d'Eu," Depaul told a French reporter.

"I have never seen a more fond and more united couple, they loved each other as if they were good bourgeois. Anxious, agitated, with a cold sweat on his brow, the count paced up and down the room next to his wife's bedroom. He came constantly to kiss her hand and to tell her to be courageous, which was not necessary."[31] As day approached on October 15, D. Isabel's eleventh wedding anniversary, Dr. Depaul decided that a forceps delivery was indispensable to prevent another tragedy. With them he delivered a baby boy, weighing over ten pounds.

The child gave no cry and appeared asphyxiated. The quick response of Mme. Soyer, the French midwife who had come with Dr. Depaul to Brazil, saved his life. She blew in his mouth, tickled his nose with a feather, and finally plunged him into the hot water brought from the kitchen by the countess of Barral herself. All appeared well until Dr. Depaul, upon examining the child twenty-four hours after the birth, noticed that he could not move his left arm. It was both hoped and expected that this defect was a consequence of the difficult delivery and that it would soon correct itself. "Bless, my dear father, our dear baby," Gaston wrote to the duke of Nemours six weeks after the birth, "and don't forget to implore the Good Lord that his little arm gets better. It is the only black spot on our happiness."[32]

After her miscarriage in 1872 and the stillbirth in 1874, D. Isabel was entranced to have a child. She lavished all her care and attention upon the baby, named Pedro de Alcântara after his paternal grandfather. "Little Pedro made with me his first visit to the church," she told her father on November 21, 1875, "and behaved like an angel." D. Isabel's life revolved around "Baby," as she generally termed her son. His physical disability simply intensified her solicitude for him. She sought to find a medical treatment that would, she kept on hoping, give him full use of both arm and hand. At the end of December she noted that "electricity was today applied to Pedro's little arm and it made him cry." For the princess her role as mother took precedence over that of wife, daughter, and heir to the throne. As the count d'Eu acknowledged in May 1876, "My wife prefers taking care of Baby to everything else."[33] D. Isabel equated her role as mother with living in Petrópolis, where she now spent more and more time each year. Residence in Petrópolis had the advantage of keeping her away from Rio City, the site of politics and public affairs.

D. Isabel tried to keep a distance between herself and the duties inherent in her role as heir to the throne, but she could not avoid that role. At the time of her son's birth, she already knew that she would shortly have to serve a second time as regent of Brazil. Pedro II's visit to Europe in 1871 and 1872 had whetted his appetite for a much longer absence abroad. The approaching centenary of U.S. independence in July 1876 offered the ideal justification for a tour that would begin in North America and continue on to Europe and the Middle East. The necessary law authorizing the emperor's absence from Brazil for eighteen months and naming D. Isabel as regent with full powers was enacted on October 20, 1875, five days after she gave birth. Late in March 1876, Pedro II and D. Teresa Cristina sailed for New York.

The task that D. Isabel assumed in 1876 was far more difficult and challenging than her first regency. In 1871, the real head of the government had been the viscount of Rio Branco, assisted by a capable cabinet dedicated to the enactment of specific reforms. With the national economy on an upswing and the country made confident by victory in the Paraguayan war, prospects looked bright. Pedro II would, it was expected in 1871, return from Europe restored and invigorated, equipped to guide Brazil on the road to progress.

Five years later the situation was very different. The mood of national self-confidence was gone. The new reforms had manifestly failed to resolve the many problems troubling Brazil. The economy was sluggish and the whole system of national government increasingly ineffective. After a prolonged absence in Europe, the British envoy reported in November 1876 "that the condition of Brazil has much deteriorated during the last three years, and that some serious crisis in her affairs cannot be far distant." Part of the problem lay at the top. The emperor had become jaded in spirit and hidebound in outlook. The set of recommendations that he wrote for D. Isabel just before his departure was consistently defensive, almost pessimistic in tone. His main concern was that his daughter should hold the line, and he presented no coherent vision of the way ahead. The cabinet in office, successor to the Rio Branco administration, lacked cohesion and energy. The youngest minister was aged thirty-nine, the oldest seventy-three. These men lacked any capacity to subordinate themselves to a much younger woman whose judgment they did not trust. The cabinet simply dug in and awaited Pedro II's return. One minister, the baron of Cotegipe, retrospectively justified the cabinet's inertia by claiming that it "could not provoke or respond to controversies; it did not embark on reforms that would excite passions, even less could it appear to abuse the credulity or experience of the Regent."[34]

D. Isabel's state of mind as she assumed the task of governing Brazil can be gauged from the first letter, dated April 14, that she sent her father after his departure.

> We have just finished with the [Good Friday] church services. I pardoned 6 criminals and commuted 2 death penalties. It is one of the few attributes of that prerogative which I enjoy! I would also like to push forward the development projects in the country, railroads, colonization, etc., etc., but the cart is very heavy and I don't know whether I will have the strength to help in the way that I can. God grant it! . . . .
>
> Your notebook [of recommendations] has been read right through and God grant that I can for the most part follow your advice.

Her words attested to her devotion to Brazil and her desire to do good, but they also show that she saw herself as caretaker during the emperor's absence. She would not strive to create her own style of governing or to embark on innovations. The cabinet would not have supported her if she had done so, and as the opening paragraphs of her letter revealed, her continuing devotion to her father, a devotion that approached dependence, prevented any such step.

> If you miss my company, I don't fail to miss yours! Those who go off don't feel the loss as much as those who stay behind! Do you recall what I told you? To be fair, however, my good Daddykins, I will say that when I made that remark I did not remember that this time I have my little child whom I lacked the last. You know, Daddy, how good it is to have a loving child, and how much one is entertained by the continuing development of a small one whom one loves, and how quickly time therefore passes. Daddy doesn't have your loving little girl there! Even if she were there the changes in a mature woman 30 years old would not supply material for daily entertainment. Anyway, each one misses the other a great deal both there and here, but not swapping your occupations for mine! . . .

Gaston has been affected by his usual ailments: liver, dizzy spells in his head, some fever at times, dyspepsia. Fortunately nothing of major concern. It did not prevent us from visiting the churches yesterday.[35]

D. ISABEL AND THE COUNT D'EU WITH PEDRO, 1876

Courtesy of the Arquivo Histórico do Museu Imperial, Petrópolis

These passages make clear where D. Isabel's priorities in life lay. Her son came first, followed by her father and her husband. Her other obligations tended to get squeezed out, as was the case with her nephews. "Pedro [Augusto] came here on Thursday and I found him in good health," her letter of April 14 remarked. "Augusto still had a slight cold. I hope to be able to visit them early tomorrow morning." The two boys were largely left to their own, looked after by a tutor, during the eighteen months their grandparents were away. This situation was not entirely D. Isabel's fault. As regent, she had to devote her time and attention to the minutiae of government, having to approve and sign all appointments and to give her assent to many routine decisions. On March 16, 1877, she wrote to her husband, then absent in the province of Minas Gerais, "I must complain to you, my poor darling, about the drudgery of these evenings. During more than an hour I have done nothing but open and dispose of letters, papers, and dispatch boxes (there was one from the minister of the Empire). I still have not had time to read even one line in the newspapers or to be present at darling Baby's supper! I hear him now talking and tapping in his bedroom."[36] Even her son had sometimes to take second place in her life.

In these circumstances, it is not surprising that D. Isabel, then thirty years old, did not aspire to play any innovative role in government during her second regency. Her goal was to keep the ship of state on an even keel and to avoid crises until her father returned, but the best-laid plans run awry. From March 1876 to September 1877 the princess lived through a series of trials as Brazil's ruler and of tribulations in her personal life. The three crises she faced as regent—the fiasco of electoral reform, a renewal of the Religious Question, and a natural calamity known as the Great Drought—lay beyond her capacity to control, but nonetheless, they served to undermine her credibility as ruler and called into question the imperial regime itself. The ordeals that the princess suffered in her personal life, a counterpoint to her difficulties as regent, contributed to weakening her public position.

In October 1875, the legislature had passed a bill designed to prevent fraud during the elections and to ensure seats to the party then in opposition. Pedro II strongly backed the law. "I believe that the ministry wants an honest implementation of the new electoral law," his memorandum for his daughter observed, but he feared what the government's representatives might do. The guarantees enacted by the law proved illusory, incapable of preventing fraud and violence in the elections held late in 1876. The ministry triumphed but at high cost. The damage to its reputation and effectiveness left it in a very weak position, hanging on to office until the emperor's return. The fiasco had larger consequences, as the British envoy pointed out. "It cannot be denied that the Emperor's popularity has greatly suffered."[37] As her father's substitute, D. Isabel shared in this loss of credibility and prestige.

The revival of the Religious Question involved the princess much more directly. In the middle of 1876, it was widely reported that the newly appointed papal internuncio to Brazil was entrusted with a special mission to insist on the expulsion of the Freemasons from the Church *irmandades*. What gave a color of credibility to this report was the recent issuing by Pope Pius IX of a new encyclical letter condemning Freemasonry. The news report set off a political tempest. The compromise of September 1874 that ended the Religious Question had settled nothing. Neither the Catholic Church nor its opponents in Brazil had abated their claims by one jot or tittle. The new internuncio, anything but a firebrand, came on no special mission, the count d'Eu told his old tutor. "But that's beside the point, the signal was given for daily diatribes, either long tirades, or caricatures, of a grossness and an untruth that would, it seems to me, be a cause for shame in any other country." As to his wife, Gaston d'Orléans added, "the princess is daily accused of sacrificing the nation's dignity to her religious beliefs that, however, she has hardly any opportunity to display."[38]

The crisis reached a climax at the start of November 1876. According to the newspapers, the minister of the Empire (Interior), supported by D. Isabel, proposed a decree banning Freemasons from the *irmandades*, a proposal opposed by the head of the cabinet and the other ministers. "I believe it to be correct," the British envoy wrote home, "that the Regent, and the Duke de Caxias [head of the cabinet] each telegraphed in accordance with their views to the Emperor at Constantinople and that his reply has been received, desiring that the Church question should not be entered upon in his absence." The count d'Eu's comment on all this was scathing. "In this whole episode there is not one word of truth; no one has ever telegraphed to the emperor; there has never been any mention of taking measures against the Freemasons in Isabel's conversations with the ministers."[39] Somewhat unwillingly, the cabinet was forced to issue an official denial of the entire story. The controversy subsided, leaving D. Isabel's reputation as a bigot confirmed and her popularity further reduced.

As these two crises developed, D. Isabel underwent severe personal tribulation. By the middle of August 1876, she had expectations of again being pregnant, her last period having been late in June. On August 26, she began to discharge traces of blood that became heavier, accompanied by intense pain. The princess took to her bed, but her condition persisted until she miscarried on September 11. Four days later she informed her husband: "The discharge, which is not really a discharge, has restarted somewhat, but not seriously, even before I got up. It has not increased since." On the 19th she reported, "since, when I wipe myself from time to time, there is always a little blood, I thought it prudent not to get up today save for my meeting with the doctor." The next day she wrote: "I am discharging more blood. I mentioned it to Feijó, who told me that it must be my period. I also believe it is, because it is regular and without any pain. He told me that following a miscarriage early in pregnancy the period restarts at the time when it would have occurred if I had not been pregnant. I am going to get up for the *despacho* that I have fixed for 2 o'clock to allow me more rest." By the middle of October the count d'Eu could at long last report that, after "a miscarriage accompanied by hemorrhages that worried us for some time," D. Isabel "is recovered, although thin and subject very easily to tiredness."[40]

D. Isabel could not depend upon her husband to carry the burden of public affairs for her during this crisis. As Gaston d'Orléans told his former tutor, he was "always subject to that state of nervous agitation, with which you are familiar." "This nervous state is aggravated by any kind of stress," he informed his father in April 1876, "and cannot be otherwise at this moment due to the excess of worry that the Emperor's absence causes." Performance of public duties exacerbated his usual bronchial infections. "During the evening of August 21 I had a fierce feverish attack and I thought I was delirious, and this condition recurred for several days. As a consequence I had to keep to my bed, or at least to my rooms, for nearly three weeks."[41] On his doctor's advice he took a two-week vacation away from Rio City and from work, even though his wife had just suffered a miscarriage.

Following the count d'Eu's return to Rio City, the couple decided, as he explained to the countess of Barral, to alter one aspect of their public life: "The princess, despite all the blood she lost for over a month, is always in the best health and goes out every day in the carriage with Baby. As for me, I carry on as best I can and I never stop coughing. We have completely given up visits to public establishments, lectures, and institutes that depress us so much. We experience sufficient pain and suffering from diplomatic receptions, audiences for the poor, and other nuisances in the household that never end."[42] This withdrawal involved no radical change in the couple's lifestyle. During the past four and a half years since the end of the princess's first regency, the couple's absence from the country in 1873 and 1874, D. Isabel's pregnancies and miscarriages, and the count's constant ailments meant that their social contacts with Brazilians had been restricted. Their isolation was also by choice. When the press polemic over Dr. Depaul was at its height in September 1875, the count d'Eu observed: "From henceforward we have decided to keep ourselves isolated, from a fear of having to discuss this disagreeable subject." The attitude toward Brazilians revealed in this comment was echoed in Gaston d'Orléans's praise for the couple's chamberlain, the count of Lajes. "His European education and his contacts with the diplomatic world . . . opened to him certain horizons much more exalted than is generally the case with his compatriots."[43] The count d'Eu's outlook marked him as an outsider, unable to accommodate himself to the culture of his wife's native land. It was no wonder that Brazilians dubbed him o francês (the Frenchman) and resented his involvement in the conduct of public affairs.

In October 1876 the count d'Eu justified the couple's decision to withdraw into private life as a positive step that would bring real advantages. "When the Princess is no longer seen every day in the streets of Rio, she is forgotten for a while and there is less temptation to denounce each of her acts and decisions to a discontented public."[44] What Gaston d'Orléans did not appreciate and probably did not want to acknowledge was that the couple's withdrawal deprived them of all opportunity to influence public opinion in their favor. By the middle of the 1870s "progressive" opinion in Brazil was increasingly dissatisfied. The country was not becoming "civilized" as rapidly as were other nations in the Western world. No network of railroads and electric telegraphs bound the country together. No system of primary schools brought education to the population. The Argentine Republic, Brazil's neighbor and rival, was making remarkable progress in all these areas, but the imperial government seemed incapable of introducing these benefits.

Republicanism as a political creed had existed in Brazil since the late colonial period. Following the troubled times of the 1830s, Republicanism had vanished as an organized movement. It did not reappear until December 1870, when the Republican Party was created in Rio de Janeiro City, dedicated to replacing the imperial regime. Republicanism appealed to elements in the younger generation, particularly to graduates of the law and medical schools, who were dissatisfied with the country's progress in comparison with the United States or Argentina. The Republican Party did not establish itself as an important political force, largely because most Brazilians continued to regard Pedro II as indispensable to the governance of the country. To attack the emperor was to undermine Brazil's reputation. Within Brazil, few men of ambition would put their careers at risk by openly attacking Pedro II and his government.

No such inhibitions protected D. Isabel and the count d'Eu. They possessed no comparable prestige. Their displeasure could blast no man's career. Respectively a woman and a foreigner, they were intrinsically outsiders. All the resentment, all the disappointment, all the impatience that Pedro II and his system of rule evoked could be vented, if deflected onto his daughter and son-in-law. The couple made ideal scapegoats, and the Republican Party and its sympathizers in the press were quick to blame them for Brazil's problems.

D. Isabel's opinion on the decision in October 1876 to give up making "visits to public establishments, lectures, and institutes" is not recorded, but the withdrawal suited her both in terms of her own health and of her child's interests. In March 1877, she wrote to Gaston d'Orleans, then absent in Minas Gerais, complaining about "the drudgery of these evenings" that prevented her from being "present at

JOÃO MAURÍCIO WANDERLEY, BARON OF COTEGIPE, IN COURT DRESS

Courtesy of the Museu Nacional Histórico, Rio de Janeiro

darling Baby's supper!" Her attention was also focused on conceiving another child. In the middle of May, she announced: "My period still has not arrived. Let us see what happens tomorrow." Her hopes were both fulfilled and put in jeopardy, as Gaston d'Orléans explained to Pedro II.

> For some days we had suspicions that Isabel is two months pregnant, and we had decided to move permanently down to the capital on May 30th,

when on the night of the 28th there appeared symptoms similar to those that preceded her miscarriage of last year. She at once decided to stay in bed where she still remains to see if she can avoid the same outcome. The symptoms have decreased but not entirely ceased. All this happened at a most awkward time. Not only were we expected in the capital on the 30th for a public audience and a *despacho* with the cabinet, but the following day was the feast of Corpus Christi, and June 1st was fixed for the opening of the new session of the legislature.[45]

Fortunately, the legislature's rules of order permitted the Speech from the Throne that opened the session to be read by the minister of the Empire (Interior), and a decree authorizing him to do so was hastily prepared. The minister sent the signed decree to his colleague, the baron of Cotegipe, for his approval.

May 31, '77

The princess is in bed and her ailment is what we inferred. It seems that everything is proceeding as it should and that her condition is excellent.

She signed the decree, but was unwilling to sign the Speech from the Throne, desiring the words "my August and Worthy Parents" be suppressed. She claims that, since she will not be reading the speech, the phrase is not suitable. I pointed out that the speech is hers, and will be read as being by her and for her, but she responded by asking us to do her this favor.

The point is of such small importance that I am going to send another speech, without these words.

I don't think that the cabinet needs to meet on this, but Y. Ex. will decide.[46]

On June 10, D. Isabel was still confined to bed and clearly worried about her condition. The lack of letters from her father intensified her depressed mood: "Daddy mine, why don't you write to me anymore? Believe me that I spent a good part of last night meditating on this and, I tell you, even in tears, thinking that perhaps Daddy may be angry with me. Tell me that you have nothing against me, that you love me as formerly so that I will be well pleased, my Daddykins! What I am told and think is that your failure to write is probably caused by the turmoil in which you live. Write to me, my goodykins, badykins. From Mummy I have always received letters."

This passage, written in pencil, revealed how deep were the emotional links that still tied D. Isabel, almost thirty-one years old, to her father. A postscript to the same letter, written in ink and so subsequent to the crisis of her pregnancy, showed the princess both at her most incisive and revealed what emotions, besides love for her father, motivated her:

> The government decided that it would not participate in any way in the [1878] Paris Exposition. The chambers have clamored so much for economies that the ministers were afraid to include an item for the Exposition in the budget. That was not my opinion, but I gave way. . . . I don't know if Brazil will gain much by a presentation of this type, because the producers, since they won't go themselves, will not be able to learn what would be most useful to them. Nonetheless, what impression will Brazil make as a civilized nation? I don't know, I cannot know, and also if the need, in effect requisite, for economy explains everything.[47]

D. Isabel rarely wrote about abstract topics but was motivated to do so in this instance because of her identification with Europe, of which the 1878 Paris Exposition would be an exemplar. It was her desire to promote a comparable civilization in Brazil that moved her to make such a strong, incisive comment.

Although bed rest prevented a miscarriage early in June, fear of what might happen kept the princess from undertaking any public role. A month later the count d'Eu went off alone to inaugurate the final stretch of the railroad linking the cities of Rio de Janeiro and São Paulo. In São Paulo, he informed Pedro II, "there exist a good number of discontented over Isabel's not going and the minister of the Empire (Interior) did everything he could to persuade her to go. But how could she subject herself to so much fatigue with the likelihood of a mishap given the state she is in?" In fact, the count's visit went without any problems, and D. Isabel was cheered up by receiving a letter from her father. "I already knew that you aren't the least bit angry with your little chatterbox! Only two months more until your return, that's fine!" she replied on July 22. Almost as an afterthought, she added, "Gaston returned yesterday from São Paulo tired but relatively well." As was her custom, D. Isabel included a brief comment on public affairs in a postscript. "Farewell, we have a terrible shortage of water. There seems to be none in the sky. My concert for the victims of the drought raised 21 contos [about $10,500] and the bazaar is producing an equally good result."[48]

The emergency to which the princess referred was the third crisis she faced during her regency. A natural calamity of unprecedented dimensions ravaged northeastern Brazil from early in 1877. The failure of seasonal rains on which the interior of the northeast utterly depended left the local population, who lived from hand to mouth, without resources. Huge numbers tried to flee the drought region, but this migration intensified the emergency, since the migrants poured into areas incapable of succoring the newcomers. Starvation and exhaustion sapped resistance to disease that became epidemic. The death rate soared. In the drought region, the existing governmental infrastructure proved incapable of handling a full-blown crisis and quite literally disintegrated. This dismal failure made plain the ramshackle nature of the imperial regime.

The Brazilian public sought by means of "Concerts, Bazaars and Theatrical Performances" to raise relief funds that, however, proved to be "a mere drop in the Ocean." Even if the funds had been much greater, they would not have solved the emergency. The lack of an effective transportation system and the collapse of governance together prevented relief from reaching the drought region. D. Isabel's response to the emergency conformed to the role assigned to women by the prevailing gender conventions. Concerts, bazaars, and theatrical performances were activities that women could organize without invading the public sphere and so contesting men's right to exercise power. The inadequacy of the relief measures, both public and private, meant that the regent was once again identified, through no fault of her own, with the incompetence or incapacity of the imperial regime. The count d'Eu told his father that "the only truly disagreeable aspects [of the regency] were the calamity of the drought, about which we could do nothing more," and the renewed Religious Question.[49]

In the middle of 1877, D. Isabel's mind was fixed not on the great drought but on her new pregnancy. The princess very much wanted the countess of Barral to be present at the delivery, as she had been in July 1874 and October 1875. D. Isabel also insisted that Dr. Depaul be brought again to Brazil. Reasonable as these two desires were, given the dangers through which the princess had two times passed, they met strong resistance, not the least from Pedro II. In July 1877, the countess of Barral wrote that, despite "what my heart has demanded since I learnt of my dear Princess's pregnancy, it's impossible, and besides I have not had a word of encouragement from the parents," with whom she was traveling in Europe. The imperial couple showed themselves equally cool toward the proposal that Dr. Depaul be once again summoned from France. "The emperor and the empress (to the latter of whom I had moreover written) have not sent one word of encouragement," the count d'Eu informed his father at the end of August. "It has made me indignant with the emperor who shows yet again the extent of his egotism in respect to his family." This lack of support was the more upsetting since the decision to employ Dr. Depaul "was very unpleasant, first because it will again make us suffer the storm of Brazilian criticisms and jealousies . . . and second because it is an enormous and exceedingly unwelcome financial sacrifice."[50]

D. Isabel's second regency came to an end when, early on the morning of September 26, 1877, Pedro II disembarked from the *Orénoque* steamer. As he had done at the end of D. Isabel's first regency, the emperor behaved as if he had never been absent and as if D. Isabel counted for nothing. The count d'Eu told the duke of Nemours: "He has never spoken to either of us, Isabel and I, either before or after the regency about politics or affairs of State. We don't complain, because we hold politics in horror. But it is all the same odd that he is not informed as to what happened on specific matters during his absence. On the day he disembarked, as soon as he crossed the threshold of the palace, he went straight to the ministers without saying a word to his daughter."[51] The emperor even arranged for a statement to be published in the principal Brazilian newspaper: "I want it to be known that throughout my entire journey of 18 months I did not send to H. H. the Regent or to any of the ministers a single telegram on the country's affairs." As the count d'Eu remarked to his father, the statement was accurate, "but this eagerness to distance himself from responsibility for everything that was done during that time has provided the subject for numerous commentaries in the press."[52]

The count wrote his comment about Pedro II's failure to consult with his daughter after the imperial couple made a brief visit to the Palácio da Princesa in Petrópolis at the end of November 1877. Shortly after his arrival, the emperor "ensconced himself in the billiard room . . . and *not one word* for at least two hours, even though he was alone with his daughter." Such was Gaston d'Orléans's complaint to the countess of Barral, and he added: "Admit that it is odd to pay people a visit in order not to talk to them." What gave the count's letter an acerbic tone was Pedro II's reaction to the information that the couple had decided to bring Dr. Depaul to Brazil for D. Isabel's forthcoming birth. "He replied to me: 'You know my opinion about that. I believe that you are wrong,' and, since I continued to make some remarks, he repeated three times 'Well, it's your affair' and broke off the conversation."[53]

The letters that Gaston d'Orléans sent to the countess of Barral did not express, he explained on September 29, his views alone. "She [D. Isabel] asks me to tell you that, when I write to you, it is from both of us, and she knows enough to understand that you won't want two letters when a single one provides the news and thoughts of both." The princess may not have written the letters, but she did read them before they were sent off. To his next letter, describing the emperor's brief visit, the count d'Eu added a revealing postscript: "I would ask you to destroy this letter since the princess finds that a good part of it has a bad tone. She is right but I don't have time to rewrite it."[54] D. Isabel may not have disagreed with her husband's comments, but she did not want them presented in a form that might give cause for a quarrel with her father.

After Pedro II's return, the princess withdrew to Petrópolis, where she resumed the quiet life that the couple preferred, and which her pregnancy made very necessary. Early in January 1878, Dr. Depaul and Mme. Soyer arrived from France. The delivery proved much easier, and the new child, a second boy, was born on January 26, 1878. He was given the name of Luís, in honor of his paternal grandfather. "The event was not without its emotional aspects," Gaston d'Orléans told the duke of Nemours, "and we feel truly happy, *so thankful and happy* (as one so often reads in the book by Q. Victoria). To have two healthy children, after so many problems that have hindered my hopes

D. Isabel, dressed for a social occasion outside the home

Courtesy of the Arquivo Histórico do Museu Imperial, Petrópolis

of being a father, surpasses what I could have dared to hope for."[55] For D. Isabel, the birth of her second son was of supreme significance. By providing her husband with healthy children, she had finally fulfilled the fifth duty laid on a wife.

D. Isabel was now entitled to pay much greater attention to her own interests. On May 1, 1878, three months after the birth, she sailed from Rio for Europe with her husband and their two children.

The couple had the emperor's permission to reside outside Brazil for two years. The ostensible reason for their voyage was to seek the best medical treatment possible for young Pedro's arm and hand. In fact, they were disassociating themselves from five years of unpleasant experiences: two miscarriages, one stillbirth, two pregnancies, eighteen months of toil as regent, and ceaseless abuse from the press. The couple was going to reside in a world with which both D. Isabel and her spouse identified, but in very different ways. Life in Europe, particularly in France, allowed D. Isabel to lead the private life she preferred. For her husband, living in France meant an end to the exile he had endured since the age of five.

The letters that D. Isabel sent to her parents during her third trip to Europe reveal her changing relationship with them. At the start she wrote every week, alternately to her mother and to her father. The frequency gradually declined to once every three weeks and finally to a single letter each month, addressed to both parents. The letters become more and more impersonal, an exercise in filling the page with what had happened since last writing. D. Isabel rarely expressed any regret at the long separation or any sense of missing her parents, and when she did, it was in response to specific circumstances. In February 1879, for example, she remarked: "I am writing in front of your superb portrait! Oh! if I could talk and my Daddykins could reply to me."[56] That her parents might feel lonely and neglected in the absence of their surviving child and of their younger grandsons does not seem to have occurred to D. Isabel. Her father and by extension her mother were no longer central to D. Isabel's emotional life. They took second place, if that, to the princess's own family, although references to Gaston d'Orléans and the two boys do not abound in the letters. The princess's letters showed the most interest and enthusiasm for her two aunts, D. Francisca and D. Januária, and above all for the countess of Barral, who figured constantly, either in regard to her activities or as a source of news.

The letters to her parents focused on D. Isabel's own round of activities, meetings with family members (mainly her own close relatives and those of her husband), participation in cultural activities, and attendance at social events. The princess paid little or no attention to public events in France or the rest of Europe. Nor did she seek to make acquaintances who might be useful to her as heir to the Brazilian throne. In June 1878, she observed to her father: "Paris is full of royalty, a true plague (speaking in general) to each other; and in this category I include myself for the others. I don't need to add that I am talking only about royalty when they are strangers to each other."[57] Since all but two of the countries of Europe were monarchies, D. Isabel was essentially isolating herself from a class to which she belonged as empress-in-waiting. She was also isolating herself in another respect. Her letters contain virtually no references to or expressions of interest in current events in Brazil. Now and then she did comment on the death in Brazil of people known to her as friends or acquaintances.

All of the evidence indicates that her residence in Europe gave D. Isabel enormous enjoyment, even fulfillment. Shortly after reaching Paris, she and Gaston rented a villa in Passy, a fashionable quarter near the Bois de Boulogne. They spent their first winter and spring there. In the summer of 1879, the family visited Aix-les-Bains, a health spa in the Alps, and then moved to Villers-sur-Mer, a seaside resort near Deauville. At the end of October they were back in their villa on the rue de la Faisanderie. In December, they made a tour through Italy and stayed at Cannes in the south of France before returning to Paris. It was no wonder that in October 1879, when they had been absent for almost a year and a half, D. Isabel informed her father: "Gaston is writing to you by this packet boat to ask you for an extension of a further year to our leave in Europe. He is giving you the reasons and you, Daddy, know that he has good sense. This request causes regret, believe me, but if we make it, it's because the future of our beloved Pedro is involved. I hold it to be necessary since later on many reasons will make it more difficult for us to return to Europe. I feel a very great deal of regret, but don't refuse me, my good Daddykins."[58] "In my opinion, frequent moves from one place to another are the worst obstacle to a serious and fruitful education," the count d'Eu told Pedro II. "I have no hesitation in binding myself, if Y. M. judges it advisable, not to request a fresh leave from Brazil until five years after the date of our return." Pedro II gave his consent to the extension requested, with a commitment on the couple's part not to travel abroad in the immediate future. "I must await my daughter for two more years," he wrote to the countess of Barral at the end of 1879. "But it is for my grandson's benefit, and that suffices."[59]

The extension of the couple's time in Europe did not bring the benefits they envisioned. D. Isabel and her husband were finally forced to accept that, no matter what treatment was applied, their elder son would never gain full use of his left arm and hand. It also became clear that, cheerful and obliging in temperament, young Pedro was not much interested in learning or in utilizing the talents he possessed. In September 1880, Gaston d'Orléans wrote to Pedro II about his grandson: "The reading lessons continue each day, but with a good deal of resistance on his part, and accordingly of patience on that of Mummy: today he got to read wolf, cow, camel." A third reason for unhappiness was the count d'Eu's increasing distaste for the whirl of engagements in which they were involved. As early as February 1879, he retreated to Orléans in order, he informed Pedro II, "to escape the busy monotony of Paris. I also avoided the great *soirée* that my father, in accord with his annual custom, must have given yesterday. . . . Isabel, who is more inclined than I to worldly diversions, stays on there in very good health."[60]

An even more compelling cause for concern was the drain that the long residence in Europe inflicted on the couple's finances. D. Isabel and her husband were by 1880 deeply in debt. They had purchased their residence at Petrópolis in 1876 for fifty contos (about $26,000). In 1877, they decided to add a front portico of six columns and a new wing, double storied. This expansion was still in process and would not be finished until 1883, at the total cost of 150 contos (about $72,000). The expense of twice bringing Dr. Depaul and Mme. Soyer from France to attend D. Isabel in her pregnancies had forced the couple to take out a loan. In essence, D. Isabel and her husband were, from 1878 to 1881, maintaining three residences—in Rio City, Petrópolis, and France. The princess was content to leave management of their finances to her husband, who became increasingly unhappy. "When I think about our stay in Paris and about the way in which we have filled the greater part of it stupidly and heinously with these futilities," he informed the countess of Barral in December 1880, "I am almost reconciled to the idea of our returning to Brazil."[61]

D. Isabel was in no position to disagree with her husband's desire to end their stay in Europe. On January 27, 1881, she informed Gaston: "I am writing to you today only to tell you that Monsieur Depaul informed me this morning that I am pregnant, more likely two and a half than two months. I am very happy and you, you will also be so, I'm sure!" The memories of the disaster she had suffered in 1874 made her determined to have the child in Paris. However, to secure the necessary permission from her father, she had to promise him a prompt return to Brazil after the delivery. "Think, my dear Father, about your little daughter who loves you so much, think also about her state of health, but above all about the suffering that she would have if due to a voyage she once again found her new hopes frustrated. I know you love me very much, my Daddy, listen to me! . . . Pedro's health fortunately no longer requires us to request a further extension, and so we will be there by the end of the year. We expect a successful delivery about August 15."[62] This appeal, which really left Pedro II with little choice but to agree, was written on April 15, 1881. The remaining weeks of the princess's pregnancy were not easy but passed with no major problems. The countess of Barral came to stay on July 22, and she sent the empress a graphic description of the actual birth, from the breaking of the first waters at four in the morning on August 8 to the successful forceps delivery of a baby boy twenty-four hours later. "The princess is doing very well and the little ones are enchanted with the arrival of another brother. The count d'Eu was as always so distraught that he could hardly contain himself. Above all, congratulations and more congratulations."[63]

With the birth of Antônio, as the baby was christened on August 27, 1881, D. Isabel became, at the age of thirty-five, a mother thrice over. The princess's three and a half years of residence in Europe gave her emotional satisfaction and stability, kept her isolated from both Brazil and public affairs, and immersed her in a way of life that answered her needs. She now entered her middle years, the age at which women acquired, thanks to their maturity and seniority, a certain standing and authority in family and society.

6

EMPRESS-IN-WAITING, 1881–1889

D. ISABEL, THE COUNT D'EU, AND THEIR THREE SONS, 1883

Courtesy of the Arquivo Histórico do Museu Imperial, Petrópolis

On December 10, 1881, D. Isabel returned to Rio de Janeiro after more than three and a half years abroad. Her years away from Brazil coincided with a marked shift in the public discourse on gender. Symbolic of this change was the slamming door that on December 21, 1879, in the Royal Theater at Copenhagen brought the curtain down on the first performance of Henrik Ibsen's play "A Doll's House." The slamming door echoed around the Western world, generating both outrage and hope. The dramatic exit of Nora, abandoning husband, children, and home, was doubly disturbing. It pointed out the unacknowledged hypocrises in bourgeois marriage, and it attested to the growing ability of women to earn a living and so to exist independently and on their own terms.

Thirty years of persistent agitation by small groups of women across North America and Europe made women's place in society a legitimate topic for public debate and, by bringing into question the most oppressive features of the patriarchal order, opened the way for "A Doll's House." Equally important were the institutions, above all in higher and professional education, which began to give women a forum for autonomous expression. The new forms of industrial capitalism, creating a more diverse economy and so a more complex social order, also opened up autonomous space for women. "According to critics across a broad political spectrum," a historian on gender and consumption has remarked, "the modern marketplace was so dangerous precisely because it provided women with the kind of financial and psychological independence that undermined their nurturing, dependent roles within the family."[1] Novel forms of consumption gave women an expanded role in the economy and allowed them to carry on social life in settings that resembled the home but lay outside it. Department stores with their myriad sales assistants and clerks, epitomized by Au Bon Marché that opened in Paris in 1876, were but one facet of the consumer and office economies that provided considerable employment for women as sources of cheap and reliable labor.

These changes made less rigid the public and private spheres as being male and female. Gender relations became, if not more equal, more complex and somewhat more flexible. Adjustments—calling them "concessions" would be misleading—were made to the legal position of women, including the Married Woman's Property Act of

1881 in Great Britain and the Alfred Naquet Law of 1884 reestablishing divorce in France. Women may have gained a sphere of autonomy, but it was highly restricted, dependent, and closely monitored. The inability of female suffrage movements to win support, much less to gain the vote, showed how tenaciously men held onto their monopoly of the resources on which the exercise of power depended. On the other side, the expansion of autonomous space (no matter how limited it may in retrospect appear), the multiplying opportunities for employment and expression, and the elimination of the most oppressive features of patriarchy satisfied the aspirations and needs of many women. In this sense, the adjustments and alterations served not to undermine but to uphold the status quo. Women who persisted in seeking radical change suffered ridicule and harassment. Feminism as a cause would not flourish until a new generation of women, who took the adjustments for granted, came of age and devoted their lives to the cause of gender equality.

During her residence in France from 1878 to 1881, D. Isabel was not directly involved in the movement for women's rights, nor did she at any time express sympathies for those rights. D. Isabel was in no way a Nora, determined to escape from "A Doll's House." Nonetheless, her style of life reflected the broader autonomy enjoyed by women, particularly in respect to daily life. Unaccompanied visits to the new department stores appealed greatly to her. Gaston d'Orléans took quite long trips away from home, leaving her in charge of the household and children. She raised no objections to this practice. In fact, she encouraged it. She wrote to him, when he was on an extended visit by himself to Algeria: "You will do well not to appear before the twenty-fifth because on the 24th there is a large party here."[2] D. Isabel had taken control of her own life, and she increasingly spent her time as she pleased, consistent with her duties as wife and mother.

Some of these same adjustments occurred in Brazil during the years of D. Isabel's absence. A decree of April 19, 1879, that remodeled teaching in the existing faculties and schools of higher education opened all courses to women. The decree was in part inspired by the career of Maria Augusta Generosa Estrela. In 1875, at the age of fourteen, Maria Augusta persuaded her father, a businessman in Rio City, to support her desire to become a medical doctor. Having perfected her English and completed preparatory schooling, she enrolled in 1876 at the New York Medical College and Hospital for Women. When business setbacks made her father unable to finance her studies, several Brazilians, including Pedro II, came to her aid, enabling her to obtain her doctorate in medicine in 1881, the first Brazilian woman to do so.

In Brazil, the first female to follow Maria Augusta's example and to take advantage of the 1879 decree was Rita Lobato Velho Lopes, who enrolled in the Rio de Janeiro medical school in 1882. She transferred to the Bahia school, where she received her degree in 1887. Her move to Bahia caused a debate among the students, one of whom contended that no man would marry a female physician, for she was "corrupted by her continual habit of going out on the streets."[3] This denunciation was aimed not at the mass of Brazilian women, who worked and lived outside the home as they had always done, but at upper-class women who, if they frequented public spaces, were still deemed to forfeit personal honor and jeopardize their family's social standing.

The unwillingness to make adjustments in respect to women that was visible among ruling groups in Brazil was motivated in part by dislike of women's rights. More important was the governing circles' perception of Brazilian women's claims as part of the growing campaign by a wide range of social interests in the Western world for socioeconomic rights and political participation. In contrast to imperial Germany, which granted male universal suffrage and instituted a form of "state socialism," including health and unemployment insurance, the ruling groups in Brazil possessed neither the resources nor the understanding to take such measures. Instead, by the Electoral Reform Law of January 1881, the franchise was withdrawn from what would now be termed the petty bourgeoisie and the upper working class of the Brazilian cities and towns. Only those who were economically "independent," in effect the owners of land or investments, could vote. The defense of class interests was of paramount concern.

Since the 1824 Constitution gave very considerable prerogatives to the emperor, the cooperation of Pedro II was indispensable in defending the status quo against attacks from below. On December 2, 1881, just before D. Isabel's return from Europe, he celebrated his fifty-sixth birthday. He now looked and behaved like an old man. He was in fact suffering from diabetes, a condition that one of the court physicians finally diagnosed around the end of 1882. The possibility of the emperor's death made D. Isabel far more an object of interest to political circles than was previously the case. She was henceforth an empress-in-waiting. Progressive opinion in Brazil distrusted the princess because of her religious views. D. Isabel's Catholicism did not, of itself, offend conservative opinion, but the fervor of her beliefs raised doubts about her reliability as guardian of the status quo. The princess was definitively not a "New Woman," but her gender and long residence in Europe, where the traditional order faced troubling changes, heightened the concern. In the years following her return, the princess did maintain the pattern of life she had enjoyed abroad. By so behaving, D. Isabel as heir to the throne set an example that did help to increase the autonomous space available to females within upper-class society in Brazil, but, for that very reason, her conduct did not strengthen her position as empress-in-waiting.

In October 1882, D. Isabel and Gaston d'Orléans celebrated their eighteenth wedding anniversary. The flame of physical love lighted during the honeymoon at Petrópolis continued to burn strong. "Farewell, beloved, I greatly hope the separation won't last very long," she wrote to him in September 1882. Long years of companionship meant that they shared a common outlook, enjoying the same activities and valuing the same friends. The recollections of their eldest granddaughter attest to the strength and stability of their relationship. "I always saw my grandparents together, but I never heard an argument or dispute between them; they shared the same rooms, and they had the air of being two good friends."[4]

In the eyes of the world, the marriage conformed to traditional expectations. D. Isabel did defer to her husband in the running of their affairs, both public and private. However, the dynamics of the relationship had shifted over the years, leaving far behind the assumptions of male superiority and female deference that originally characterized their union. In February 1882, two months after the couple's return to Brazil, Gaston d'Orléans confessed to the countess of Barral: "I have just torn up four pages of my journal-letter. My wife, having found in it some words that displeased her, first harassed me on the

subject and then started to erase them. That infuriated me and I tore
up the letter in a fit of anger. So here, nonetheless, are the fragments,
which will allow you at least to see that we have not hidden anything
from you."⁵ Three months later, D. Isabel wrote to inform her husband that the emperor wanted him, if so willing, to participate in an
inspection tour on May 31. That day was also the culmination of the
cycle of devotions celebrating "the Month of Mary" in the church at
Petrópolis. "I would very much appreciate, my beloved, if you would
on that same day join me in the devotions [to the Virgin Mary]. But
don't fuss over the point. If so many commitments on the same day
upset you, I won't speak further of it."⁶ D. Isabel had become the
more resilient partner in the marriage. Her activities no longer depended upon her husband's prior approval. Understanding each other's
strengths and weaknesses, the spouses accepted the other's needs and
desires and accommodated them.

Following their return to Brazil at the end of 1881, the couple
spent most of their time in the Palácio da Princesa in Petrópolis. If
either of them had obligations to fulfill in Rio City, she or he would
go down for the day rather than stay there. The completion in 1881
of a direct railroad link between Rio and Petrópolis facilitated such
daily trips, which were mostly undertaken by the count d'Eu. He
continued to attend meetings on military matters, but more and more
his activities were concerned with educational and charitable organizations aimed at social improvements. This round of activities tired
him from time to time, but they also gave him a new psychological
satisfaction and self-confidence. On September 2, 1884, the twentieth anniversary of his arrival in Rio, Gaston d'Orléans remarked to
his father: "Although I have become much thinner and more wrinkled
since I left Europe and life in Rio increasingly seems very tiring, I
nonetheless have found this year much less painful than the previous
ones."⁷ After his return to Brazil in 1881, Gaston d'Orléans developed a way of life that did not demand more of him than he could
give.

Much of D. Isabel and the count d'Eu's time and energy were
devoted to the upbringing and education of their children. "They are
all three doing very well," the princess informed her father-in-law,
"and my first pleasure is to take care of them."⁸ She went riding with

them in the morning, took them for walks, and taught them music. The count d'Eu was no less involved in his children's upbringing, giving them French lessons. Shortly after the family's return to Brazil, he selected a preceptor, or director of studies, Dr. Benjamin Franklin Ramiz Galvão. The choice was somewhat unexpected. Not only was Ramiz Galvão at that time simultaneously a professor at the Rio medical school and director of the National Library, but he was in belief a follower of Auguste Comte's Positivism and politically a Republican. To D. Isabel, as a good Catholic, his philosophical views can only have caused concern, but her father strongly approved his son-in-law's choice. "Doctor," as Ramiz Galvão was known by the family, proved to be an excellent selection, someone who could induce his pupils to study without losing their affection. The emperor appointed him the princes' *aio* (supervisor) in September 1882.

During the 1880s, Pedro II and D. Teresa Cristina were markedly less involved than previously in the lives of D. Isabel and her family. The princess continued to be a dutiful daughter, but her family took precedence. She was much less willing than formerly to accommodate her schedule to that of her parents. "Gaston would also very much like to know where and when Daddy will embark on Wednesday to go to Ponte d'Areia for the ship launching," she wrote from Petrópolis in June 1883. "I would also like to know if Daddy will need the steam launch and if his trip there is going to complicate my return to Petrópolis."[9] Pedro II continued, as had long been his custom, to see his daughter every Sunday evening, when he first read aloud to her and then dined with the family. It was, however, he (with D. Teresa Cristina in tow) who came to her residence in Rio or Petrópolis, not she to his. The princess could afford to be fairly offhand in her attitude because the element of tension previously existing between her husband and her father was much reduced. Gaston d'Orléans was more accepting and less competitive. He no longer resented the emperor's dominance, as he had in the first years of his marriage.

The emperor himself had become less formidable and omnipresent. He was visibly slowing down, and his health was uncertain. Gaston d'Orléans reported to the countess of Barral: "I found the emperor looking tired and breathless. He has a slight cough and he complained to his daughter about fits of shivering." These presages of mortality did not of themselves prompt D. Isabel to take a larger role in public affairs. As she explained to her father-in-law, her first pleasure was taking care of her children "and next of my house and my garden." The extensions to the Palácio da Princesa in Petrópolis were finally completed in 1883. "Our house here is entirely finished and is comfortable," she commented. "The bedrooms are now large and on the second floor." Her letters to the duke of Nemours also mention an activity that had become a principal interest in her life. "I am always busy with music and I study with great pleasure both piano and violin," and "I continue with great joy and benefit my lessons with Mr. White." José White, a Cuban of African descent, was a talented violinist who had trained in Paris. Through music, D. Isabel was clearly able to find satisfaction and fulfillment. As her eldest granddaughter recalled, "the sessions [with José White] stood apart from ordinary life."[10]

D. Isabel's interest in music was bound up with her devotion to religion, which maintained its central role in her life. "I continue with great joy and benefit my lessons with Mr. White, and on Fridays with the other ladies both old and young we sing in church the Stabat [Mater] of the Way of the Cross. I very much miss Vespers here." She took as her confessor "a very good Brazilian priest who has inherited almost all the clientele, if I may dare to use that word, of the former curate who was French."[11] She also spent much time and concern in overseeing her sons' religious instruction, of which a high point was Pedro's first communion.

The princess's love of music was one of the bridges that linked her home to outside life. She and the count d'Eu were constant patrons of the opera and of concerts. Recalling "the happy hours" she had spent with her father-in-law at the opera in Paris, the princess commented, "What we have had here this year has been mediocre."[12] Operas and concerts were social events at which the princess and her circle of friends could meet and enjoy themselves. The couple acted as sponsors of concerts that raised funds for the organizations they supported. D. Isabel became sufficiently self-confident of her performance on the piano to play at the parties that she and Gaston d'Orléans occasionally gave after their return to Brazil.

The emperor and empress no longer did any entertaining. The court no longer served as a social center, a lack that the diplomatic corps deeply resented. To fill the void, D. Isabel and her husband were persuaded to offer during the winter months (May to October) a soirée every two weeks at the Paço Isabel in Rio. A retired Austrian diplomat, visiting Brazil in August 1882, attended one of these receptions and described the evening in his diary:

INTERIOR SCENES OF THE PAÇO ISABEL

Courtesy of the Biblioteca Nacional, Rio de Janeiro

> They live in a beautiful house in Botafogo. . . . The vestibule serves as salon and it separates two rooms also used for the reception. In the room to the left, the ladies are seated along the wall. The Empress and the Princess were there. The men filled the two other rooms and the study of the count d'Eu. There were not many people present. . . . The Princess played music. She played the piano accompanied by a violinist from Havana, three quarters African. After the concert, the dances began, and at that moment I withdrew.[13]

As this description makes clear, the soirées were not elaborate or very exciting, and they tended to attract only those who were already friends of D. Isabel and her husband.

The princess's love of plants provided a second bridge between her home and outside life. As early as 1868 she had begun to collect several dozen species of orchids, and these she acclimatized in the gardens of the Paço Isabel in Rio City. In 1875, she and the count d'Eu helped to organize the first horticultural exhibition in Brazil, held at Petrópolis. A special building, manufactured in France, was erected to house the shows, and "the Crystal Palace," as it was known, is now a heritage site of Petrópolis. In 1882, the couple patronized a public concert in favor of the Horticultural Association of Petrópolis. In March 1886, the count d'Eu noted that his wife "today is personally busy, along with the ladies who are her friends, in arranging the flowers and other plants displayed at the Horticultural Exhibition at Petrópolis."[14]

Good works also linked D. Isabel's home life to the outer world. Charity, especially when it was associated with religion, lay with the private and so female sphere, according to the traditional views. Through charitable work, women could, as one historian has observed, "embody feminine moral superiority in practical ways and . . . set an example for the rest of society."[15] D. Isabel's campaign to raise funds for the construction of a new parish church in Petrópolis fell into this category. Charitable work also gave women an opportunity to participate in the public sphere without arousing adverse comment. After her return to Brazil, the princess moved from being involved in charitable work on an individual basis to acting as sponsor of organizations dedicated to social betterment. At the start of 1882 she became patron of the Comissão das Senhoras da Instrução Pública (Commission of Ladies for Public Education). She named her friend Amandinha de Paranaguá Doria to be the commission's president. Similarly, she served as patron of the Associação da Infância Desamparada (Association for Neglected Children), sponsoring a concert on its behalf in 1884. These activities reflected not a commitment to social reform so much as a desire to bestow benefits on the unfortunate in life with the intent to make them both happy and virtuous.

Every one of D. Isabel's activities outside her home involved a circle of female friends. Female friendships gave women a space that males did not dominate, in which they possessed autonomy, and in which they could express their minds and their feelings. Within this network, women gained knowledge and support to manage their daily lives. The emotional edge that at times characterized these female relationships has caused them to be termed "romantic friendships."[16]

What women did within their own sphere, that of private life, aroused in husbands neither curiosity nor concern. In an age in which heterosexuality was axiomatic and other sexual orientations ill-defined and unacknowledged, romantic friendship between women, married or unmarried, could be intense without arousing any guilt or alarm. Only women who openly contravened convention by dressing and behaving like men were subject to public scorn and ostracism.

D. Isabel between "my two closest," Mariquinhas Tosta and Amandinha Doria, Petrópolis, 1884, at the Horticultural Exhibition opening

Courtesy of the Arquivo Histórico do Museu Imperial, Petrópolis

D. Isabel's principal friends, whom she termed as *minhas duas primeiras* (my two closest), were Maria Amanda de Paranaguá Doria, baroness of Loreto, and Maria de Avelar Tosta, baroness of Muritiba.[17] As the photograph of the three holding hands at the opening of a horticultural exhibition at Petrópolis indicates, her relationship with Amandinha and Mariquinhas can be aptly termed a romantic friendship. Both women were younger than the princess and had known her since childhood. Both were married but had no offspring. They were accordingly able to spend a great deal of time with the princess, and to use the phrase that D. Isabel applied to Gaston during her first regency, they "did the chores" in respect to the charitable and social activities she supported.

The circle of friends, both female and male, that surrounded the princess and the count d'Eu after their return from Europe was not large. Six lists of "Visitors at Petrópolis" that Gaston d'Orléans sent the countess of Barral from January to June 1886 record about seventy-five names a month. Included were members of the diplomatic corps and wives, a good number of the *semanários* (those in personal attendance on the emperor during a weekly turn of duty), members of court families, individuals involved in church and charitable work, some members of the financial world, artists, and local Petrópolis worthies. Notably absent were politicians, with one or two exceptions, such as the marquis of Paranaguá, Amandinha's father, who as a court chamberlain was often in service on the emperor.

This distance from the political world and from public affairs was due in large part to the emperor's continued monopolization of power but also to the couple's experiences during D. Isabel's second regency. Less than a month after their return from France, Gaston d'Orléans commented to the countess of Barral that, "despite our utterly quiet life, time is no more available at Petrópolis than at Paris, even without taking into account public affairs to which we are at present, thank God, complete strangers." Not until the middle of 1884 did he modify his attitude. Believing that "we needed to get away from this Petrópolis routine, torpid in several respects," he proposed that the entire family should visit Brazil's southern provinces. "The emp., the ministers, and every one want me to go," he told the countess, but he refused to travel alone.[18] D. Isabel expressed strong objections when the plan was broached to her. Eventually, not wishing to be separated from her spouse, she agreed, and early in November they all left Rio City by train for São Paulo province.

This new willingness to take a public role on the part of the count d'Eu and, less willingly so, by D. Isabel may have been connected to the growing importance in public affairs of the issue of abolition. The Law of Free Birth, enacted in 1871 during D. Isabel's first regency, created an emancipation fund designed to finance large-scale manu-

mission, thus bringing slavery to a rapid end. The fund proved ineffective, freeing very few slaves. This failure, together with Spain's elimination of slavery in its Caribbean colonies and a growing belief that
the continued existence of slavery was holding back Brazil's progress,
produced during the early 1880s an organized and energetic abolition movement. This movement secured converts from the ranks of
the Liberals, in office since 1878, and the opposition Conservatives.
In both parties, and among the Conservatives above all, the opponents to any action on slavery were entrenched and resolute.

By June 1884 the abolitionist movement had achieved such
progress in mobilizing public opinion that Pedro II appointed a new
Liberal cabinet committed to accelerating the end of slavery. The
measure introduced by the new ministry proposed to free all slaves
aged sixty and over, to prohibit the interprovincial slave trade, and to
increase the funds available for the freeing of slaves. When the bill
was defeated in the Chamber of Deputies, the cabinet refused to resign and, with the emperor's consent, dissolved the legislature. Although D. Isabel and the count d'Eu played no role in these events,
politicians believed that the couple sympathized with the abolitionist
cause. In 1869, when serving as commander in chief in Paraguay,
Gaston d'Orléans had secured the immediate abolition of slavery in
that country. As regent in 1871, D. Isabel had sanctioned the Law of
Free Birth. The cabinet, anxious to cultivate support by the heir to
the throne and her spouse, welcomed the count d'Eu's proposal for a
tour of the southern provinces.

D. Isabel kept a diary throughout the tour, from November 1884
to March 1885, for her parents' perusal. Its entries provide good in-
sight into the princess's mature character. As might be expected, the
text contains many references to religion (usually comments on specific churches) and to music. It also describes endless receptions and
visits to charitable institutions, schools, churches, and *fazendas*. On
November 15, she toured the *fazenda* Santa Gertrudes, near Rio Claro,
in São Paulo province.

> Visit to the Fazenda, which the count of Três Rios [its owner] told me is
> much superior to what it was when my parents visited it. Indeed, it is
> very well organized, excellent machinery from the firm of MacHardy,
> and good order everywhere.

THE COUNT D'EU WEARING A PONCHO, RIO GRANDE DO SUL, 1884

Courtesy of Isabelle, comtesse de Paris

The Fazenda contains everything, cattle, swine (enormous pigs), ducks, teals, turkeys, goats, beans, maize, rice, fruit trees, and even a reservoir with fish.

The coffee plantations are the most beautiful I have seen, and I believe I do not exaggerate when I say that I saw trees four meters [thirteen feet] high with huge canopies.

The Fazenda contains 600,000 coffee trees and last year they yielded 60,000 arrobas [971.5 tons] of coffee. There are also fields of cane and manioc, which provide sugar and meal to feed the establishment.

The count told me that he only needs to buy salt and dried meat for the Fazenda. There is a brickyard, sawmill, and the foundations of a house for immigrant workers.[19]

Although the princess's diary does not evaluate the characters of the women and men she met, it is clear that she enjoyed encountering so many new faces. "As you know, it cost me a lot to leave my dear parents, my tranquil home, several friends whom I left in Rio, and my dear music, but I am very pleased to have decided to come," she confessed to her father-in-law in December. "I am at present pleased with everything that I have seen, and with the warm reception given us everywhere."[20]

The receptions included a "visit to the Town Hall" of Itu, in São Paulo, where "I handed out 14 letters of manumission, paid for through the emancipation fund. The owners seemed more happy than the freed themselves."[21] D. Isabel perceived the manumission of fourteen slaves as similar to the alms (gifts of money) that she, as a good Catholic, distributed to the poor during her visit. She was happy to present the deeds of freedom, but the topic, as her remarks about the demeanor of owners and former slaves show, was not one in which she felt herself personally engaged. That attitude was soon to change. In the elections held on December 1, 1884, the cabinet that had introduced the bill to accelerate abolition narrowly failed to gain a majority of seats. The agitated state of public opinion and the determination of the abolitionist movement made continuation of the status quo impossible. The passage of a law freeing slaves over sixty was unavoidable. Despite its determination to maintain slavery, the new Conservative cabinet headed by the baron of Cotegipe finally enacted the bill in September 1885.

Among the measures employed by the abolitionist movement to mobilize public support for the general ending of slavery was the creation of private emancipation funds that attempted to purchase the freedom of all slaves within a specific district. The emancipation fund was exactly the type of public activity that appealed to D. Isabel. It was charitable work, designed to aid the unfortunate and to make them both happy and virtuous. It was personal in that it dealt with individuals and their fate. It combined good works with opportunities to socialize with her circle of friends. Above all, it was a pious undertaking that carried out the predicates of Christianity and was approved by the Church. Traditionally, the Catholic Church in Brazil condoned, even supported, the existence of slavery. The increasing influence among Brazilian Catholics of ultramontanism, concerned to establish the Church as a strong, independent force in public affairs speaking with moral authority, led to a marked change in attitude. Several bishops now declared themselves in favor of abolition on moral grounds.

On March 14, 1886, the empress's sixty-fourth birthday, D. Teresa Cristina presided over a gala meeting at which she presented 176 former slaves with their letters of manumission. The funds had been raised through a private emancipation fund organized by the Rio de Janeiro municipal council. The Rio council, seeking to accelerate the ending of slavery within the city, asked D. Isabel to give her patronage to this campaign and specifically requested her to nominate a committee of ladies who would raise funds to this end. On April 7, the count d'Eu wrote to the minister of the Empire (Interior) on the subject. "We would not wish to give a definitive response, without knowing what the Imperial Government's attitude is to this idea, which otherwise appears laudable to me, and whether it intends to approve the resolutions taken by the Municipal Council." The minister at once referred the matter to the cabinet, which, committed to protecting slavery, decided that the municipal council had exceeded its mandate in advocating such a project. As to the municipal council's specific request, "the cabinet does not recommend that Her Highness the Princess Imperial lend it the great prestige of her position and of her virtues. Rather it respectfully requests, for the good of the State's service, that in a question of this nature Her Imperial Highness maintains the neutrality that is in every respect required of individuals in exalted positions exempt from all responsibility for their acts."[22]

Although gender did not directly intrude in this exchange, it underlay both the request and the response. It was the count, not D. Isabel herself, who wrote to the minister of the Empire. His letter voiced not her but "our" desire, and it observed that the idea "appears laudable to me," not to her. The terms of the discourse, which concerned the exercise of power, were entirely male. The minister's response conveyed a double rebuke to D. Isabel. The heir to the throne should not become involved in the question. In addition, as a woman, she should not employ her "virtues," by definition feminine qualities and so restricted to the private sphere, in what was essentially a public matter. She should not intrude upon "the good of the State's service," an arena of action reserved to men.

The ministry's response, which in effect denied women any role in the public sphere, was of a piece with its very reactionary approach to slavery. The Cotegipe cabinet, despite having enacted the 1885 law freeing sexagenarian slaves, was resolved to keep slavery in existence by every means available to it. As its response to the count d'Eu showed, the ministry freely used its powers to harass the abolitionist movement and to restrict its activities. Initially successful, this policy soon proved self-defeating. Moderate opinion was alienated by the harassment. The abolitionist movement was radicalized and adopted bolder tactics, such as promoting mass flight by slaves.

D. Isabel and her spouse played no part in this drama that dominated public affairs during 1886. Their attention was fixed on a private matter. In 1879, in order to persuade Pedro II to grant them an extension to their leave in France, they had promised to remain five years in Brazil from the date of their return. In December 1886, that commitment expired. The count d'Eu had informed his father on the twentieth anniversary of his arrival in Rio, "As for me, while I have as you know no desire to end my days in Brazil, I have recently become much more reconciled."[23] In his own mind, he was still a foreigner.

One factor that reconciled the count d'Eu to life in Brazil was the prospect of regular visits to Europe. Early in September 1886, four months before the couple were free of their pledge, Gaston d'Orléans informed the countess of Barral: "We have decided to go to Europe at the end of this year for six months only, including travel time. The emp. immediately consented to the idea." Since their eldest son, almost eleven years old, could not be taken out of his school at Petrópolis for very long, half a year was the maximum time the family could be absent. On January 5, 1887, the couple and their children sailed, leaving the emperor and empress alone in their summer palace at Petrópolis. "The departure of my children and little grandsons caused me much pain," Pedro II commented two days later.[24]

The visit started well with a stay with the count's relatives who lived outside of Seville, but when D. Isabel and her family moved to a villa at Nice in the south of France, problems began. The children, particularly Antônio, the youngest, suffered from chronic bronchitis. On February 23, an earthquake struck at six in the morning, forcing everyone out of their beds to take refuge in the garden. "The princess displayed great sang-froid during the whole affair and the count d'Eu (who is usually upset by the smallest thing) took the cataclysm almost as a joke, making fun of the others' terror," reported the countess of Barral, adding "Baby Pedro [was] very distraught and crying, Luís unmoved."[25] No harm was done, and a short visit to Italy restored everyone's good humor.

Another disruption soon followed. On March 2, 1887, the princess received telegrams informing her that Pedro II was sick. A week earlier, while attending a conjuring show, the emperor suffered a headache so fierce that he had to leave. A cycle of sickness, which his physicians could not diagnose or treat, continued throughout the months of March and April. D. Isabel was called back to Brazil, arriving in Rio on June 6, after a five-month absence. Pedro II's physicians desired that he should go to Europe to seek the best medical advice and treatment, but he resisted leaving the country. Not until June 30 did he depart, with his wife and eldest grandson Pedro Augusto, in an intensely emotional atmosphere. Some feared that he would never return. Others believed that he could never recover his health sufficiently to rule again. All were conscious that a turning point had been reached. As regent, D. Isabel was ruling in her father's name and on his behalf, but it was entirely possible that June 30 marked the real beginning of what was termed "the Third Reign."

D. Isabel, shortly before her third regency, 1887–88

Courtesy of the Fundação Grão Pará, Petrópolis

    That the regent and her spouse were conscious of this possibility is indicated by a symbolic act they took immediately after the emperor's departure. D. Isabel and her family moved into her parents' residence at Rio, the palace of São Cristóvão. "It is from Mummy's room and table that I am writing to you both," the princess informed her parents two days after their departure. "Our installation here is very convenient and even this solitude of São Cristóvão (made happy by the children) is good especially during these first days."[26] An even more decisive assertion of their autonomy and their right to exercise power was their decision to put in order and store in chests the masses of letters and documents that were strewn around Pedro II's study and libraries in the palace. Neither the move nor the task was made with the emperor's prior knowledge and approval.

Upon becoming regent, the princess was content to let stand the political status quo. "The ministry offered me its resignation that I did not accept," she recalled a year and a half later. "The baron of Cotegipe seemed to me to be able to maintain himself in office, and I was aware of his strong propensity to support religion, a propensity that was unfortunately rare." She and her husband applied themselves systematically to state affairs, but they did not warm to the business of ruling any more than they had done in 1871 and 1872 and again in 1876 and 1877. Writing to the countess of Barral in the middle of July, the count d'Eu commented: "As for the ministers, they are as yet hardly a nuisance. Meetings with them have been rare and short; in the emperor's absence politics are naturally asleep. The worst work is that of examining the petitions for pardons and the never-ending *requerimentos de esmolas* [requests for alms]."[27]

This sense of detachment, this unwillingness to take the initiative, did not last. The issue of slavery was the cause. The Cotegipe ministry's attempt to interpret the provisions of the 1885 sexagenarian law in a restrictive, retrograde sense and its use of force to discourage abolitionist meetings were self-defeating. "The ministry as a result is once again weakened morally," the count d'Eu commented to his father, "and my advice would be to replace it when occasion offers and when there is no suggestion of illegal pressure."[28] The cabinet's position was further weakened when an abolitionist defeated the new minister of the Empire (Interior) in a by-election. The landowners of São Paulo province, the leading coffee-growing area, began to abandon the cause of slavery, certain that they could maintain production by employing immigrant labor.

"The abolitionist cause advanced; its ideas every day gained ground with me," D. Isabel later recalled.

I read every publication on the topic and I became ever more convinced that some action had to be taken. When I said so to the baron of Cotegipe, he retorted that he could not go beyond the Saraiva law [that of 1885], because he had had a share in it. But he could arrange for it to be interpreted so that the interval before freedom would be much shortened. He mentioned 3 or 4 years as the length of time needed. With this the legislature closed [in October 1887], and the baron promised to study the question during the recess. Each day that passed convinced me the more than he would do nothing.

D. Isabel's impatience grew. Reporting on the festivities for Pedro II's birthday on December 2, she told her father: "The Municipal Council freed 62 slaves through its fund. I have already planted the idea of a major festival to this end upon your return! It is to be hoped that everyone follows the example of the São Paulo planters! Rio de Janeiro is at present very stubborn but sooner or later it will be forced to do the same as the others."[29]

By the start of 1888, the abolitionist cause had ignited in D. Isabel an unprecedented interest in public affairs and resolve to govern. "You see, my dear, that I don't concern myself solely with *frivolities!*" she told the countess of Barral on January 11. "I can think well, I want to achieve the best possible for my country. I will receive widespread recognition later, after I have ruined my health, just like poor Daddy!" Three days later, determined to force the cabinet into action, she called the baron of Cotegipe to a personal meeting. "She at once said to me that it seemed to her that the ministry was losing prestige," the baron of Cotegipe noted in a memorandum made after the meeting. He asked for her reasons. "H[er]. H[ighness]. replied referring to the question of abolition of slavery." Cotegipe retorted that "the ministry was studying the question and in April would give its opinion, whether it would do something or not." D. Isabel then "said that she thought it best if the cabinet made some type of pledge immediately. I replied that, in the absence of a plan, to do so would show a lack of judgment and that we would explain our actions only to the legislature."[30]

In accord with the prevailing views of women, the baron of Cotegipe in his narrative refused to treat the regent as autonomous. "H[er]. H[ighness]. seemed to be inspired by the count d'Eu, since he either approved of what she said, or he added his own observations." Among these was a suggestion that the cabinet "could consult the council of state or convoke a conference of *lavradores* [farmers]. (Respect prohibited me from making an appropriate response to this odd proposal.)" In his memorandum, Cotegipe reported the final exchange with D. Isabel. "My sense of loyalty required me to advise H. H. that she should leave this matter and political questions to the political parties, as Queen Victoria did. On this point she asserted her rights, which I did not contest save for the use that she made of them in questions that separated the parties. Both H. H. and the count d'Eu observed that Queen Victoria had already lost or was losing by this neutrality."[31] By referring to Queen Victoria, Cotegipe indicated to the regent that it was inappropriate for her as a woman to exercise powers that it was perfectly proper for her father to employ. The chief minister's memorandum concluded: "In view of this, it seems to me that H. H. has been influenced, since never before has she spoken so clearly and emphatically. She has previously expressed a desire for some kind of action, but she has never before put in question the ministry's continuance as she did now. We will have to consider what must be done." Accustomed to treating the regent and her husband with disdain, Cotegipe had used his verbal skills to outtalk the princess, heedless of the consequences. On her side, D. Isabel viewed the meeting as a failure. "The baron seemed to understand nothing, and with many fine words and guile he was once again shrewder than I."[32]

Refusing to be discouraged by Cotegipe's stalling, D. Isabel repeated to the entire cabinet what she had said in private to the first minister. Once again, she received only fair words. By the end of February, her patience was exhausted, as a letter to the countess of Barral revealed.

Gaston has written to you. He has sent you the boys' little newspaper [*Correio Mirim*] where you will note everything that is being done for the emancipation of the slaves in Petrópolis. As I have already told you, it is almost foolish to spend money on freeing slaves, but we see that we can thereby give immediate liberty to those who will be free anyway in a year and a half (which is my conviction and that of the majority). To do this is in any case a great act of charity. Besides, what most influenced us was the prospect of giving a boost to the idea of abolition in the near future, which seems to be on everyone's mind, save on that of the stubborn who must be woken up. Either they wake up or they will be swept away. May God protect us, and may this revolution or evolution of ours occur as peacefully as possible.[33]

The baron of Cotegipe remained adamant in his refusal to accommodate in any way to the regent's concerns. He gave her no indication of the cabinet's future course. "From the little I did get out of him and out of Sr. Belisário [Soares de Sousa, the minister of finance] and from the ministry's attitude I was convinced that they would do nothing." The breaking point was reached over the issue of the Rio City police's maltreatment of those participating in street demonstrations in favor of abolition. D. Isabel sent a lengthy explanation of the outcome to her father, still recuperating in Europe:

> In respect to the [Cotegipe] cabinet, you will have learned from the newspapers what happened. The most recent confrontations very much saddened me. For some time my ideas diverged from those of the ministry. I felt that the government had lost a great deal of moral standing. I had said something to this effect a good many weeks ago and did so now with considerable firmness and in writing, at the same time blaming the police in large part for what happened—the police or rather the attitude adopted by the police authorities for some time past. My observation about the loss of moral standing and the fact that I insisted on the dismissal of the Chief of Police caused the ministry's fall. I do not regret what I did. Sooner or later I would have done it; I admit that a blind irritation took hold of me. In good conscience I could not continue with the ministry, when I for my part felt and was convinced that it did not meet the aspirations of the country in the existing situation. God help me, and may the question of emancipation soon reach the final stage that I so much want to arrive. A great deal needs doing, but this most of all![34]

D. Isabel personally selected the head of the new cabinet. She gave her choice, João Alfredo Correia de Oliveira, who had served in the Rio Branco ministry of 1871–1875, entire freedom to select his fellow ministers. She also gave him a free hand as to the cabinet's program. "I let days and weeks pass without daring to ask directly what the ministry planned; I wanted to give it entire liberty."[35] However, the princess did voice her objections to the idea that former slaves should be forced to give work service for a further two years.

Such a requirement, it became clear, could not be enforced, and public opinion shared D. Isabel's desire for an immediate and total end to slavery. When the new legislative session opened in May 1888, the minister of agriculture accordingly presented a bill for unconditional abolition. A wave of popular enthusiasm for the measure secured its enactment in seven days. D. Isabel contributed by coming down from Petrópolis the very same day, Sunday, May 13, in order to sign the bill into law.

The scene in the City Palace, where the princess received the official deputation presenting the bill for signature, was a delirium. The palace was packed with excited people of all classes, women and men, and the mood was one of unrestrained rejoicing. Three days of public celebrations followed, during which all business was suspended and joy reigned supreme. This triumph was marred for D. Isabel by a family crisis. Her father, who had been convalescing in Europe since the middle of 1887, showed himself to be the worst type of patient. When D. Isabel signed what was termed "the Golden Law" (A Lei Aúrea), Pedro II had just suffered a severe crisis in health. A few days later a new collapse of his physical system occurred. On the very edge of death the emperor's body suddenly rallied. A prolonged convalescence followed.

"Today would be one of the most beautiful days of my life, if it were not that I knew my father to be sick. God grant that he may come back to us in order to make himself, as ever, so useful to the country."[36] The wording of this statement, which D. Isabel made when she received the text of the Golden Law on May 13, indicated that the central part she played in securing immediate abolition did not signify any change in her relationship with her father. He continued to serve as her model for her acts as regent. She followed the course he had set in terms of policy and administration. She was simply standing in for him until he came back. The account justifying her recent actions, which D. Isabel wrote in December 1888 (see In Her Own Voice below), made clear that the princess perceived her conduct as exceptional. She had been driven to act by her conscience and by a conviction that abolition would be best for the nation. God had guided her.

In Her Own Voice

December 1888

How did the abolitionist viewpoint gain ground so quickly in me? The concept, already innate within me, was intrinsically humanitarian, moral, generous, great, and supported by the Church. Slavery was essentially an imposition. The owners had profited too long from this imposition. What if they had paid wages from the start?! It is true that if they had, they would have had resources they could have disposed of, and thus some would not have collapsed so helplessly. However, the evil was done, and it could not help but be eradicated. Besides, they ought to have made preparations or rather they never did prepare. Their slaves fled, and there was no means of preventing that. (What surprises me is that they did not flee much sooner.) The country was in agitation. Should I not have taken all this into account, and should I not have confronted with a clear conscience the alienated, whether small in number or rather the many that in fact there were? And the question of compensation? Despite never having stated my opinion on this idea prior to the proposal for it being made, I could not grant it as being either advisable or just. A number of scruples stood in my way, despite my pushing them away. First, the country could have compensated only in an illusory fashion, since it would have to be provided by taxes that would have fallen on those who had no connection with the question. The emancipation fund, financed by taxes, the only one applicable for this purpose, would have been less than sufficient. And whom would it aid? Those who had not voluntarily freed their slaves. It would be only to pay off overdue debts with no benefit to agriculture, and it would be better spent on projects that would serve the general good of farming, which would be most just. Besides this, as I have already noted, the idea of the injustice of slavery and the excessive time that the owners had exploited their slaves could not fail to influence my spirit.

My children, should you later on read this paper, please realize that if your mother acted thus in the great question of abolition, it was out of a conviction that it would be best for the nation, which she had a duty to watch over, and for you all, to whom she would leave her reputation as mother and the throne free of any blemish of egotism or of weaknesses. God aided me, my children, in acting entirely in accord with my conscience. I debated with myself again and again, but I did everything with ease, to the extent that, later on when all was concluded, I was amazed at the encomiums I received for my courage, the wisdom I showed, the greatness of the undertaking. . . .

Always act as God instructs you, your conscience and your spirit will be calm, everything will be easy for you, and if this is not the case, it is because God judges you fit for the struggle as a way of making you yet more worthy of gaining eternal life.[37]

D. Isabel's experiences as regent in 1887 and 1888 certainly made her far more conscious than she had previously been about government as a mechanism for achieving change and improvement. Writing to her father in March 1888, she commented, "a great deal needs doing, but this [abolition] most of all."[38] It was, however, one thing for the princess to be concerned about what needed to be done and quite another for her to set out specific policies that would achieve those ends. Her father had not made practical training in the exercise of power part of her education. During her first regency she had been a novice, content to leave the business of government to the viscount of Rio Branco. The conjuncture of personal and public circumstances during her second regency in 1877 and 1878 had made it very difficult, if not impossible, for D. Isabel to strive for change and improvement. Now, in 1888, the challenges facing anyone (monarch or president) ruling Brazil were so formidable as to challenge the capacity of the most experienced male ruler.

Pedro II arrived back in Brazil in August 1888, far sooner than anyone expected following his sickness at Milan. His doctors decided that as long as he was physically within reach of the attractions of Europe, he would never restrict his activities. Only in Brazil, restricted to his familiar routine, could he be managed. Reporting the emperor's arrival, the count d'Eu perceptively commented:

The avidity and the enthusiasm of the public for the emperor have been very great, more even more marked, it appears to me, than on his previous arrivals. But it is a totally personal homage; because, as I think I have already written, the republican creed has made since his departure last year enormous advances that impress everybody; and, notwithstanding the economic prosperity during the present year, never, for the past 40 years, has the situation of the Brazilian monarchy appeared more shaky than today.[39]

Gaston d'Orléans clearly understood that, notwithstanding the prestige Pedro II still enjoyed among Brazilians, changing conditions in the country had deprived the imperial regime of its viability.

In this same letter, Gaston d'Orléans informed his father of a scheme, "proposed by [the viscount of] Nioac and Mota Maia," to extend D. Isabel's regency despite her father's return, so that his health would not be compromised by the task of governing. Pedro II would be no more than emperor in name. On being sounded out by Nioac on this proposal, Pedro II showed himself, as might be expected, less than enthusiastic. On the day following the emperor's return, João Alfredo, the cabinet's head, went to transact business with Pedro II. Many years later, when talking to Tobias Monteiro, a historian, the chief minister recounted what then transpired.

When João Alfredo arrived at São Cristóvão, the princess received him on the veranda. On his inquiring about what was afoot, she replied that Mota Maia was with the emperor and that he would learn from him what was his [Pedro II's] frame of mind. Shortly thereafter, Mota Maia appeared and declared that the emperor had said that he did not understand the role of honorary emperor. Thereupon the princess raised her hands and said: "I thank God that my father feels that he has the strength to govern and removes this great responsibility from me." João Alfredo remarked that she said this with an air of fierce sincerity.[40]

If this account is accurate, it shows how little her third regency had influenced D. Isabel, how indifferent she was to the exercise of power, and how strong was her sense of filial duty. As long as her father desired to reign, the princess was more than content that the government should remain in his hands.

D. Isabel's attitude had the drawback of leaving the government adrift. Pedro II's life as a semi-invalid meant that official business could not be allowed to disrupt his routine or to cause him fatigue. D. Isabel collaborated with the count of Mota Maia, her father's personal physician, and João Alfredo, the chief minister, in an elaborate scheme to disguise the extent to which Pedro II was being managed. The emperor may have not appreciated what was happening, but the public did, as the count d'Eu pointed out in November 1888. "The monarchy's decline has only become yet more obvious, the public not having been slow to understand that the emperor with the best will can no longer, due to the restraints that his state of health requires, govern in the way he used to do before his illness."[41]

THE IMPERIAL FAMILY AT PETRÓPOLIS EARLY IN 1889

Courtesy of the Arquivo Histórico do Museu Imperial, Petrópolis

The whole system of government, which for over forty years had depended upon the emperor for direction and inspiration, drifted along in the months following Pedro II's return. The princess did not maneuver to replace her father. Her own children, then aged thirteen, ten, and seven, were too young for them to do so. The seat of power was in effect empty, and Prince Pedro Augusto nourished, it now became obvious, ambitions to place himself there. The prince, D. Isabel's eldest nephew, had come to Brazil in 1872 with his younger brother, Augusto, to be brought up by their grandparents. Prior to the birth of D. Isabel's first son in 1875, Pedro Augusto was the ultimate heir to the throne. The somber course of his childhood—loss of his mother at the age of three, separation from his father at the age of six—continued as a lonely and restricted adolescence in São Cristóvão palace. The two boys received little attention and affection from their aunt and uncle during their grandparents' absence from Brazil in 1876 and 1877. Pedro Augusto's antipathy toward D. Isabel and the count d'Eu may have dated from this time.

As a young man, Pedro Augusto was good-looking, personable, and intelligent. His visit to Europe in 1887–88 in his grandparents' company gave him a certain polish. He was above all male. For Brazilians who did not like D. Isabel but did not desire a republic, Pedro Augusto appeared an ideal successor to Pedro II. The prince possessed a liking for intrigue and a large fund of resentment. His sense of reality and even his mental stability seem to have been weakened by a serious illness he suffered during his stay in Europe. After his return to Brazil, now aged twenty-two, he began to dream in earnest of the throne and, to achieve his ends, did not hesitate to foment discontent against his aunt and uncle. His ambitions attracted no significant support and further weakened the monarchist cause. The futility of Pedro Augusto's maneuvers caused his younger brother to rebuke him with the memorable phrase: "Leave it alone, for the succession does not belong to her [D. Isabel], nor to the maimed [Pedro], nor to the deaf [the count d'Eu], nor to you either."[42]

Pedro Augusto's ambitions to occupy the throne may have been vain, but his intrigues certainly contributed to the fierce antipathy toward D. Isabel and her husband. The prospect of her succession to the throne aroused deep resentment in many quarters. "I am convinced that the Third Reign will be a disgrace and I find this opinion spreading and deepening every day, and it cannot but be so," a writer commented at the end of 1887. Even those who supported the imperial regime recognized this fact. "The princess does not enjoy popularity and, unhappily, she lacks many other qualities needed to occupy her father's position, and, above all, prudence and judgment," the editor of the *Jornal do Comércio*, the leading newspaper, reported in

February 1889.[43] Since D. Isabel's role in securing an end to slavery had won her widespread popular support, the editor's assessment of the situation requires explanation.

The passage of the Golden Law had indeed made D. Isabel popular among the mass of Brazilians who termed her *A Redentora* (the redemptress). At the same time, her role in abolition made her disliked, even scorned, among the classes that controlled Brazil's wealth. The planters in particular could not forgive her for supporting abolition without any compensation for the "property" they had lost, for so they regarded their former slaves. The *fazendeiros*, having recovered from the shock of the Golden Law, clamored for compensation, and their campaign explains D. Isabel's observations in her account of the abolition crisis (see In Her Own Voice, this chapter). The princess's gender intensified the planters' dislike. Property rights they identified with maleness. That a woman should exercise power was reason enough for outrage, but that she should use power to strip them of property was the ultimate insult to their masculinity.

The planters' campaign for compensation was strongly backed by the Republican Party, which (heedless of ideological inconsistency) sought to enlist in its ranks all interests aggrieved with the imperial regime. The core of the Republican Party lay in the intelligentsia, men who were educated but who lacked wealth and family connections. The intelligentsia drew its inspiration from France, where the Third Republic was then locked in fierce conflict with monarchism and the Catholic Church. French Republicans had little or no concern for the rights of women, whom they saw as the allies and agents of the altar and the throne. "If the franchise were given to women tomorrow," a leading politician wrote, "France would all of a sudden jump back into the Middle Ages."[44] The Brazilian Republicans shared this view of women's rights. The *Gazeta da Tarde*, a radical newspaper, proclaimed early in 1886:

> In conclusion, the countess d'Eu is not fit to occupy the throne of a country where the democratic tide is daily mounting. The reign of the princess and her entourage will bring disgrace to her family, disaster to the cause of liberty, and tremendous calamity to Brazil. The Palácio Isabel is in a constant state of conspiracy, not against the emperor, but against the progress and development of a noble people and their legitimate as-

pirations. She can only reign as a reactionary, and I don't believe that the people would in any circumstances submit to government by the sacristan and the speculator.[45]

D. ISABEL'S THREE CHILDREN AT THE
PALÁCIO DA PRINCESA, PETRÓPOLIS, 1889

Courtesy of the Fundação Grão Pará, Petrópolis

The princess's habitual withdrawal from the public scene and the people's lack of firsthand acquaintance with her facilitated the attacks by the radical politicians and press. They therefore experienced an exceedingly nasty shock when D. Isabel as regent not only took the lead in the struggle against slavery but also achieved its abolition in a matter of months. She had in effect outflanked the progressive forces in Brazil and established her popularity among the very people whom the Republicans claimed to represent. The Republicans, educated and elitist, did not in fact feel much sympathy for the mass of the population, illiterate and unenlightened. The new alliance between the princess and the people made the "Third Reign" suddenly appear far less illusory or inviable than they assumed it was. They therefore redoubled their attacks on the princess in the months following her regency.

As for D. Isabel, she resumed her customary life after her father's return, once again withdrawing from public affairs. For her to have maintained her new popularity, she would have had to find the means of keeping close contact with the ordinary people of Brazil. For her to have done so would have meant a direct challenge to her father and his authority. The princess's character and her pattern of life prevented any drastic change in behavior. She continued to devote her time to her family and friends, her music, her plants, and religious duties. Her sole intrusion in public affairs only served to enhance her reputation as a religious zealot. In recognition of the princess's role in ending slavery in Brazil, Pope Leo XIII sent her a gift, the Golden Rose, bestowed on rare occasions on meritorious members of the laity. In a ceremony held on September 28, 1888, at the Imperial Chapel in Rio City the papal internuncio presented the gift to the princess, who gave a pledge of obedience to the pope.

D. Isabel's religion was a central facet of her existence. To her, a gift from the head of the Christian Church was an honor to be received in public with the utmost reverence. Believing as she did in the pope's infallibility in matters of faith and morals, she naturally promised him obedience. To her foes, the public ceremony and the pledge justified everything they argued against D. Isabel. In 1886, the *Gazeta da Tarde* had proclaimed: "The princess is unfortunately a *beata* [religious fanatic]; this fatal quality is one of the most dominant aspects in the life of the future empress."[46] The Golden Rose ceremony also served to seal D. Isabel's fate in the minds of the ruling politicians. Fervent piety on a woman' part was acceptable if kept within the private sphere. Isabel now insisted on intruding religious zeal into the public sphere. In the politicians' view, no woman could take the initiative or impose her views on males, but twice in 1888 D. Isabel had done precisely that. She used the monarch's prerogative to dismiss the Cotegipe cabinet in favor of one willing to enact abolition, and now she subordinated herself, as empress-in-waiting, to the pope. Already, during her third regency, she had tried to insist that a crucifix be hung in every schoolroom. Politicians simply could not trust D. Isabel to protect the status quo. They viewed her as dangerous, unpredictable in her actions, and likely to be guided not by them but by her husband and, for all they knew, by the pope as well.

The attacks on D. Isabel extended to her husband. Since his arrival in Brazil a quarter century before, Gaston d'Orléans had never captured the people's sympathy. He commanded no respect in public life. On the contrary, he remained deeply unpopular. First and foremost, his deafness that had grown worse with age cut him off from Brazilians. His accent reminded anyone who talked to him that he was a foreigner. *O francês* (the Frenchman) lacked physical presence and social graces. "He is not handsome, he is not elegant, he is not likable [*simpático*]," the *Gazeta da Tarde* remarked in 1886.[47] Any slander against him found easy acceptance. He was a slum landlord, supposedly renting his properties in Rio City at exorbitant rates. He was closefisted and had stashed away money in France as a precaution against the future. Despite his year's achievements as commander in chief in Paraguay and his service in improving the army's equipment since then, the count d'Eu had no support among either officers or enlisted men. The common assumption was that, being a man, he would in effect be in charge of Brazil when D. Isabel succeeded her father. He did not have the public's confidence.

In the face of constant press attacks, it is no wonder that the count d'Eu finally became, in his own words, "tired of being used as a scapegoat by the press, ostensibly responsible for everything without having in reality either voice or influence in anything." He began to take a role in public affairs. In March 1889, when a yellow fever epidemic broke out in the port town of Santos, he led a medical mission there to aid the sufferers. "It was fortunate that the count d'Eu decided to go there, showing an interest in the people," the editor of the *Jornal do Comércio* commented, "and I would wish that the princess too had shown the same in respect to this capital."[48] In May, Gaston d'Orléans broached to the João Alfredo ministry the idea that he should undertake a long public visit to the northern provinces of Brazil.

"The president of the council [of ministers] and the emperor both greatly applauded the idea, but in addition suggested that the princess would also do well to make the trip. This suggestion Mota Maia [Pedro II's personal physician] was opposed to, because of the emperor, so it had to be abandoned."[49] The point of the objection was that since Pedro II might die at any moment, his heir should not be far away from Rio for several weeks. Justifiable as the objection was, its effect was to deprive the plan of much of its efficacy. D. Isabel's remaining in Rio de Janeiro, enjoying her usual life, while the count undertook a public tour of the north, confirmed the prevailing impression that once the "Third Reign" began, it would be he, the empress's unpopular consort, who would be Brazil's real ruler.

The proposed tour was almost aborted by a political crisis that flared up days before his departure. The Liberal Party and the disaffected (pro-compensation) wing of the Conservatives united to defeat the sitting cabinet. João Alfredo requested a dissolution of the legislature. In keeping with his new activist role, the count d'Eu asked Pedro II for an interview in which he argued against granting a dissolution. "It is the first time that I have talked politics to him. He let me speak for about half an hour without saying anything, a bit vexed I think. After a pause he said that he would think about it," Gaston d'Orléans told the countess of Barral. "The Princess had promised to be present at this discussion, but, delayed by her devotions in church, she only arrived when we were concluding."[50]

As was his custom, the emperor kept his daughter and son-in-law totally excluded from the ensuing political maneuvers. Even at this stage in his reign, he could not envisage sharing authority with anyone, least of all with a woman. The ministry, denied a dissolution, resigned, and the feuds between the two wings of the Conservative Party prevented a replacement from being formed from its ranks. Pedro II turned again to the Liberals, and the viscount of Ouro Preto headed the new cabinet. In it he included, as minister of justice, the baron of Loreto, Amandinha's husband. The minister of war was the viscount of "Maracajú, my greatest confidant during the Paraguayan war," commented the count d'Eu. "You will say that these are excellent choices: Oh, well! I am only faintly pleased. I fear that all that will smack too much of the court [áulico] and won't carry conviction in the eyes of the country." He would have preferred, he told the countess of Barral, a ministry espousing the most radical ideas. "If the new ministry is going to appear, as did its predecessor, as the vehicle for the princess's desires, nothing will have been truly gained."[51]

The viscount of Ouro Preto selected the baron of Loreto to be a minister with the goal, it was widely believed, of securing D. Isabel's goodwill and of ensuring that, should her father's death bring her to the throne in the immediate future, she would maintain the cabinet in office. For these same reasons, Ouro Preto encouraged the count d'Eu to proceed with his tour of the northern provinces. The trip that lasted from June to September was a success, demonstrating that the monarchy still commanded considerable support within the country. The one cause for concern was a speech that Gaston d'Orléans made at Recife in August, when he referred to the fact that if a republic should through the will of the electorate replace the monarchy, the imperial family would have to leave the country.

On learning of this speech, D. Isabel wrote a letter expressing her disquiet and remarking, "I well understand that, should there be another form of government, we would perhaps be perforce obliged to withdraw, but I don't like saying that. I am attached to the country, I was born there, and everything in it reminds me of my 43 years of happiness!" When the moment came to send this letter, the princess substituted for it another text that avoided any direct mention of her dissatisfaction with the speech. In fact, other commentators shared D. Isabel's unhappiness. "The count d'Eu made in Pernambuco a speech that was politically of small prudence," the editor of the *Jornal do Comércio* wrote at the end of August. "I increasingly disbelieve in the peaceful transfer of power on the death of the emperor who, fortunately, looks very well."[52] Gaston d'Orléans in no way disagreed with this opinion. Earlier in the year he had remarked to the countess of Barral: "I appreciate that you are concerned about the political situation in Brazil. Who would not be? However, I believe it *impossible* that Father might ever be exiled. As long as he survives nobody will push matters to an extreme. But afterwards? That is terrible to contemplate. I don't understand what *precautions* you would wish us to take! We don't have the means to undertake them in any form."[53]

When D. Isabel and her husband were reunited at Rio in the middle of September 1889, the political situation appeared far more favorable to the monarchy than when the count d'Eu had departed on his tour. Several developments accounted for this improvement. On the night of July 15, when the imperial family was leaving the theater, they were greeted with cries of "Long live the Republic," and a revolver shot was fired at their coach. During this incident, D. Isabel behaved, as did her parents, with great coolness and good sense. The whole affair served to discredit radicalism and induce caution. The new cabinet began to shower financial and political concessions on

THE IMPERIAL FAMILY AT THE PALÁCIO DA PRINCESA, PETRÓPOLIS, LATE IN 1889

Courtesy of the Arquivo Histórico do Museu Imperial, Petrópolis

the discontented. On August 31 the Liberal Party won an overwhelm-
ing majority in the elections for a new Chamber of Deputies. At the
same moment a heady stock market boom began. "The economic
and political situation of the country appears to me to be promising,"
the editor of the *Jornal do Comércio* remarked; "however, I fear the
adventurous and somewhat rash nature of the v. of Ouro Preto." He

"does not always consider the future effects of the measures that he somewhat hotheadedly adopts, or deliberately avoids considering their impact."[54]

Ouro Preto's rashness was not checked or controlled by the emperor, who spent most of his time at Petrópolis and who only occasionally came down to Rio, and certainly not by the heir to the throne. For D. Isabel and the count d'Eu the most important event at this time was the celebration of their silver wedding anniversary, held in the Paço Isabel on October 15, 1889. Supporters of the ruling cabinet used the celebration as the occasion for demonstrating their loyalty to the heir to the throne and her husband. "The greater part of the press on that day showed a friendliness to which we are not accustomed," Gaston d'Orléans told his father, "and the dissenters confined themselves to silence."[55] The next month a number of festivities were organized in honor of a Chilean warship's visit to Rio de Janeiro. Among them was a lavish ball, on November 11, on the Ilha Fiscal, an island in Rio de Janeiro bay. The next day D. Isabel began to prepare the Paço Isabel for an evening party to be given on November 19 in honor of the officers of the Chilean warship.

Under this calm surface an explosion was preparing. The Republican Party, which the viscount of Ouro Preto had prevented from securing any seats in the newly elected Chamber of Deputies, abandoned all hope of replacing the imperial regime by peaceful means. The radicals in the party took control. A weapon lay to hand. The officer corps, particularly the junior officers who were often Republican in outlook, was highly discontented and in a state of open indiscipline. Ouro Preto had made no attempt to conciliate the armed forces and rapidly became the focus of the officers' discontent. Plans for a military uprising took shape, and a leader was found in General Manuel Deodoro da Fonseca, a senior military officer who had his own reasons for disliking Ouro Preto. The immediate goal was to oust the cabinet, but many of the conspirators hoped and intended that the rising might bring down the imperial regime as well. During the night of November 14–15, the officers led the garrison troops out of their barracks and marched on the army headquarters in the center of Rio City. The cabinet, forewarned, gathered together what forces it could and barricaded itself in the army headquarters. A brief face-off followed, but the cabinet's forces would not open fire in its defense. Resistance crumbled. The rebels entered the building. The ministers were forced to resign. General Deodoro da Fonseca, exhilarated by the course of events and persuaded by the younger officers, embraced the cause of a republic of which he would be the first president.

"It was ten o'clock in the morning of November 15, 1889, when the viscount of Penha and the baron of Invinheima [two senior military officers] appeared at our house, telling us that, as they said, part of the army had revolted and that, at Lapa [close to the Paço Isabel], there was a battalion reinforced by students from the Military School, both armed." Thus D. Isabel, some days later, described the events in an account she entitled "Memoir for My Children."[56]

> The news we received was such as to seem exaggerated to us. Miguel Lisboa offered to go to the Campo d'Aclamação to find out what was happening. He returned reporting that the Ministry was besieged in the headquarters and Ladário [the minister of marine] said to be dead.
>
> We telephoned the arsenals of the Navy and War and they answered that they knew nothing.
>
> I did not wish to leave the Paço Isabel. I feared that if matters were not as stated, they would later accuse me of fear, which however I have on no occasion shown.
>
> Shortly afterwards we received news that peace was restored, there was nothing more to fear, but the united army had imposed and achieved the ministry's resignation. Gaston exclaimed: "The monarchy is finished in Brazil." Still credulous, I judged that such a remark was too pessimistic. We are also informed that Deodoro [da Fonseca] had beside him Quintino Bocaiúva and Benjamin Constant [two leaders of the Republican Party] and that he had proclaimed a provisional government.[57]

At this point in the drama, the main concern of D. Isabel and her husband was to get in contact with her father in order to persuade him to stay in Petrópolis, where he could organize a response to the rising. But the central telegraph agency was already in the rebels' control. The couple decided to send their three sons to Petrópolis in the care of Dr. Ramiz Galvão, their *aio*. "It was a way of informing Daddy and also of getting the boys out of harm's way," the princess observed.

During the boys' journey by boat and train, "our presence was scarcely noticed," the middle son Luís later recalled. "I remember perfectly that our travelling companions discussed with indifference the day's news, not regarding it, it would seem, as important."[58] This indifference in fact typified the public's reaction to the regime's overthrow.

To return to D. Isabel's narrative of events: "Shortly after midday we received a telegram from Mota Maia saying that Daddy was leaving Petrópolis and traveling by the Northern railroad. We resolved to go and meet him." They boarded a launch to make the trip by water, but "on the way, Gaston saw in front of the Misericórdia [hospital] Daddy's coaches. We went to the Pharoux quay and there we learned that he was, in fact, already in the City Palace. We disembarked and stayed there with him and Mummy."[59] During the anxious hours that followed in the City Palace, both D. Isabel and the count d'Eu tried to persuade Pedro II to take action. He could regain control of the situation, they suggested, by entrusting the formation of a new cabinet to a politician who commanded the sympathies of the armed forces. The emperor did nothing. He would not even consent to summoning a meeting of the Council of State, composed of senior politicians. The princess and her husband finally took the initiative and sent out, in her name, summons to the councilors. Not until 11:30 at night did Pedro II at last agree to meet with the council, which advised the formation of a new cabinet. By then, events had moved far beyond any possibility of reversal. General Deodoro da Fonseca had proclaimed himself president of the new republic and appointed a ministry. The only consolation, and that an important one, for D. Isabel was the receipt of a telegram from her sons' *aio* announcing that they had reached Petrópolis in safety.

The next day, the members of the imperial family saw the City Palace being surrounded by cavalry patrols. They were held close prisoners. At two in the afternoon a delegation of army officers informed Pedro II that he and the rest of the imperial family had to leave Brazil within twenty-four hours. "It is impossible to recount what we felt in our hearts! The idea of leaving friends, the country that I love so much and that recalls a thousand happinesses I have enjoyed, made me break into sobs."[60] These sentiments D. Isabel embodied in a public message, responding to the order to leave:

It is with my heart riven with sorrow that I take leave of my friends, of all Brazilians, and of the country that I have loved and love so much, and to the happiness of which I have striven to contribute and for which I will continue to hold the most ardent hopes.

Rio de Janeiro, November 16, 1889

Isabel countess d'Eu[61]

In reality, D. Isabel was not required to leave behind all her friends, since both Amandinha Doria and Mariquinhas Tosta, with their husbands, decided to accompany the imperial family on their voyage into exile. Both couples went off to pack their bags and set in order not only their own affairs but also those of the princess. For D. Isabel a principal concern was to ensure reunion with her three children, still absent in Petrópolis. There, "cooped up in the palace, we were left for two long days in the most complete ignorance of what was happening outside," the middle son recalled.[62]

During the night of November 16–17, the members of the imperial family were awoken well before dawn and informed they must embark at once. They were taken on board the *Parnaíba* gunboat anchored in Rio de Janeiro bay, and there they remained until midday. One fear was removed during the morning when "the boys, whom on the previous day we had ordered to come from Petrópolis, arrived, thank God." In the afternoon, the gunboat steamed out from the harbor and, about eight o'clock in the evening, met with the *Alagoas* packet boat that had been designated to carry the exiles to Europe. The transfer of the imperial family from one vessel to the other took place with some considerable difficulty. "In truth there was danger, above all for Daddy and Mummy and for the young ones."[63] On the steamer, D. Isabel found her two friends with their husbands, who had hastily completed preparations for the journey. At midnight the *Alagoas* got up steam and set a course for Europe. The years of exile had begun.

7

HER OWN WOMAN, 1889–1921

D. ISABEL IN FRANCE DURING HER EXILE FROM BRAZIL

Courtesy of the Arquivo Histórico do Museu Imperial, Petrópolis

The voyage into exile marked the turning point, the grand climacteric of D. Isabel's life. The fundamental change she experienced at midpoint in adulthood can be compared to the advent of menopause in a woman's life cycle. A late nineteenth-century medical study, based on the histories of over 1,000 women in England and France, found their average age at menopause to be forty-five years and nine months. Although no evidence exists to show precisely when D. Isabel experienced change of life, her exile from Brazil took place at the age of forty-three, very near to the average age of menopause.

D. Isabel's reproductive cycle paralleled her public career in Brazil. The ceremony on July 29, 1850, recognizing her as heir to her father, occurred about the same time as menarche. Her marriage took place a few weeks after her majority, the legal age at which she could ascend to the imperial throne. During her first regency, D. Isabel was increasingly anxious to fulfill her assigned role of producing a child and eventual heir to the throne. Regent for the second time five years later, she was occupied with looking after her infant son and becoming pregnant again. By the time of her third regency, a decade later, she had three young sons and so had fulfilled her role as mother. A writer on women and medicine in the Victorian age has argued in respect to menopause that "once her childbearing capacity was lost, a woman's world was characterized by a loss of meaning."[1] In parallel fashion, the coup of November 15, 1889, deprived D. Isabel of her role as empress-in-waiting. She would live on in France for another three decades, but nothing she did merited, in the judgment of both contemporaries and posterity, attention.

Even though most medical texts and advice books of the nineteenth century agreed in viewing menopause as the end of a woman's life course in terms of her physical, intellectual, and social worth, these male authors' opinion reflected entrenched gender attitudes rather than female experience. It is true that during the Victorian era, only a minority of young women could expect to live to the age of menopause and beyond, but change of life was not of itself a cause of death. What killed most women or shortened their lives were the perils of pregnancy and childbirth. Women who did live to experience menopause could expect thereafter to enjoy better health and to survive longer than did men of similar age. Of course, external circumstances still shaped women's existence. At best, a middle- or upper-class woman could anticipate being a well-to-do widow, heading her own household and deferred to by her offspring. At worst, she would have to manage on meager resources an invalid husband or aged parent. Nonetheless, after menopause women could make their own lives to an extent that had not previously been possible. They did indeed become their own women.

After November 15, 1889, D. Isabel very much became her own woman, even though during the long voyage into exile, the prospects did not appear bright or promising. On the *Alagoas*, she spent much time writing down her reactions to recent events. In these notes, most of which she eventually incorporated into a "Memoir for My Children," she vented her strong feelings about the coup, "the greatest unhappiness of our life." First and foremost, she blamed the politicians who, in her view, had failed in their duty. "How was it that the ministry, especially the ministers of War, Marine, and of Justice and, through them, the president of the Council knew nothing? Imprudence! and more imprudence! carelessness or what? Once the entire armed forces were on the side of the insurgents none of us nor anyone else could have done other than what we did."[2] If Pedro II and the count d'Eu had been informed of how matters really stood, both would have positioned themselves in Petrópolis, she claimed, and would not have let themselves be led into a trap in Rio City. Her father had been ill served by those whom he had most reason to trust.

In her notes D. Isabel portrayed herself as calm and resolute. When Gaston wanted to withdraw to Petrópolis, she had resisted the suggestion. "As for me, since I always see everything in the best terms, I was far from thinking that what happened would happen. Accordingly, I was much influenced by the idea that we should do nothing that would later on make our position less easy, laying us open to accusations of cowardliness. . . . I did not want to leave the Paço Isabel immediately. I was concerned that if things were not as they stated, I might later on be accused of fear, of which, however, I have never given a sign."[3] Her words were indirectly a denial and so a rebuttal of the prevailing perception of women as weak mortals unable, as men were, to outface danger or respond coolly to challenges. Her narrative also makes clear that she did not perceive herself as in any way responsible for the monarchy's overthrow. "Talking [to the commander of the *Parnaíba* gunboat] about the events that gave rise to the crisis, and about the accusations of meddling leveled against us, we stated that we never involved ourselves in affairs of state."[4] Consistent with D. Isabel's attitude toward politics and public affairs, her memoir contains scant mention of the causes for the regime's overthrow, nor does it evaluate the reasons why events took the course they did.

D. Isabel's indifference to power and her tendency to accept the world as it existed explain why her memoir expresses little or no sense of loss or deprivation. Her regrets at ceasing to be heir to the throne had to do with her being forced to leave, without any certainty that she would return to, the land of her birth. Deeply upset by her last sight of Brazil on November 23, D. Isabel vented her feelings on paper: "One cannot be entirely happy in this world! My truly good times are already over! May God let me keep, at least, my loved ones! The country of my truest affections is at every moment receding from sight! God protect it! The memory of happy hours both upholds me and depresses me!"[5] Yet the situation was not so simple. D. Isabel's life in Brazil had always been defined by her role as heir to the throne, a role that brought her little satisfaction. Since her marriage in 1864, she had spent no less than six years in Europe, where she had lived as the countess d'Eu, virtually a private person. In November 1889, she was simultaneously going into exile and returning to a familiar way of life. All her relatives lived in Europe, none of them in Brazil. If she had to leave behind a circle of friends, the two she cherished most were traveling with her. France, where the imperial family would settle, possessed no fears and no dangers for D. Isabel. Her command of the language was excellent. She was bicultural and bilingual. In France she could practice her religion without restriction or reproach, ensuring that her sons received a Catholic education.

The voyage on board the *Alagoas* dragged on from November 18 to December 7, 1889. Pedro II, who maintained his customary self-control, spent his days reading aloud and in intellectual conversation. He avoided any mention of recent events or of his plans for the future. D. Teresa Cristina, emotionally devastated by her exile from Brazil, became increasingly ill. Pedro Augusto, unbalanced by the sudden reversal of his fortunes, developed an acute persecution mania that for some days made necessary his confinement in his cabin. As D. Isabel noted, "we had serious concerns about his sanity."[6] The count d'Eu busied himself by providing his sons with what school-work and physical exercise he could. D. Isabel passed most of her days in the company of the Dorias and the Tostas. It was not a cheerful time.

In contrast to the former emperor, who refused to discuss his plans, D. Isabel and the count d'Eu had no choice but to consider their future life. Place of residence and finances were of particular concern to them. In respect to the first, D. Isabel's love for her parents and her sense of duty constrained their choice. At least during the first few months, the entire family would likely have to reside together. More urgent was the problem of finances. The imperial family took no money with them into exile, and they held no assets in Europe. D. Isabel and her husband spent much time, in the early part of the voyage, writing letters and instructions for the management of their property and affairs in Brazil. Since both the princess and her parents were heavily in debt, they were entirely dependent upon the income received from the Brazilian treasury. The provisional government had promised to continue this income for the time being. It had also issued a decree granting the deposed monarch the sum of 5,000 contos (six times the amount of his annual income). Not until November 27, when the *Alagoas* was approaching the Cabo Verde islands, its first stopping point, did the former emperor consider this offer. "My opinion had been to accept it, if it were handed over, as a guarantee for the benefits that the laws assign to the imperial family," Gaston d'Orléans told the countess of Barral. It was D. Isabel who stood on principle. "But the princess objected to this, supported by Tosta and Doria, and it was also learned that the emperor had said to Mota Maia that he wanted to receive none of it."[7] D. Isabel's narrative makes no mention of this matter. The draft of the declaration declining the grant is, however, in her handwriting. A fair copy signed by Pedro II was mailed to Brazil from the Cabo Verde islands.

Two moments of satisfaction were granted to D. Isabel on the final leg of the voyage into exile. "On the 1st [of December] my heart leapt up to see hoisted, as we left São Vicente [in the Cabo Verde islands] our flag, which had not been flown on the steamer since our

departure. I could not prevent myself from clapping my hands and
I had a moment of great joy. It seemed to me to be a good omen!
I recalled so many moments of true happiness!"[8] The following day,
December 2, was her father's sixty-fourth birthday. D. Teresa Cristina was laid up with influenza, but the other family members and
the entourage gathered to celebrate the day. At a special dinner
champagne was served. "We drank to Daddy's health, and he replied
to us with a toast: 'To the prosperity of Brazil!' Everyone warmly
took part in our rejoicing, and the commander and the crew showed
themselves particularly willing to express their sympathy in every possible way. . . . All the entourage wrote tributes, which, signed, we saw
given to Daddy. I was very moved when, that morning, I went to
embrace him!" The tribute that the princess wrote on behalf of herself
and her husband echoed these sentiments. "After so much anguish,
may your birthday, our beloved Daddy, serve as the dawn of less
unhappy days. May this hope, which December 2 awakens, come
true; may all of us, at least for many, many years to come, spend this
day, so dear to us, at the side of our beloved Daddy whom his children love so wholeheartedly."[9] As these words indicate, the events of
November 15 had not caused D. Isabel to falter in her devotion to her
father.

Early on the morning of December 7, the *Alagoas* dropped
anchor at Lisbon. The exiles were received with royal honors by
Pedro II's great-nephew, King Carlos I, newly ascended to the
throne of Portugal. Public interest naturally focused on the deposed
emperor, whose calm and dignity aroused much admiration. Little
attention was paid to the count d'Eu and even less to D. Isabel. A
Portuguese journalist wrote: "Good-natured and courteous, somewhat
deaf, His Highness the count d'Eu spent much time talking with us.
He received us with much satisfaction, wishing to learn the latest news
from Brazil, asking us about the smallest details of the news that we
were giving him and that we knew from the telegrams received at
Lisbon." After summarizing his conversation about the events of
November 15, the journalist continued:

> We were talking with the count d'Eu when Her Highness the Princess
> Imperial approached us.

"Tell me," the countess d'Eu asked us, "what is that horrible thing next to the Tower of Belem?"

"It is a gasometer, belonging to the new gas company," we replied.

"It is a pity to have thus spoiled that beautiful monument."

"His Majesty the emperor is going to stay in Lisbon? Is he going to establish his residence in our country?"

"I don't know; but I am sure that he is not. The emperor is going to live in Cannes. Tell me, has the new Brazilian flag already been adopted?"

"The most recent telegrams," we said to her, "say that until the constituent assembly meets, the old flag is retained."

"That makes me happy. I found it repulsive that by the wish of two or three men a new flag has been imposed on the country."

And we spoke further about Brazilian matters that are unimportant.[10]

For the journalist, and indeed for those who read his report, D. Isabel was not someone whose opinions carried weight. She existed as an adjunct to her father and her husband.

For ten days the imperial party stayed in Lisbon. D. Isabel with her family, Pedro Augusto, the Tostas, and the Dorias then left on a visit to southern Spain, while the former emperor, D. Teresa Cristina, and their attendants toured northern Portugal. The two parties planned to rendezvous in due course in northern Spain and to travel on to France. D. Isabel and her party embarked on a round of sightseeing that brought them to Madrid two weeks later. Amandinha Doria recounted what followed.

On our journey we learned that our most beloved empress was sick. They did not wish to give us immediately the fatal news, since everyone in Spain knew that Her Majesty, on the 28th at 2 in the afternoon, had died at Porto of a heart attack.

Still ignorant of this sad event, we went to the 11 o'clock Mass at the church of Saint Ignez.

Returning to the hotel, the prince [count d'Eu], opening some telegrams sent to him, discovered in them the terrible news and at once Their Highnesses and all of us broke into sobs and tears, since we loved our empress very much.[11]

The influenza the former empress had contracted aboard the *Alagoas* had worsened after her arrival in Portugal, in part because Pedro II refused to take notice of his wife's condition or abandon his usual round of activities for her sake. In Porto, on the morning of her death, when she asked for a priest to be sent, her husband had gone out to see the sights of the city. D. Teresa Cristina died almost alone. Pedro II's remorse over what he had done resulted in intense grief and physical prostration. He turned to his daughter for consolation.

D. Isabel and her party rushed to the city of Porto, arriving there on December 30. In the hotel, D. Teresa Cristina's corpse was lying in state. On seeing her mother's body, D. Isabel fainted. Her relationship with D. Teresa Cristina had been complex. In her childhood, the two were clearly close, but D. Isabel was quickly drawn to the more dominant of her parents. The countess of Barral's appointment as *aia* in 1856 further diminished D. Teresa Cristina's standing. After her marriage in 1864, D. Isabel tended to use her mother as a provider of food, clothing, and services, yet she did feel protective toward the empress. The princess's own partnership with Gaston d'Orléans could not but make her aware how starved of affection and support her mother had been over the years. Compounding the grief and confusion caused by D. Teresa Cristina's death was the news that the provisional government of Brazil had on December 21, 1889, abolished the annual income received by the imperial family and banished the former emperor and his descendants from Brazilian soil. The knowledge that she could never return to her adopted country was probably a contributing cause of the former empress's death.

The Portuguese government offered a state funeral for D. Teresa Cristina at Lisbon with the date set for January 9, following the ceremonies held to celebrate King Carlos I's accession. Until then, Pedro II, his family, and his entourage had to remain in Porto at the hotel where the empress had died. Virtually no money was available to meet expenses of this stay and the costs of the funeral. The count d'Eu informed his father: "As for the financial situation, it is at this moment reduced to *zero* as much for him [Pedro II] as for us."[12] A large loan was arranged on the former emperor's behalf with a leading merchant of Porto who had made his fortune in Brazil. In this transaction, D. Isabel and her husband played no part, but knowledge of it made them, already heavily in debt in Brazil, determined to keep their own expenses to a minimum.

D. Teresa Cristina's death and the decree of banishment altered the dynamics of D. Isabel's relationship with her father. She did not love Pedro II the less, but he lost the ability to command. Instead of his daughter serving as a diversion and relaxation from his duties, she now became a necessity, a central point of his existence. For D. Isabel her ties to her father constituted but one dimension of her life. Her attitude continued to be one of filial devotion, but increasingly, her main goal was to coax her father into doing what she thought to be best for him. This system of management had in fact begun in August 1888 on the emperor's return to Brazil. D. Isabel was already accustomed to cooperating closely with the count of Mota Maia, her father's physician and companion in exile.

On the day following the funeral and interment at Lisbon, the imperial party left by train for Cannes, chosen by Pedro II as their place of residence. The changing relationship between D. Isabel and her father was manifest when the travelers broke their journey to visit the shrine at Lourdes. D. Isabel had visited the shrine in October 1873 and again during her residence in France from 1878 to 1881, when she had dedicated a plaque that read: "Thanks to God and to Mary, July 28, 1874–October 15, 1875–January 26, 1878," the dates of the births of her first three children. Pedro II, who had previously disdained the devotions favored by D. Isabel, not only attended Mass in the Church of the Grotto but also made his communion. He noted in his diary: "I have liked Lourdes."[13]

At Cannes the entire party settled into the Hotel Beau Séjour. One of D. Isabel's first responsibilities was to unpack, assisted by Amandinha Doria, the luggage that the empress had brought with her from Brazil. To members of the entourage she gave mementos from her mother's possessions. All was not sadness, however. Many of D. Isabel's relatives came to visit. Especially welcome were the countess of Barral and her daughter-in-law, who was Amandinha Doria's sister. "We live the most frivolous life possible," Amandinha noted in her diary on January 25, "imitating the fashionable who live for enjoyment, visiting the shops and drinking tea or eating pastries in Rumpelmeyer's, the most renowned confectionery shop in Cannes."[14]

D. Isabel and her husband set about resuming their own, autonomous life. They enrolled their three sons in the College Stanislas run by the Jesuit order. The boys' fluency in French facilitated their adjustment to the school. D. Isabel, often accompanied by Amandinha Doria, began looking for a villa to rent. The princess, as Amandinha noted on January 28, "wants to convince the emperor that he should reside, with the princes, in a house and stop living in a hotel, which is extraordinarily expensive, the rooms alone costing a thousand francs a day." She added: "His Majesty has objected to the idea, saying that he prefers the hotel." On the last day of the month, D. Isabel with Amandinha inspected the "Villa Beau Site, or Villa d'Ormesson, splendid, magnificent views, excellent facilities, near to the Hotel Beau Site, which belongs to the owners of the property, . . . with a beautiful garden, or English park, including a *lawn tennis* court, the fashionable game. The price is 500 francs for the remainder of the season."[15] D. Isabel and her husband decided to rent the villa, which they could afford, since Gaston d'Orléans's father agreed to provide them with a monthly allowance until their financial situation improved.

Once again, D. Isabel tried to convince her father to move in with them. "Question of where to reside," Pedro II wrote in his diary on February 4; "I decided not to leave this hotel. It is not easy traveling with others." Since the Villa Beau Site lay at the opposite end of Cannes from the Hotel Beau Séjour, the former emperor was by his decision depriving himself of easy contact with his daughter and her family. "It is a shame that H. M. does not at least have under the same roof his offspring and their children (today his only consolation), and equally sad that the princess is so far from her beloved father," Amandinha Doria recorded. "She has shed copious tears, although she intends to make frequent visits to see him in the Beau-Séjour and she is sure that, for his part, the emperor will be every day in her house."[16]

D. Isabel's change of residence coincided with the departure of relatives and friends visiting Cannes since the middle of January. The Tostas accompanied the princess in her move to the Villa Beau Site, where the couple took up residence. The Dorias, however, did not stay in Cannes. Amandinha and her husband left on a prolonged tour of Europe, which they had not previously visited. Pedro II made his first visit the next day: "I went to the Villa d'Ormesson to which my daughter with her family has moved. It has a good view."[17] On the following Sunday he resumed his accustomed habit of dining with his daughter at her house. However, as his diary entry for that day reveals, he discovered that the world was not quite what it had been.

> After having my coffee I am going to my daughter's house for dinner. 4h 20' I did not find her there and in fact I passed her on the road and she was going, as Gaston told me, to a fête at the College Stanislas. It is difficult to travel with someone who makes us lose time. Mota Maia [his physician] went to tell her I was here, and in the meantime I will read. 6h 25' . . . I started my reading of Pe. Bernardes' *Luz e Calor* to Isabel. 10 1/2 I dined well at Isabel's house.[18]

As this diary entry makes clear, D. Isabel, in her new life, did not allow looking after her father to take precedence over her own family's interests. Every Thursday the five of them went to dine with Pedro II. After the meal, Gaston took the children home, and D. Isabel stayed with her father until about 10 o'clock. In all other respects the two establishments kept to themselves, as Gaston d'Orléans informed the countess of Barral in the middle of March. "We know less than ever about what is being cooked up there [in the Hotel Beau Séjour] concerning finance or politics. It is remarkable! but, after all, consistent with what has always been the case." This letter contained his comment that not since his residence in England in 1870 had he felt so secure and contented as he did now. "It is even a great pleasure that our expenses are slightly less than the budget established by Papa, whereas down there [Brazil] one of my miseries was that for the last 25 years I was always spending more than I could afford."[19] The residence at Cannes continued until the end of July, when the school year closed and the lease on the Villa Beau Site expired. The imperial family then embarked on a round of visits.

The first stop was a stay of two weeks with the countess of Barral at Voiron, outside Grenoble, in the French Alps. The Dorias also came to Voiron at the end of their European tour. For D. Isabel, who had known the countess and Amandinha for over thirty years, these two weeks were an opportunity to recall her youth. It was a happy time, but it was also a moment of change and farewell. "We did not stay longer in Europe, my husband and I," Amandinha recalled in old age, "because he had to return to Brazil to make his living. We were not rich."[20] When the Dorias left Voiron on August 3, there was no certainty that D. Isabel would ever see her friend again. The same was true of the countess of Barral, now seventy-four and well into old age.

THE IMPERIAL FAMILY AND OTHERS AT VOIRON, FRANCE, AUGUST 1890

Courtesy of the Arquivo Histórico do Museu Imperial, Petrópolis

At the next stop in their itinerary, the German spa of Baden-Baden, D. Isabel took charge of her destiny. She and the count d'Eu decided that they would make their permanent home on the outskirts of Paris, close to a suitable school for their sons. They hoped that Pedro II would agree to reside close to them, if not with them. The count d'Eu left Baden-Baden first, to be followed on September 10 by his wife. Pedro II noted: "Isabel has already come, some time ago, to say good-bye to me, since she is going to Paris for some days in order to see a house in the suburbs for the winter."[21] From Versailles, just outside Paris, D. Isabel wrote a long letter to her father's physician.

Sr. Mota Maia,

It is on the dining room table that I am writing to you. We have spent the whole day running from pillar to post. We have inquired everywhere, we have left no stone unturned, but as of now we have only found two 1st floor apartments that could be suitable for Daddy.

For us, it's impossible to find anything save a villa. There is one that suits and which is not far from the apartment in Passy. In Auteuil there is nothing suitable. The most reasonable solution for so much difficulty and complication is Versailles, unless one wants to put Daddy into apartments in the center of Paris, which is less advisable.

This, then, is what I propose to you, and I earnestly beg you to speak to Daddy and equally to [the count of] Nioac so he talks to Daddy in this sense. I count on your dedication and friendship. Tell Daddy that I can't move into my villa immediately and that we propose that we all go to the Hotel des Reservoirs in Versailles. From there, when I move into my villa, Daddy would go to Nioac's house, for about two weeks, and he would return, when he wanted to, to Versailles, which we can't leave, in view of the boys' education. I judge the Hotel des Reservoirs (which is sheltered) to be more suitable and better for Daddy, rather than the apartments in Passy or Auteuil (the ones I found) that are not, and I saw everything that there was.[22]

D. Isabel's letter made plain that, much as she wanted her father to take up residence close to them, no refusal on his part would block the decision she had made. Pedro II agreed to visit her new villa near Versailles. He stayed in Paris itself but made several visits so that he could enjoy "the almost constant company of my offspring and small grandchildren."[23] No persuasion could, however, make him change his plans. Early in November, Pedro II with his entourage went back to Cannes.

This departure meant that D. Isabel was now finally and entirely her own woman. She could make her life as she wanted within the conventions that she herself accepted and supported. It was an existence that focused, as it had done in Brazil, on her family, her religious duties, and her social activities. Gaston d'Orléans continued to receive D. Isabel's love and concern. Although he found great pleasure in taking trips and seeing new places, D. Isabel preferred her own home and a domestic life. The letters she wrote when apart from him were full of comfort and support, with phrases such as "I am above all sad to see you so distressed!" A comment by Pedro II shows how the two accommodated to each other, each pursuing their preferred activities. "Gaston came here with the grandchildren after lunch. Isabel went to Paris to look at the shops and will only be here this evening. I don't care for these excursions without Gaston who does not enjoy going shopping."[24]

Having settled down on the outskirts of Paris, D. Isabel was able to participate in a wide range of cultural and social events in the French capital. Her closest and most constant companions were Mariquinhas Tosta, baroness of Muritiba, the childhood friend who shared her exile, and Eugenia da Fonseca Costa, daughter of the viscount of Penha, a Brazilian who moved to Paris after November 15, 1889. These two served, in effect, as D. Isabel's ladies-in-waiting, and indeed Eugeninha Penha, as D. Isabel usually referred to her, was the great-niece of the viscountess of Fonseca Costa, D. Teresa Cristina's lady-in-waiting and confidante. Since D. Isabel was still treated as royalty by the circles she frequented, her social life was little affected by her being in exile.

Both the princess and her husband made their main object of concern their children. At the time the family took up residence in their villa outside Versailles, their eldest son Pedro celebrated his fifteenth birthday. Luís was two years his junior, and Antônio or "Totó," as he was commonly called, was aged nine. The three boys were quite distinct in character. Pedro was friendly and good-natured but not quick to learn and often clumsy. Luís was strong-willed, very active, and acute. In March 1890, their father commented on "Baby Pedro, always notable for laziness and ineptness," while "Luís does the identical course work all by himself with admirable distinction and capacity." The ease with which Luís outshone his older brother and his parents' censorious attitude probably made Pedro the less willing to compete, inhibited as he already was by the disability in his left arm and hand. Totó was very much the youngest child, somewhat indulged, in part because of his constant ill health and in part because of his engaging personality. "Totó," as his grandfather observed, "is very cute."[25]

Although now residing far from Pedro II, D. Isabel did not neglect her father. The two of them constantly wrote letters and exchanged telegrams. She made several visits to him in Cannes, spending a month there during February and March 1891. This long stay helped

Courtesy of the Museu Nacional Histórico, Rio de Janeiro

to console him for a common loss, the countess of Barral's death on January 14. As soon as she learned of the countess's sickness, D. Isabel had rushed to her bedside. "We returned yesterday from a sad pilgrimage, which filled me with sorrow, but which we were pleased to undertake in order to make one last act of homage to our most beloved countess of Barral," the princess wrote to a childhood friend in Brazil. "Unfortunately we only arrived at Grande Garenne after her death; we were able to accompany her to her last resting place and to pray for her beside her body." Sad as was the countess's death for D. Isabel, it was a much more severe blow for her father, who very much needed his daughter's comfort during the long and severe winter of 1891. During the school vacations in January and April, Gaston and the children also came to visit. When they all left on April 10, Pedro II wrote in his diary: "I will be very, very much alone until the start of May," when he moved from Cannes to Versailles. Due to his diabetes, he was much less active than previously, with a limited ability to walk. On May 13, the former emperor celebrated with his daughter the third anniversary of the abolition of slavery. "I gave a beautiful bouquet to Isabel in celebration of today's anniversary."[26] Only two others, one of them the son of the viscount of Rio Branco, were present at this modest ceremony. A month later, Pedro II left Paris for a stay in Vichy, where his health took a disastrous turn for the worst. D. Isabel paid him a week's visit late in June and, accompanied by her son Antônio and Eugeninha Penha, spent six weeks with him in August and September.

An incident during this second stay pointed up D. Isabel's independence from her father. On Sunday, August 16, Pedro II noted in his diary: "Excellent visit with the bishops of Rodez and Rennes, especially with the former, more intelligent than the other." Two days later D. Isabel wrote to her husband:

> Tell Marguerite that Monseigneur Gonindard [coadjutor bishop of Rennes] is here, that he preached, that I had a long conversation with him on Sunday (he came to see us with the bishop of Rodez), that he strongly urges me not to fail on this occasion to go to Paray-le-Monial, that he will arrange matters there for me, and that perhaps I may be able to enter the cloister and stand where Our Lord showed His heart to Saint Marguerite-Marie [Alacoque]! I would be so happy if I could! How I would pray there for all those who are dear to me!

D. Isabel at once began to arrange her pilgrimage to the shrine dedicated to the Sacred Heart. On August 20, Pedro II noted in his diary: "I had a discussion with Isabel who intends to go to Paray-le-Monial, which will increase her reputation as a fanatic [*beata*], prejudicing her in public opinion. But there is no harm in it and she is going." The next day he commented: "I have just said good-bye to Isabel; despite what I advised, she insists on going." On the evening of August 22, following her return, he simply wrote, "10 1/2 My daughter and Totó as well as Eugeninha Penha." The next day D. Isabel sent an ecstatic letter to her husband. "What shall I say to you about Paray-le-Monial? When we got back to Moulins, it seemed to us as if we had fallen from Heaven to earth. I left that holy sanctuary with many *saudades* [regrets]. When there I consecrated Totó to the Sacred Heart. That it may protect him!" In sum, D. Isabel had finally outgrown her father. She no longer sought to engage in the pursuits that he favored. On September 12, Pedro II recorded, "Isabel came to wish me good night. She had not enjoyed the theater. I gave her the news of Peruzzi's death, whom she clearly did not know, despite having frequently seen his name in the letters I wrote to her during my time in Italy."[27] A former diplomat, writer, politician, and stalwart of Italian unification, Ubaldino Peruzzi was exactly the type of person whom Pedro II admired but who did not in the least interest D. Isabel.

An improvement in the former emperor's health allowed him to leave Vichy in the middle of September. After a stay in Versailles, he moved to Paris, where D. Isabel and Gaston visited him at least three times a week. Early in November, politics suddenly intruded. Manuel Deodoro da Fonseca, the president of Brazil since November 15, 1889, lost patience with the opposition in the Congress. He dissolved it, taking dictatorial powers. His act brought the country to the brink of civil war. For a few days the restoration of the imperial regime seemed possible. In Paris, a small group of monarchists consulted with Pedro II as to what action should be taken. The plan seems to have been that Pedro II and D. Isabel would both renounce their rights in favor of Pedro, now aged sixteen. The young prince would return to Brazil accompanied by his grandfather, who would act as regent until Pedro reached his majority in October 1893. Both D. Isabel and her husband would remain in Europe in order not to prejudice the success of this scheme. D. Isabel was not involved in these discussions, but the plan was not viable until she consented to it. She was consulted on November 12, and as Pedro II cryptically noted in his diary, "the result was what I feared."[28]

The ostensible reason for D. Isabel's refusal was her unwillingness to let her son, still an impressionable youth, return to Brazil where the political and intellectual atmosphere was, as the princess well knew, hostile to Catholicism. The new republic had deprived that faith of its status as the state church, and nobody, the bishops included, wished to reverse this step. If made emperor, Pedro would therefore rule over a lay state, surrounded by irreligious advisers. In D. Isabel's opinion, her eldest son's faith would be in danger. In the event, D. Isabel's refusal to consent was of no consequence. On November 21, the Brazilian Navy revolted against Deodoro da Fonseca who, faced with the prospect of bloodshed, resigned. The vice president assumed office, and the legislature was restored. The immediate crisis was over.

These developments in Brazil were soon overshadowed by events in Paris. Pedro II picked up a cold that developed into pneumonia. His diabetic condition made recovery impossible. In the early hours of December 7, 1891, he died in the Hotel Bedford, just behind the Madeleine church in the heart of Paris. Present in the room were D. Isabel, her husband, and her nephew Pedro Augusto, together with the former emperor's physician Mota Maia, his chamberlain Aljezur, the Tostas, and some twenty other Brazilians. Those present first kissed the hand of the deceased and then that of D. Isabel, in formal recognition of her new position as claimant to the Brazilian throne. As such she was treated in the days following her father's death. The French government gave Pedro II a state funeral, with official honors in the Madeleine church. The coffin, accompanied by D. Isabel and her entire family, went by train to Lisbon for a second state funeral. Pedro II's remains were interred next to his wife in the royal mausoleum.

In the course of two years, D. Isabel had lost both her parents. Now, at the age of forty-five, she became the senior member of her family, able to chart her own course. The property her parents owned in Brazil was sold, and she inherited half the proceeds. She was financially independent, although much of the inheritance went to repay the huge debts that Pedro II had incurred during his two years in exile. D. Isabel and her husband were able to acquire their own house, a large villa in the Paris suburb of Boulogne-sur-Seine, where they lived a conventional and fairly frugal existence. They devoted their time to their sons' upbringing and to caring for Gaston d'Orléans's father, the duke of Nemours, then in old age. Except for the fact that D. Isabel was, in the eyes of monarchists, the true ruler of Brazil, there was nothing to distinguish her in outlook and behavior from a thousand other ladies of the French aristocracy.

At the time of the overthrow of the imperial regime, its return seemed an impossibility. At the very end of 1889, the editor of the *Jornal do Comércio*, the leading newspaper, had commented, "in my opinion, the idea of a monarchical restoration should be banished from the mind of all sensible men. To attempt anything in this direction would today be madness and even a crime against the country, which would be plunged into bloodshed and never again be what it was."[29] The specter of civil war first haunted Brazil in November 1891 but was averted by Deodoro da Fonseca's resignation as president. His replacement, General Floriano Peixoto, was far more ruthless in purpose and resilient in character. Floriano's autocratic style of rule provoked widespread opposition, particularly among his rivals in the armed forces. He dealt mercilessly with dissent.

In November 1892, a group of monarchist supporters sent an urgent appeal to D. Isabel. "The reaction to the state of affairs established on November 15, 1889, is spreading profoundly and extensively across all the provinces, and in the province of Rio Grande do Sul is ready to break out into armed resistance. For the complete success and unquestioned triumph of the cause of which Y. I. M. is the first and sole representative, a cause that the majority of the Nation espouses, there is a need for financial resources that, given the present circumstance of the country, cannot be found there."[30] The conspirators wanted D. Isabel to sanction promises on their part that a restored monarchy would repay with interest all moneys lent in support of the rebellion. They also asked her to sanction the rebellion because, "if this present occasion be lost, it will be difficult to find another to re-establish order, liberty, legality in the ill-fated country threatened by the most terrible ills."

D. Isabel's reply was worded so as to avoid giving offense to the authors of the appeal, but the terms it employed made her attitude fully clear. "My father with his prestige would probably have rejected civil war as a means of returning to the country. . . . I would regret anything that arms brother against brother. . . . I do not consider it to be the role of the royal prerogative [*poder moderador*] to be involved in such a struggle, particularly when its success appears to be little more than possible. I cannot fail to point out that in the event of failure the present attempt will make more difficult another one with better chances."[31] She would not forbid the attempt, but she would not sanction it. In a private response sent to João Alfredo, who had served as head of the cabinet during her third regency, D. Isabel was more forthright in expressing her opposition. "In no way do I wish to encourage such a war, the more so since I don't see it as having a strong base or likely success. . . . When will politicians stop resorting to means that diminish the moral stature of peoples and individuals? It is thus that everything is lost and we will ourselves lose. You however know my sentiments as a Catholic and a Brazilian!"[32]

The monarchist chiefs' appeal and D. Isabel's response, both public and private, reflected a gender divide. For the monarchists a resort to arms was a necessity, not just because of Floriano Peixoto's oppressive rule but also because men in such circumstances had to show their resolution, courage, and willingness to act boldly. Violence was the appropriate masculine response. Armed rebellion appeared much less justified to D. Isabel, who viewed the use of force as incompatible with Christianity. The glamour of battle meant nothing to the princess, whose first thought was for the maimed, the widows, and the orphaned children. "How preferable it would be if moral persuasion alone enabled us to return there! . . . It grieves me to think that perhaps the only result will be to swell the number of unfortunates."[33]

The promised insurrection broke out in February 1893, and the civil war lasted until August 10, 1894. In the end the acting president triumphed. As D. Isabel had foreseen, the conflict had not achieved a restoration. The monarchists failed to mobilize sufficient popular backing, and they could not win over the armed forces. To do so the cause would have had to be led by a warrior prince—dashing, brave, and resourceful—resembling Prince Alfonso, who had in 1874 overthrown the Spanish Republic and ascended the throne as King Alfonso XII. No such savior was available in Brazil. D. Isabel's eldest son Pedro came of age in October 1893, but he showed no desire or capacity to take up the cause. His cousin Pedro Augusto, D. Isabel's eldest nephew,

THE COUNT D'EU IN LATE MIDDLE AGE

Courtesy of the Biblioteca Nacional, Rio de Janeiro

was certainly willing, but after Pedro II's death, his conduct became increasingly unbalanced, and in October 1893 he attempted suicide. Pedro Augusto's father was forced to commit him to an asylum, where he spent the rest of his life.

D. Isabel's refusal to countenance a civil war in Brazil did not mean that she played no role in the conflict. Her reply to the monarchists' appeal she had signed simply as "Isabel," signifying her claim to be monarch. The political interests backing Floriano Peixoto stressed that a monarchist restoration meant accepting D. Isabel as empress, using this fact to denigrate the rebels and to rally support for the regime. All the gender prejudices associated with the exercise of power were mobilized against D. Isabel, who was portrayed as a political reactionary and a religious fanatic.

D. Isabel and the count d'Eu, accustomed to press attacks and public hostility, were shielded by distance from this new campaign launched against them. They suffered no personal loss from the failure of the monarchist cause. Their life in France maintained its quiet rhythm as the years sped by. In September 1894, D. Isabel thanked her husband "for your good letter of the 2nd, written thirty years after we saw each other for the first time! It seems as if it were only yesterday that I saw you, my darling, in Mummy's cozy room at São Cristóvão!"[34] Late in June 1896, the duke of Nemours died, and his legacy gave his son and daughter-in-law financial security. A month later, D. Isabel celebrated her fiftieth birthday.

During the 1890s, D. Isabel's three sons entered adulthood and embarked on their own lives. In September 1893, she sent news of her eldest to a childhood friend in Brazil: "On the 25th Pedro is going to Vienna. It is clear that he must do something and a military career seems to us the only one he should follow. He is going to study in the military school at Wiener Neustadt," near Vienna. "Separation from him will cost me a lot." His two brothers followed Pedro to the same military school. "On the 18th Pedro was promoted to officer," his mother wrote in August 1896, "having completed his three years at the academy with the highest marks. The ceremonies were beautiful and touching. I now have the three of them with me, which is a great consolation for the prince [the count d'Eu] and me." Six years later D. Isabel commented: "Here I am back in Boulogne[-sur-Seine], having traveled a great deal. At this moment I am alone, Antônio having left yesterday with the prince for Austria. Fortunately, the prince will come back to me on the 15th."[35]

To fill the void left by her sons' departure from home, D. Isabel threw herself with zeal and dedication into all types of charitable work organized by the Catholic Church. A passage from the sermon delivered at her funeral gives, despite its hyperbole, a good idea of her daily

D. Isabel's eldest son, Pedro, as an officer in the Austro-Hungarian army

Courtesy of Isabelle, comtesse de Paris

D. ISABEL ENTERING HER CARRIAGE AT THE CHÂTEAU D'EU, FRANCE, with Dr. Francisco de Sousa Melo and Mariquinhas Tosta's husband, the baron of Muritiba

Courtesy of the Arquivo Histórico do Museu Imperial, Petrópolis

rounds. "Her hands gave bounteously both to the poor and to the glory of God. Her charity knew no limits save those imposed by a fortune too small for her rank, for the generosity on a royal scale that her compassionate heart dreamed of. At Boulogne-sur-Seine, priests, heads of charities, male and female, competed in soliciting her high patronage for their collections, their subscriptions, and the charitable fêtes. She never refused."[36]

In 1905, Gaston d'Orléans purchased the château d'Eu, located in the town of that name, near Le Tréport on the Normandy coast. The castle, a favorite residence of King Louis Philippe, stands in the heart of the town on a broad bluff overlooking the river Bresle. Three years earlier a fire had considerably damaged the castle, really a large country house dating from the sixteenth century. "We are going to fix the exterior. As to the interior, we will only take care of the chapel. The rest is not necessary, and it is very expensive to restore," D. Isabel told Amandinha Doria.[37] Thereafter the couple spent the winters and spring in their villa at Boulogne-sur-Seine and the summers and fall at Eu. To the castle's vast rooms were moved the imperial family's possessions—furniture, pictures, papers—received from Brazil in the early 1890s and mostly in storage since then. D. Isabel's private apartments faced the formal gardens laid out by André Le Nôtre, the celebrated landscape architect. In them she planted several hundred roses of different varieties, and their scent invaded the very castle itself.

Gaston d'Orléans's purchase of the castle from which he took his title as count was part of a larger dynastic plan. In 1909, he made an agreement with his cousin, the duke of Guise, pretender to the French throne, that he and his descendants would constitute a separate, independent branch of the French royal family. "The count d'Eu desired to tie his son Pedro to Eu in order to make him a French prince," Pedro's eldest daughter commented in the late 1970s. "To gain that end, he acted somewhat as a tyrant over my father who, out of filial love, let him do so. Even the count d'Eu's will was drawn up with the purpose of tying Dom Pedro to Eu."[38] What gave Gaston d'Orléans the opportunity to force his eldest son to accept his plan was the latter's choice of a spouse.

In February 1889, the count d'Eu had described Pedro as being "just as incapable and heedless in this [playing billiards with Pedro II] as in everything else," yet in 1896 Pedro completed, in his mother's words, "his three years at the academy with the highest marks."[39] This transformation is not really surprising. At Wiener Neustadt academy, for the first time in his life, Pedro lived free from his parents' oversight and recriminations. At the military school he struck up a friendship with the four Dobrzensky de Dobrzenicz brothers, barons of the Austro-Hungarian empire and descendants of the ancient Czech nobility. Pedro visited the family's estates at Chotebor, southeast of Prague, where he made the acquaintance of their sister Elizabeth. Just as D. Isabel during her first visit to England in 1865 discovered a way of life that satisfied her, so now her eldest son found an existence that suited him: unassuming, spontaneous, domestic. The growing attraction that he felt for "Elsi," as she was known, was bound up with this discovery, but the couple was well suited in character and outlook. As their eldest daughter phrased it: "Often surprising, my parents' behavior could cause considerable astonishment. However, their simplicity, joined to their naturalness, meant that they never scandalized anyone."[40]

In contrast, Pedro's younger brother Luís was an activist, being ambitious and strong-willed, viewing the world as his to conquer. He took up mountaineering and in September 1896 ascended Mont Blanc. A visit to southern Africa was followed by a long and very challenging tour through central Asia and India. All three experiences, Luís wrote about and published. D. Isabel and the count d'Eu regarded their second son, not Pedro, as the person capable of maintaining the monarchist cause in Brazil. Writing in April 1904 to a leading monarchist in Brazil, D. Isabel remarked: "I would also like you to be convinced that I in no way make a question of my own person. Somebody who is younger could be more in a position to be useful, and if I have not yet given up the reins, it is because youth can be rash."[41]

After his return from his adventures, Luís embarked on exactly that type of project. He decided to visit Chile on a steamer that stopped at Rio de Janeiro. He intended by his presence to challenge the decree of banishment enacted against the imperial family by the provisional government. Luís's sudden appearance in Rio de Janeiro revealed how slight the appeal of monarchism had become in Brazil. The hand of time lay heavy on "venerable leaders of our party," as he noted when they came on board his steamer. "How their faces had grown old, how much white hair!"[42] No new generation of monarchists existed to advance the cause. The national government enforced the decree of banishment, and Luís was not allowed to set foot in his native land.

LITHOGRAPH OF THE IMPERIAL FAMILY, sent out as a Christmas card

Courtesy of the Fundação Grão Pará, Petrópolis

He eventually related his experiences during this journey in *Sob o cruzeiro do sul*, published in 1913.

Luís was, however, to receive one consolation for his disappointed ambition. His brother Pedro was adamant in his desire to marry Elizabeth Dobrzensky, but D. Isabel and the count d'Eu withheld their consent because of the intended bride's lack of royal descent. Even

Elizabeth "Elsi" Dobrzensky de Dobrzenicz, 1908

Courtesy of Isabelle, comtesse de Paris

after Emperor Francis Joseph made Elizabeth Dobrzensky's father a count in 1906, D. Isabel and the count d'Eu would not agree to the marriage until their second son had found a spouse. In 1908, following Luís's engagement to his cousin, Maria Pia of Bourbon-Naples, D. Isabel and her husband finally consented to Pedro's marriage, provided that he renounce his rights to the Brazilian throne in favor of his brother. This act forwarded the count d'Eu's plan to make his eldest son the head of an independent branch of the Orléans family. Pedro, who had no interest in becoming monarch, signed the renunciation on October 30, 1908. The marriage of Luís and Maria Pia took place on November 4 and that of Pedro and Elizabeth ten days later.

In the interval between the two marriages, D. Isabel wrote to the Monarchist Directorate in Rio de Janeiro.

> Pedro will continue to love his country and will give his brother all the support he requires and of which he is capable. Thank God they are very much united. Luís will actively take charge of everything that relates to the monarchy and what is good for our land.
>
> Without desisting from my rights, I want him to be cognizant of everything, in order to prepare himself for the position that I desire with all my heart he will one day reach.
>
> Please will you therefore write to him as often as you judge necessary, making him aware of what is happening.
>
> My strength is not what it was, but my heart is the same in its love for my country and for all those who are dedicated to us.
>
> With my friendship and trust in you,
>
> Isabel Countess d'Eu.[43]

This letter was written nearly two decades after D. Isabel's exile from Brazil, and its language is revealing. She continued to live according to the standards she had absorbed in her earliest years. The claimant to the Brazilian throne must marry a wife of equal status. By designating Luís as heir to her rights and as her agent, D. Isabel distanced herself from the role that had been hers since her father's death in December 1891. She no longer signed as "Isabel," reverting to the familiar "Isabel countess d'Eu," which identified her as a private person. This change in status did not imply, she stressed, any waning of her love for Brazil. Symbolic of this love was the Amazonian macaw, a present to the family, which had accompanied them into exile. "The princess asks me to tell you that the beautiful Pará parrot," the count d'Eu had informed the donor in 1895, "is still with us and is in good health. The boys won't leave it behind even during their vacation travels." In her recollections, "Joies et Tristesses," written toward the end of 1908, D. Isabel referred to "our dear little parrot from Pará, our faithful companion of twenty years, which died only recently."[44]

One delight that her sons' marriages gave D. Isabel was grandchildren. "I am awaiting the birth of my third grandchild produced by Pedro," she wrote in August 1914 to João Alfredo. "I am sending enclosed a photograph of myself with my grandchildren by Luís. Pedro Henrique [Luís's eldest] is growing continually and is a very intelligent child. His grandparents have a particular love for their darling little grandchildren." Marie Isabelle, D. Isabel's eldest granddaughter, recalled: "My grandmother adored me and I was very proud of this love; I now ask myself whether I returned it sufficiently. She spoiled me so much." "I was the cherished granddaughter of my grandparents . . . I had a kitten's consuming love for my grandmother and an immense tenderness for my grandfather."[45] The causes for the couple's devotion to their first granddaughter, with her blonde locks, harked back almost forty years. She was the reminder, almost the reincarnation of their own daughter, also blonde-haired, who had died in her mother's womb.

After marrying, Pedro and Luís continued to reside with their parents, moving between the villa at Boulogne-sur-Seine and the castle at Eu. Proximity to her grandparents allowed Marie Isabelle to observe them with the sharp eyes of childhood.

> My grandmother was a "woman with personality," as individuals difficult to categorize are termed. Physically, she was small, blonde, with blue eyes. Her hair was swept up in a mass of small curls, a style originally adopted out of necessity following an attack of typhoid fever. She was not very pretty, but she was charming, intelligent, and assertive. Her voice was soft, and she did not speak with a Brazilian accent but with the intonation peculiar to the Bourbon-Naples family, which endured even after its members were scattered across the face of the globe. Besides, the empress Teresa Cristina, her mother, was a Bourbon-Naples. I found the voice of my grandmother very melodious and I liked the tone in which she called me "Bébelle." She was, further, a woman of generous even if strongly held ideas.

D. Isabel, in her granddaughter's words, "knew how to express her authority in a very specific form." When her grandchildren dared to pick blooms from the rose beds underneath the windows of her rooms at the château d'Eu, she would call out: "You naughty little things, please don't ruin my roses!"[46]

The villa at 7 boulevard de Boulogne, Boulogne-sur-Seine, was "a beautiful mansion of the Napoleon III period with its large garden, lawns, stables, kitchen-garden, and greenhouses. On the first floor there was a little chapel, its walls covered with red cloth and hung with reliquaries, and on a column, in one of the corners, the celebrated Golden Rose." D. Isabel spent her mornings in her study with her secretary, keeping abreast of her correspondence with family and friends and planning her activities. "Two things alone impassioned her: Brazil and the conversion of the godless," her eldest granddaughter recalled. "For many years, she made vain attempts to save, among others, the soul of Marshal Joffre who often came to see her at Boulogne." Her visitors included many Brazilians, both visitors to France and residents there. Notable among the latter group were Mariquinhas Tosta, baroness of Muritiba, and her husband, who had accompanied the imperial family into exile. The Muritibas and others, such as the baroness of São Joaquim, continued in service with D. Isabel and constituted the last vestiges of the imperial court. Another figure from the past was her old music teacher, José White, the Afro-Cuban violinist who, like D. Isabel, had moved from Rio de Janeiro to Paris. "He came several times a month and for several hours you could hear music coming from the salon to which no one was admitted. The children alone occasionally had permission to enter this sanctuary; this salon was filled with curios, photographs, marble statues, and there was never a single flower."[47]

D. Isabel's placid round of life abruptly changed with the outbreak of World War I in August 1914. The invasion of France by Germany gave Luís, who was in his own words "a soldier heart and soul," an outlet for both his idealism and his activism.[48] He and his younger brother Antônio rushed to defend the country of their ancestors. Since a law forbade them, as members of the French royal family, from serving in that nation's forces, they both enlisted as officers in the British army. For the duration of the war, D. Isabel and her husband lived in the castle at Eu, where they both served, visiting the wounded and feeding refugees from Belgium and northern France. On October 15, 1914, the couple celebrated, in the company of three sons, two daughters-in-law, and six grandchildren, their golden wedding anniversary. The photograph taken on that day was the final occasion for unalloyed happiness.

The trials and sorrows that followed struck D. Isabel in her very identity as a woman. In 1915, while serving in the trenches of Flanders, Luís, her second and prized son, contracted an ailment that left him

THE GOLDEN WEDDING POSTCARD SENT BY D. ISABEL AND THE COUNT D'EU, OC-TOBER 1914. Left to right, standing, Luís, Antônio, Pedro; seated, Maria Pia, D. Isabel, the count d'Eu, Elizabeth, with grandchildren. The count d'Eu is holding the hand of the future comtesse de Paris

Courtesy of the Fundação Grão Pará, Petrópolis

debilitated and barely able to walk. Antônio, her youngest-born, who had been in the thick of the war, survived it without harm. After the Armistice, on a flight from Paris to London, his plane crashed in northern London. Left critically wounded, he died on November 29, 1918. "Blond, not very tall, with a jutting jaw, I found him very handsome and in fact he had an undeniable charm," his eldest niece recalled. "He was truly an original loved by all and adored by women." His death was a devastating blow to D. Isabel, as her letter to her husband, written on the day after she received the news, shows (see In Her Own Voice below). In the agony of her loss, she turned as she had always done since her sister's death in February 1871, almost half a century before, to faith, "the only consolation for such a loss."[49] Yet, even as she suffered, she did not forget her spouse, hoping by her words of consolation to lessen his sorrow.

In Her Own Voice

November 30, 1918, Boulogne-sur-Seine (Seine)

My poor beloved darling!

What grief! My heart and my head are shattered! Our good and gallant Totó! Pray that my head keeps intact. I prayed so much for Totó's recovery that if God has not granted it to me it is because He has judged it better so. This dear, dear darling has gone to God at the height of his strength and his beauty, in radiance and strengthened by the sacraments of our Holy Catholic Church! For him it is splendor, for us the hard trial that we will face with submission, through God's aid! It is a great comfort to think that he is happy. But I will never see him again in this world! That's appalling. I will keep him close by me at all times, this dear, dear Totó! How much I am also thinking of you, my most beloved, and of this dear Pedro who is so obliging in everything! Luís and the two daughters-in-law join me in my grief, as does everyone around. This morning our excellent parish priest came to say Mass here for Totó and we all took communion in his honor, including Puppe and Bonbon. Louis gave me to read his very beautiful article on Totó in today's *L'Action Française*. Oh! My God! My God! Yesterday evening I went out of my mind, but the Good Lord restored it.

In tears I embrace you with all my heart, darling, darling!

Yours, utterly for you, hoping that I can soften your grief!

Is[50]

Some months after this tragedy, D. Isabel lost her second son, Luís. The ailment he had contracted in the trenches resisted every form of treatment. His condition slowly, relentlessly declined until death claimed him in March 1920. In addition to these heavy personal blows, D. Isabel found her own health deteriorating because of a heart condition (perhaps inherited from her mother) exacerbated by her increasing weight. She found walking more and more difficult, having to use a cane. Eventually, she was confined to a wheelchair. In July 1919, just after his wife's seventy-third birthday, the count d'Eu reported that D. Isabel, "in spite of going out regularly with her usual courage, feels at times quite exhausted, mainly at the end of the day." Immobility worsened her condition. "I am not doing too badly," she wrote to her husband in January 1921, "but my legs and ankles have recently been very swollen."[51]

D. Isabel's immobility denied her one final consolation: her own return to her native land to witness the reburial of her parents. She had been adamant that she would not, as long as a republic existed in Brazil, permit her parents' bodies to be removed from Lisbon. However, the overthrow of the Portuguese monarchy in October 1910 caused her to change her mind. In response to a formal request from the monarchist leaders, she authorized the return if the government so requested and the banishment was revoked. The World War intervened, preventing action. In May 1920, the president of Brazil sent to the Congress a bill revoking the banishment and authorizing the return. The law was promulgated on September 7, and four months later, on January 8, 1921, a Brazilian warship carrying the bodies of the emperor and empress entered Rio harbor. On board were the count d'Eu and his surviving son Pedro, but not D. Isabel, by then virtually bedridden. Her husband sent back letters addressed to "*Chère bien aimée*" (Dear beloved), giving D. Isabel long and moving accounts of the voyage, the disembarkation in Rio, and his subsequent days in Brazil, including a visit to Petrópolis.[52] She had to be satisfied with this substitute for the fulfillment of her dream of one day going back to the land of her birth.

On October 15, 1921, D. Isabel and Gaston d'Orléans celebrated at the château d'Eu the fifty-seventh anniversary of their marriage.

D. Isabel's effigy tomb, Petrópolis cathedral, with those of her husband and parents

Author's personal collection

Three weeks later she contracted influenza, and she soon realized that her end was near. "I never felt myself so weak," she told the parish priest. "Prepare me for death. I would have liked to have lived some more time in the midst of my family, but I ask for nothing. The Good Lord knows better than we what we need." On November 14, she lost consciousness and her body ceased to struggle. Her parish priest arrived in time to administer the last sacraments of the Church, with the members of her family kneeling around her. Five days later the count d'Eu wrote to Amandinha Doria in Rio de Janeiro: "These are the first lines that I have written to Brazil since the terrible blow, and I am in no condition to give you details." The letter ended: "You can imagine the desolation in which we live and you can feel sorrow for the calamity inflicted on your old friend, Gastão d'Orléans."[53]

Four years older than D. Isabel, Gaston d'Orléans did not long survive her. Invited with his surviving family to attend the centennial celebrations of Brazil's independence, he died on the way to Rio on August 28, 1922. His body was returned to France to be buried next to his wife's in the crypt of the Orléans family at Dreux. In 1953, their coffins were brought to Brazil, with the intention that they should be reinterred alongside Pedro II and D. Teresa Cristina in the cathedral at Petrópolis. Not until 1971, the 150th anniversary of Brazil's independence, were the bodies moved to Petrópolis.

D. Isabel's effigy tomb now stands in the imperial chapel within the cathedral at Petrópolis. It is sited to the left of Pedro II's tomb and is set well back so as not to compete with his effigy. Gaston d'Orléans's tomb is separated from his wife's, standing to the right of D. Teresa Cristina's. The chapel contains no recognition of the indispensable role that D. Isabel's faith and determination played in the cathedral's construction. Outside, the vendors catering to tourists have no pictures of D. Isabel among the postcards they sell. In death no less than in life, D. Isabel remains subject to the assumptions about gender that so shaped her existence.

8

REFLECTIONS

D. ISABEL IN PARIS IN LATE MIDDLE AGE

Courtesy of the Arquivo Histórico do Museu Imperial, Petrópolis

All human beings are born with a capacity for agency—for desiring, for forming intentions, and for acting. Agency, as action, often involves getting another individual or a group to do something that the other would not otherwise do; it involves exercising power. Agency, as desiring and forming intentions, is shaped by individuals' personal qualities, by the culture in which they live, and by their access to resources. William H. Sewell Jr. explains that "part of what it means to conceive of human beings as *agents* is to conceive of them as *empowered* by access to resources of one kind or another."[1]

Although "some measure of . . . resources are controlled by all members of society, no matter how destitute and oppressed," Sewell points out, "the agency exercised by different persons is far from uniform." Agency requires an interplay between individual human beings and the cultures and resources of the societies in which they live. In any society the prevailing culture favors some and disadvantages other individuals. Some scholars, such as James C. Scott in his work on peasant resistance, argue for a considerable degree of individual autonomy and so agency, regardless of larger circumstances. Recent scholarship on Spanish America goes further. Florencia E. Mallon postulates that autonomy and agency among peasants can involve not just resistance but an active role in the shaping of culture and events. Other scholars, including French social scientist Pierre Bourdieu, with his concept of *habitus*, consider that the dominant culture and distribution of resources form a structure or framework so strong and so pervasive that "even the most cunning or improvisational actions undertaken by agents necessarily reproduce the structure."[2]

Sewell acknowledges the existence of autonomy and agency but emphasizes the influence of "social positions—as defined, for example, by gender, wealth, social prestige, class, ethnicity, occupation, generation, sexual preference, or education."[3] D. Isabel's life exemplifies the ways in which gender as a structure has shaped and constrained human agency and so the exercise of power. Gender did so even among women apparently best positioned to possess autonomy. In the Western world of the nineteenth century, nine women served as monarch or regent of their country. Since these women wielded the prerogatives granted to the sovereign, it might be assumed that they were able to exert a considerable influence on the conduct of public affairs.

Gender was fundamental to these nine women's lives. They had to carry out their duties as ruler within cultures that assumed the incompatibility of femininity and the exercise of power. Men were the norm. All but one of the nine were quite young when they began to act as rulers and so were at a period in their life courses when they were expected to assume and did fulfill multiple and cumulative female obligations. They were expected to be women and rulers at the same time in societies, like that of Brazil, where their lives were, by virtue of their gender, enormously constrained by the array of assumptions intended to limit their public role.

Gendered assumptions have systematically denied women access to resources and participation in the public sphere. Norms of behavior have been so pervasive as to deprive both women and men of the ability to conceive of alternative belief sets and behavioral forms, the necessary first step to enabling women to exercise power openly in what men have called the public sphere.

D. Isabel's life (1846–1921) spanned the years of what is customarily termed "the first wave of feminism." During the princess's lifetime, women in many countries of the Western world began, in the face of savage ridicule and harassment, to conceptualize an alternative framework of gender relations. By their actions, they secured the removal of the formal bars to their ownership and use of resources. They widened the area in which they possessed autonomy and agency, gaining access to higher education and entry into the professions. Just prior to D. Isabel's death, women in some countries of the Western world achieved the right to vote and to run for election in national politics. The pace of change was extremely slow and the gains made were as much a matter of form as of substance. Women were not liberated in respect to their access to resources. The patriarchal system of gender relations existing across the Western world remained dominant and entrenched.

From 1850 onward, D. Isabel was princess imperial, in effect empress-in-waiting. As heir to the Brazilian throne, she possessed privileged access to the resources upon which the exercise of power depends. During adulthood she enjoyed a considerable income, and she was always treated with deference. Her education and her frequent voyages to Europe endowed her with an array of cultural attributes unusual among men in Brazil and almost unprecedented among Brazilian women. As regent the princess held full control of the monarch's prerogatives. Yet, in the view of posterity, she acted decisively only once on a single issue: the immediate abolition of slavery on May 13, 1888.

It may appear contradictory, even deplorable, to us that D. Isabel did not assert herself. Access to the resources underlying power is not, however, sufficient of itself to give agency. The mix of cultural attributes absorbed by D. Isabel through her relationships with her father, *aia*, and husband, the way of life that her marriage imposed on her, and the conditions in which she served as regent were each and all inimical to her developing a strong sense of autonomy and a desire for agency. During her life, D. Isabel did not pursue goals that she chose for herself. Instead, along with many other women in the nineteenth century, particularly those of the upper class, she played the roles that others assigned to her. Those roles were, in succession but also cumulatively, those of daughter, bride, wife, mother, and empress-in-waiting. She did not give up any of her existing roles when assigned a fresh one, adding the new burden to those she was already carrying. D. Isabel was expected to perform all of her roles simultaneously, regardless of whether the roles were mutually compatible or excessive in total. The princess did not rebel against her lot in life, and rarely did she express discontent with it. She learned from her first years what were the duties of women. In sum, although the princess did enjoy access to the resources underlying power, her personal circumstances inhibited her from exercising power.

It is not surprising that D. Isabel never showed much zest for her fifth and historically most important role, that of empress-in-waiting, for it required gender characteristics quite different from those demanded by her other roles. The princess spent her childhood and adolescence in an environment that was highly patriarchal in its structure and its attitudes. As Chapter 2 explains, the whole world revolved around Pedro II, and his every wish was law. As a father, he was not harsh or inconsiderate, but with his daughters as with everyone else, he was accustomed to getting his way. The emperor's treatment of his offspring had a profound impact on D. Isabel. Jeanne H. Block's study, written in the early 1980s, has concluded that in the

D. ISABEL AS A VERY YOUNG WOMAN

Courtesy of the Arquivo Histórico do Museu Imperial, Petrópolis

formation of gender identity, "the father appears to be a more crucial agent in directing and channeling the sex typing of the child, both male and female." Far more than mothers, fathers treat daughters differently from sons. Fathers encourage their daughters to develop and maintain close interpersonal relationships. "They are encouraged to talk about their troubles and to reflect on life, are shown affection physically, and are given comfort and reassurance." A daughter is, in other words, raised to be "unambiguously a woman," which, as Carolyn G. Heilbrun has pointed out, "means to put a man at the center of one's life and to allow to occur only what honors his prime position."[4] So it was between D. Isabel and Pedro II. It was a relationship on both sides of mutual pleasure and satisfaction, enhanced by D. Isabel's willingness to banter with her father. This feistiness did not lessen the reality that she was never more than his "little chatterbox," unwilling to confront him on any matter of principle lest she risk losing his love.

This dependence was reinforced by D. Isabel's having had, during her childhood and adolescence, very little contact with the world that lay outside her family and the two palaces. Life as experienced by the vast majority of Brazilian women did not constitute any type of viable alternative to D. Isabel's status as heir to the imperial throne. She was trapped and confined within an assigned role that, as her father shaped it, was devoid of any autonomy and agency. Like Henrik Ibsen's Nora, she lived in a doll's house. Pedro II sought to ensure that his two daughters' "education should not differ from that given to men, combined with that suited to the other sex."[5] Education he defined in its narrowest sense: the bestowing of abstract knowledge. He made no attempt to integrate this abstract knowledge with experience of the larger world or combine instruction with practical application as actual preparation for his daughter's ruling Brazil. As a consequence, D. Isabel perceived the world of learning and even education itself in gendered terms, as the perquisite of her father in particular and of men in general.

Even at the time, some appreciation existed that the princess's upbringing might be inadequate. Writing to D. Isabel after her marriage, her former *aia* recommended three goals for the education of her offspring. D. Isabel should "surround them much earlier with people competent to raise them, so as not to produce a conflict in affections, should not heap on so many subjects to study simultaneously, and should introduce the children much earlier to the social world where they can develop their intelligence from what they hear."[6] The countess of Barral put her finger precisely on the principal flaws in the princess's upbringing. She had not been given outside instructors early on, had been overwhelmed with disorganized knowledge,

D. Isabel as a mother, 1883, with her three sons and the countess of Barral, during the countess's last visit to Brazil

Courtesy of the Fundação Grão Pará, Petrópolis

and had been denied experience of the external world. These weaknesses explain as much as anything does why D. Isabel's education neither encouraged nor prepared her to think autonomously and to act in innovative ways.

A weakness in the princess's upbringing not mentioned by her former *aia* was that it did nothing to prepare her for life as a Brazilian. D. Isabel was taught to be well-dressed and well-behaved, fluent in French, English, and German, pious and punctual in her religious duties, busy with family and good works, educated but not an intellectual, and devoted to upholding the social, cultural, and gender status quo. Through the influence of both Pedro II and the countess of Barral, she was brought up to be bicultural and bilingual, with France vying with Brazil as her model. The princess had a deep love for her country, but that love was primarily for the physical—for Brazil's plants, animals, and landscapes. In childhood and adolescence, D. Isabel had very little contact with any Brazilians, apart from servants, and the situation did not greatly improve after her marriage. Almost one-third of the years from the count d'Eu's return from Paraguay at the end of April 1870 to the couple's exile in November 1889 were spent outside Brazil. Only in 1884 and 1885, during her visit to the southern provinces, did the princess have any prolonged contact with her future subjects, and the diary she kept during the trip suggests that she spent much, perhaps most, of her time with men of her own class. It was not just absence abroad that prevented D. Isabel from identifying with Brazilians in general and Brazilian women in particular. Her condition as royalty made it difficult for her to see herself as belonging to any larger group. She certainly did identify with her female friends, but these were upper-class women, most of whom she had known from childhood. The conditions of her daily life prevented D. Isabel from developing any sense of autonomy conducive to the exercise of political power.

By marrying his daughter to a non-Brazilian, Pedro II confirmed and increased the gap existing between D. Isabel and her fellow Brazilians. The honeymoon trip that she and Gaston d'Orléans took to Europe in 1865 was, as Chapter 3 pointed out, a key episode in the princess's life. The trip revealed to her the type of existence that gave her the most satisfaction, one that she did indeed enjoy for over thirty years after 1889. She built up the bicultural and bilingual identity that her upbringing gave her. The one side, Brazilian and Portuguese-speaking, linked to her status as heir to the throne and empress-in-waiting; and the other, European and French-speaking, linked to her husband. Since conventions of the day dictated that a wife leave contact with the outside world to her husband, D. Isabel's marriage at the age of eighteen intensified her isolation from her fellow Brazilians. As Chapter 4 explains, D. Isabel's social life was extremely restricted. Neither the Paço Isabel in Rio de Janeiro nor the Palácio da Princesa in Petrópolis ever became important centers for socialization among the ruling groups of Brazil.

D. Isabel's marriage in October 1864 was an arranged match, against which she did not protest. She fell deeply in love with her husband, and her love remained constant to the end of her days. Playing the culmulative roles assigned to her did cause the princess considerable problems. She was a dutiful daughter to Pedro II who would not, as was often the case with fathers in the nineteenth century, abandon his paternal claims upon her. She was also a loving bride and good wife to Gaston d'Orléans, who from the start needed a great deal of support and understanding. D. Isabel became caught in a triangle, both physical and cultural, between the two men, with Pedro II and the count d'Eu across the top and she at the bottom. The burgeoning tensions between the two men, with Gaston d'Orléans seeking to assert his power in Brazil and Pedro II trying to emasculate him in order to prevent him from becoming a competitor for power, left D. Isabel caught in the middle. She would not chose sides, instead pretending that no conflict existed. The tension was resolved by the nervous breakdown that the count d'Eu suffered as commander in chief in Paraguay. This experience and his chronic ill health ended any desire to compete with his father-in-law.

Prior to her first regency in May 1871, D. Isabel took no part in affairs of state. Beyond the memorandum on governing Brazil that her father wrote for her just before his departure for Europe, the princess had received virtually no preparation and no exposure to public affairs. The tensions between the count d'Eu and her father gave D. Isabel ample reason to avoid involvement in current affairs, as Chapter 4 explains. The prevailing mode of raising daughters tends, according to Jeanne H. Block's 1984 study, "to foster proximity, discourage independent problem solving, restrict exploration, minimize contingency experiences, and discourage active play and experimentation in the physical world." As a consequence, "females are more likely to rely on existing structures in processing new inputs, finding it more difficult to modify premises, restructure experience, and forge new psychological structures." This observation might have been written specifically to describe D. Isabel's first term as regent of Brazil. As her letters to her father and to her father-in-law show, she did not adjust her mind frame to accommodate fresh experiences. The regency was something that she undertook as a favor to her father. She was quite willing to let Gaston "do the greater part of the chores," so that "I have more than enough time to sleep as much or more than previously, to take walks, and even to read novels."[7]

D. Isabel's attitude toward power cannot be ascribed to lack of intelligence or to any inability to apply herself to the topic at hand. The letter she wrote to her father on June 4, 1871, describing her first *despacho* with the ministers (see In Her Own Voice, June 4, 1871, in Chapter 4), is shrewd and hardheaded in its observations and assessments. Her creation of an orchid collection, described in Chapter 4, points to her resource, energy, and intelligence in handling topics that interested her. It is revealing that in her correspondence D. Isabel speaks about "our" orchids, but her husband always refers to "my" orchids in his letters. It is also significant that this piece of botanical research, for such it was, had no visible outcome beyond the private sphere. As a woman and a princess, D. Isabel had no means of systematically pursuing her investigations or of sharing them with the larger scientific community.

During her first regency, D. Isabel was still young, in her mid-twenties. Increasing age and the knowledge of the world that it brought might have made the princess more engaged in the affairs of government during her second regency five years later, had it not been for the burden that her role as mother, discussed in Chapter 5, imposed upon her. In May 1871, after nearly seven years of marriage, D. Isabel gave for the first time indications of being pregnant. Those hopes were dashed at the start of August. Thereafter, she suffered a miscarriage in October 1872, a stillbirth in July 1874, a very difficult delivery in October 1875 (causing permanent physical damage to the child), a miscarriage with hemorrhaging in September 1876, a difficult delivery in January 1878, and a fairly easy delivery in August 1881. This horrendous history, for no milder adjective suffices, caused D. Isabel to turn in on herself and made her children her most precious possessions. As Gaston d'Orléans told his former tutor in May 1876, during the second regency, "my wife prefers taking care of Baby to everything else."[8] Her offspring, acquired at a very high personal cost, commanded first claim on her time, attention, and energy. Everyone else took second place, and affairs of state did not even compete.

The one area in which D. Isabel's behavior did from 1872 onward distinguish her from her father was in respect to religion. The emperor was punctilious in complying with the observances prescribed by the Catholic Church, but piety was not a mainspring of his life. Three events—her sister's death in February 1871, her miscarriage in October 1872, and the stillbirth in July 1874—made her faith an indispensable support for D. Isabel. Without it she could not have persisted in the multiple roles she had to play. Particularly after the stillbirth, the princess turned to religion, in which she found a profound consolation, a place of refuge, and a source of meaning in life. Her zeal for the devotional practices and dogmas associated with ultramontanism, unfamiliar to most Brazilians, made D. Isabel suspect and confirmed what males wanted to believe: she was not exempt from the weaknesses inherent in women. The campaign of invective against the princess during the renewed "Religious Question" in 1876 revealed how little respect she commanded among the dominant (and male) sectors of public opinion. That opinion did not understand that without the aid of religion, D. Isabel could not have played her multiple and cumulative roles as well as she did. Her faith gave her the resilience to meet the challenges in life, including the events of November 1889, the journey into exile, and the death of her parents. As her letter of November 30, 1918, shows (see In Her Own Voice in Chapter 7), religion enabled her to withstand the shock of her youngest son's sudden and tragic death. Religion was indispensable to her.

D. Isabel's strong faith, placing her life unreservedly in God's hands to do with it as He pleased, explains her willingness, after the stillbirth of 1874, to risk further pregnancies, but her strong sense of female duty also contributed. She accepted that, as a woman, she must produce offspring to secure the future of the imperial dynasty and to fulfill her assigned role. Her aunt, Queen Maria II of Portugal, is reported to have responded, when warned of the risks of yet another pregnancy: "If I do die, I will die at my post!" By her willingness, the princess was in essence giving a similar response, but she did so at a considerable personal cost. She seems to have been subject from time to time to phobias and nervous attacks. In March 1880, she wrote to her father from Paris: "I don't know why my nerves are in such a horrible state but the fact is that my fear of mad dogs has become as intense as it was 8 years ago. It's a martyrdom."[9] Her successful third pregnancy appears to have given her a greater self-assurance.

In the development of D. Isabel's character, the three and a half years spent in France from 1878 to 1881 marked a period of transition, as Chapter 6 explains. The birth of Antônio in August 1881 brought the cycle of childbearing to an end, so lightening the burdens she bore. Her relationship with Gaston d'Orléans had matured into a partnership of equals in which she was the stronger personality. The partnership allowed her to adopt the more open, autonomous way of life that she experienced during her time in France. Integral to it was involvement in organizations devoted to charitable work, bestowing benefits on the unfortunate in life with the intent to make them both happy and virtuous. Following her return to Brazil in 1881, the princess continued these activities, assisted by her circle of female friends. D. Isabel's years of residence in France did encourage a sense of autonomy and agency.

This sense of agency had the potential to expand into D. Isabel's public role. Not until 1884, three years after her return to Brazil, did she reenter public life, when she undertook a four-month trip through the southern provinces. By then her youngest son Antônio was three years old, and the birth of another child unlikely. Not only did the princess find the trip a pleasant experience, but it aroused her interest in the condition of Brazil. What intensified this interest was the sympathy she felt for the abolitionist movement. The abolitionist cause was, in her own words, "intrinsically humanitarian, moralistic, generous, great, and supported by the Church."[10] What thrust D. Isabel into the center of public affairs was her third regency, made necessary by the crisis in her father's health and his departure for Europe.

D. Isabel's conduct as head of state during her first and second regencies had conformed to what the gender attitudes of the time deemed seemly in a woman. The baron of Cotegipe, the central figure in the cabinet during the second regency, conceded as much in a memorandum he wrote in the early 1880s. "It is my duty to declare that H. H. was in the conduct of her constitutional duties what Queen Victoria is said to be in England." D. Isabel had not, however, made the politicians feel secure, nor did she command their trust and confidence during her first two regencies. The cabinet, Cotegipe remarked, "could not provoke or respond to controversies; it did not embark on reforms that would excite passions, even less could it appear to abuse the credulity or experience of the Regent."[11] This comment revealed how totally the politicians identified the governing of Brazil with Pedro II as emperor. Major questions could be decided only when he was present, with his advice and consent. If D. Isabel had been a man, she might have been able to subvert this dominance, to initiate a different style of governance. As a woman, expected to be subordinate, supportive, and deferential toward males, specifically the politicians, she had virtually no choice but to conform to her father's style of rule.

These conditions did not exist during D. Isabel's third regency in 1887 and 1888. The condition of Pedro II's health at the time of his departure for Europe made it clear that, at worst, he would never return and, at best, he could no longer play his accustomed role in governing Brazil. As regent, D. Isabel became, as the title of Chapter 6 indicates, empress-in-waiting. She was far more willing than she had previously been to take an active part in affairs of state. Her involvement in charitable works and her deep religious faith underlay her resolve to achieve the immediate abolition of slavery. Her experience during the regency convinced her that other reforms were also necessary. As she wrote to her father in March 1888, after the fall of the Cotegipe cabinet, "may the question of emancipation soon reach the final stage, that I so much want to arrive. A great deal needs doing, but this most of all!"[12] The end of slavery came two months later, coinciding with the crisis in Pedro II's health in Europe. If he had then died, the princess would have become empress at the moment when her popularity stood at unprecedented heights. As Isabel I, she would have possessed the opportunity to press for reforms, the urgency of which she recognized. This opportunity did not occur, since her father survived the crisis.

D. ISABEL AND THE COUNT D'EU, OCTOBER 1919, still in love on their fifty-fifth wedding anniversary

Courtesy of the Fundação Grão Pará, Petrópolis

D. Isabel was aged forty-two when Pedro II returned to Brazil in August 1888. Her upbringing as a dutiful daughter meant that, while her father lived, she would do nothing to contest his right to manage the affairs of state. She withdrew once again into her accustomed roles, and there she continued during the next thirty-three years, until her death in November 1921. Neither the overthrow of the monarchy in November 1889, nor her father's death two years later, nor the civil war that plagued Brazil from February 1893 to August 1894 tempted her to take up a public role. During the last decades of her life she deeply regretted not being able to return to her native land. A reference to Brazil could, as her eldest granddaughter discovered, bring tears to her "beautiful blue eyes, so clear and so smiling."[13] These regrets apart, D. Isabel's final years gave her satisfaction and fulfillment, save for the loss of two of her three sons just before her death.

In terms of gender, D. Isabel lived an existence that was subordinate, exploited, and restricted. It is remarkable how well the princess adapted and how successful she was in shaping the constraints binding her into an acceptable and satisfying way of life. Despite her privileged position in respect to the resources that underlie power, her gender meant that she did not develop a sense of agency in public affairs until she was almost forty years old. The paradox in D. Isabel's life is that her single use of that agency, her principal exercise of power by which posterity alone remembers her—securing the Golden Law of May 13, 1888—contributed to her exclusion from public life and her banishment from her native land. However, as she herself proclaimed to her lifelong friend Amandinha Doria on November 16, 1889, a day after the empire's overthrow: "If abolition is the cause for this, I don't regret it; I consider it worth losing the throne for."[14]

NOTES

Chapter 1, pages 1–17

1. Tamara K. Hareven, *Families, History, and Social Change: Life-Course and Cross-Cultural Perspectives* (Boulder, 2000), 327, 331.

2. William H. Sewell Jr., "A Theory of Structure: Duality, Agency, and Transformation," *American Journal of Sociology* 98, n. 1 (July 1992): 7–8.

3. Joan Wallach Scott, "Gender: A Useful Category of Historical Analysis," *American Historical Review* 91, n. 5 (December 1986): 1053–75, republished in J. W. Scott, *Gender and the Politics of History* (New York, 1988), 28–50. The passages quoted are from p. 43.

4. Sewell, "Theory," 20.

5. Simone de Beauvoir, *The Second Sex*, trans. and ed. H. M. Parshley (New York, 1993), 281.

6. Natalie Z. Davis, "Women's History in Transition: The European Case," *Feminist Studies* 3 (1975): 90.

7. Thomas Ewbank, *Life in Brazil; or the Land of the Cocoa and the Palm* . . . (London, 1856), 80.

8. The text of the 1824 Constitution is reprinted (pp. 481–505) in José Antônio Pimenta Bueno, *Direito público brasileiro e análise da constituição do império*, 2d ed. (Rio de Janeiro, 1958). The passages cited are on pp. 189, 460, 481, 498.

9. Public Record Office, Great Britain, Foreign Office (hereafter PRO FO), series 13, Brazil Correspondence, v. 161 William Gore Ouseley, chargé d'affaires, to Viscount Palmerston, foreign secretary, confidential memoir, dated July 30, 1840, enclosed in dispatch n. 54, Rio de Janeiro, July 30, 1840.

10. Arquivo Grão Pará, Petrópolis (hereafter AGP) XXXIX - 1 D. Teresa Cristina to Pedro II, Naples, December 2, 1842.

Chapter 2, pages 19–50

1. AGP XXXIX - 1 D. Teresa Cristina to Pedro II, Santa Cruz, July 19, 1844.

2. T. Ewbank, *Life in Brazil*, 146.

3. AGP XXXVIII - 14 Draft of Pedro II to D. Maria II, Rio, December 21, 1846.

4. AGP XXXVIII - 10 Draft of Pedro II to D. Amélia, Rio, July 11, 1847. D. Afonso in fact died on June 11, not June 4.

5. Arquivo Histórico do Museu Imperial, Petrópolis (hereafter AHMI), Coleção Pedro d'Orléans e Bragança (hereafter POB), Catalogo (hereafter Cat.) A, Maço 207, Documento (hereafter Doc.) 9335 Recollections entitled "Joies et tristesses," written in French by D. Isabel (hereafter cited as "Joies et tristesses"). Internal evidence dates the draft to the last months of 1908.

6. AGP XL - 2 D. Isabel to her parents, São Cristóvão, July 2, 1887.

7. Pedro II to Joaquim Teixeira de Macedo, transcribed in Sérgio Teixeira de Macedo, "D. Pedro II, esposo e pai," *História* I, n. 1 (September 1939): 2.

8. The appointment was unusual in that, by custom, the imperial physicians' turn of duty at court lasted only one week. See Arquivo Nacional do Torre do Tombo, Lisbon (hereafter ANTT), Caixa 734, Cepilha 136, Doc. 1 Pedro II to Maria II, Rio, September 13, 1852.

9. "Joies et tristesses." The wording is heavily amended so that it is difficult to establish a definitive text. The translation tries to convey the slight awkwardness of the writing.

10. AGP XL - 2 D. Isabel to Pedro II, São Cristóvão, April 11, 1856, Paço Isabel, January 19, 1869, Petrópolis, October 18, 1874. [In Condessa de Barral, *Cartas a suas magestades 1859–1890* (Rio de Janeiro, 1977), which prints letters from D. Isabel, the words "mª Rosa" are wrongly transcribed as "Maria Rosa."] On May 29, 1875, D. Isabel wrote from Petrópolis to her father: "Our good Rosa is 70 years old today!"

11. AHMI, POB, Cat. B, Maço 20, Doc. 1046 Undated draft of D. Pedro II to D. Amélia, [Rio, November 14, 1853]. The letter's date is mentioned in D. Amélia's reply, Lisbon, January 11, 1854, now held in AGP; see Lourenço L. Lacombe, *Isabel a princesa redentora (biografia baseada em documentos inéditos)* (Petrópolis, 1989), 22–23.

12. Entry for December 31, 1861, in Hélio Vianna, ed., "Diário de 1862," *Anuário do Museu Imperial* (hereafter *AnMI*) 17 (1956): 17; AGP XXXVIII - 3 Pedro II to D. Teresa Cristina, "7 3/4," undated [dated by internal evidence to 1851].

13. James F. McMillan, *France and Women, 1789–1914: Gender, Society and Politics* (London, 2000), 41, 42. Entry for June 12, 1862, in H. Vianna, "Diário de 1862," 133. Pedro II made this comment during a discussion about the marital discord existing between the count of Iguaçu, his (illegitimate) half-brother, and the countess of Iguaçu.

14. J. F. McMillan, *France and Women*, 42.

15. *Jornal do Comércio*, April 13, 1854; AGP XL - 2 D. Isabel to Pedro II, undated [São Cristóvão, early October 1864].

16. Article 14 of Pedro I's draft instructions, printed in Lourenço L. Lacombe, "A educação das princesas," *AnMI* 7 (1946): 245; Marquis of Itanhaem to Aureliano

de Sousa e Oliveira Coutinho, Rio, August 1, 1834, printed in *Mensário do Arquivo Nacional* V, n. 6 (June 1974): 25; T. Ewbank, *Life in Brazil*, 151.

17. Bibliothèque Nationale, Paris, Nouvelles Acquisitions Françaises 6644 Pedro II to Frederica Planat de la Faye, Rio, May 22, 1874. Mariana Velho da Silva's father served as acting *mordomo* (steward of the household) to the emperor from 1847 to 1854.

18. See AGP XL - 2 and XL - 3.

19. AGP XL - 2 D. Isabel to Pedro II, São Cristóvão, October 6, 1859.

20. AGP XL - 2 D. Isabel to her parents, Petrópolis, March 3, 1857.

21. AGP XL - 4 D. Isabel to Louis, duke of Nemours, Petrópolis, December 26, 1876.

22. AHMI POB Cat. B Maço 29 Doc. 1046 Undated draft of D. Pedro II to D. Amélia, [Rio, November 14, 1853].

23. J. F. McMillan, *France and Women*, 50, 58.

24. Undated draft document, in D. Teresa Cristina's handwriting, entitled "Attributes of the Governess" (*Atribuições da Aia*), original in AHMI POB and printed in L. L. Lacombe, "Educação," 250. Internal evidence dates this document to about April 1857.

25. See footnote 22. Pedro II's preference for a German probably refers to the supposed characteristics of that nation: neatness, cleanliness, industriousness, and interest in learning.

26. Countess of Barral to D. Teresa Cristina, [Petrópolis,] February 1, 1860, original in AGP and printed in Condessa de Barral, *Cartas*, 53.

27. Document from the archive of Paulo Barbosa da Silva, printed in Américo Jacobina Lacombe, "A condêssa de Barral," *AnMI* 5 (1944): 16.

28. Countess of Barral to D. Teresa Cristina, undated [São Cristóvão, October 18, 1859,] original in AGP and printed in Condessa de Barral, *Cartas*, 29.

29. On the use of these endearments, see AGP unnumbered Countess of Barral to D. Isabel, October 30, 1864; Countess of Barral to Pedro II, [Petrópolis,] July 13 [1875,] original in AGP and printed in Condessa de Barral, *Cartas*, 117; AGP unnumbered Countess of Barral to D. Isabel, "Dia de S. Pedro!" [June 29, 1863].

30. Countess of Barral to D. Teresa Cristina, [São Cristóvão,] November 6, 1859, [Petrópolis,] January 7, 1860, originals in AGP and printed in Condessa de Barral, *Cartas*, 31, 49; AGP XL - 3 D. Isabel to D. Teresa Cristina, [São Cristóvão,] October 6, 1859.

31. AGP unnumbered Countess of Barral to D. Isabel, 88 Boulevard Haussmann, [Paris,] October 19, 1865.

32. Entry for Dec. 31, 1861, in H. Vianna, "Diário de 1862," 15; AHMI POB Cat. B Maço 37 Doc. 1057 Entry in Pedro II's diary for August 8, 1891.

33. AGP XL - 2. Both exchanges are undated, but the princesses received their first lesson in political economy late in 1863.

34. AGP XL - 3 D. Isabel to D. Teresa Cristina, [São Cristóvão,] October 8, 1859. The fascination with sewing is perhaps explained by a later letter (January 3,

1860), in which she pleaded: "Mummy, please give us permission to use the sewing machine at night."

35. AGP XL - 2 D. Isabel to Pedro II, Claremont, England, February 20, 1865.

36. J. A. Pimenta Bueno, *Direito público*, 494.

37. AGP XL - 1 Passage dated August 10 in D. Isabel to Gaston, count d'Eu, São Cristóvão, August 7, 1865.

38. AGP XL - 2 D. Isabel to Pedro II, undated [from internal evidence, probably written between October 1, 1859, and February 11, 1860].

39. Mozart Monteiro, "A Familia Imperial," *Revista do Instituto Histórico e Geográfico Brasileiro* (hereafter *RIHGB*), v. 152 (1925): 78. The evidence presented in Pedro Calmon, *História de D. Pedro II* (Rio de Janeiro, 1975), 2: 571, dates this accident to the middle of 1862. AGP unnumbered Countess of Barral to D. Isabel, "Dia de S. Pedro!" [June 29, 1863].

40. AGP XL - 1 Passage dated August 10 in D. Isabel to Gaston, count d'Eu, São Cristóvão, September 17, 1869.

41. M. Monteiro, "A Familia Imperial," 76-77; AGP XLI - 4 Gaston, count d'Eu, to Marguerite d'Orléans, Rio, September 20, October 8, 1864.

42. Quotation in J. F. McMillan, *France and Women*, 58; AGP Folder of draft documents Pedro II to François, prince of Joinville, Rio, September 21, 1863, copy in the hand of D. Teresa Cristina.

Chapter 3, pages 51–82

1. Edward Shorter, *The Making of the Modern Family* (New York, 1975), 15.

2. Queen Victoria to Princess Victoria, Windsor Castle, April 10, 1858, in Roger Fulford, ed., *Dearest Child: The Letters between Queen Victoria and the Princess Royal, 1858–1861* (London, 1964), 87. The "family" was the house of Saxe-Coburg-Gotha.

3. J. A. Pimenta Bueno, *Direito público*, 481; Countess of Barral to D. Teresa Cristina, Petrópolis, February 1, 1860, original in AGP and printed in Condessa de Barral, *Cartas*, 54, 55; Archduke Maximilian to Emperor Francis Joseph, Salvador da Bahia, February 12, 1860, original in the Osterreich Historisches Staatsarchiv, Vienna, and quoted in P. Calmon, *Pedro II*, 2: 627.

4. AGP XL - 3 D. Isabel to D. Teresa Cristina, [Petrópolis,] January 30, 1860; D. Isabel's remark is mentioned in D. Amélia to Pedro II, Lisbon, December 12, 1860, now held in AGP, and cited in L. L. Lacombe, *Isabel*, 61; AGP Folder of draft documents, Pedro II to François, prince of Joinville, Rio, September 21, 1863, copy in D. Teresa Cristina's hand.

5. J. F. McMillan, *France and Women*, 37.

6. AHMI I - DBM - 6.4.865. - Pl. B. c. 1-27 Pedro II to the countess of Barral, Caçapava, August 17, 1865, printed in Raymundo Magalhães Jr., ed.,

D. Pedro II e a condessa de Barral através da correspondência íntima do imperador, anotada e comentada (Rio de Janeiro, 1956), 52.

7. J. A. Pimenta Bueno, *Direito público*, 496; AGP Folder of draft documents, Pedro II to François, prince of Joinville, Rio, September 21, 1863, copy in D. Teresa Cristina's hand.

8. AGP Folder of draft documents, Pedro II to François, prince of Joinville, Rio, September 21, 1863, copy in D. Teresa Cristina's hand.

9. AGP XXIX - 1 François, prince of Joinville, to Pedro II, Claremont, England, November 6, 1863, December 6, 1863, February 7, 1864.

10. AGP Folder of draft documents, Pedro II to François, prince of Joinville, Rio, January 7, 1864, February 8, 1864, copies in D. Teresa Cristina's hand; AGP XXIX - 1 François, prince of Joinville, to Pedro II, Claremont, England, May 4, 1864.

11. Speech of May 3, 1864, in *Fallas do throno desde o anno de 1823 até o anno de 1889 acompanhadas das respectivas votos de graças* (Rio de Janeiro, 1889), 503; AGP XXIX - 1 François, prince of Joinville, to Pedro II, Vienna, October 28, 1864.

12. AGP Folder of draft documents, Pedro II to François, prince of Joinville, Rio, May 23, 1864, and August 23, 1864, copies in D. Teresa Cristina's hand.

13. AGP XLI - 4 Gaston, count d'Eu, to Marguerite d'Orléans, Rio, September 6, 1864. The text is in French but "decidedly" is in English.

14. AGP XL - 1 D. Isabel to Gaston, count d'Eu, São Cristóvão, September 1, 2, 3, 5, 1865. The reference to "my diary kept last year" is in a letter of September 12, 1865. All the letters that D. Isabel wrote to the count d'Eu are in French, with occasional words and phrases in Portuguese.

15. AGP XL - 1 D. Isabel to Gaston, count d'Eu, São Cristóvão, September 5, 7, 8, 11, 1865.

16. Royal Archives, Windsor, England (hereafter RA), VIC Y 51/66, Louis, duke of Nemours, to Queen Victoria, Claremont, Esher, October 19, 1864.

17. AGP XL - 1 D. Isabel to Gaston, count d'Eu, São Cristóvão, September 18, 1865.

18. AGP XLI - 4 Gaston, count d'Eu, to Marguerite d'Orléans, Rio, September 20, 1864.

19. AGP XL - 2 D. Isabel to Pedro II, October 15, 1864. Twelve months later she told Gaston, "last year I found it so good and at the same time so odd to be alone with you in the carriage to Petrópolis"; AGP XL - 1 D. Isabel to Gaston, count d'Eu, São Cristóvão, October 15, 1864.

20. AGP XL - 2 D. Isabel to Pedro II, October 15, 1864.

21. AGP XL - 1 Passages dated October 15 and 16 in D. Isabel to Gaston, count d'Eu, São Cristóvão, October 14, 1865; XLI - 1[1] Gaston, count d'Eu, to Pedro II, October 17, 1864. The letter to the emperor is written in French. Gaston d'Orléans thereafter used Portuguese when writing to the emperor.

22. AGP XLI - 4 Gaston, count d'Eu, to Marguerite d'Orléans, Petrópolis, October 22, 1864. The word "cottage" is in English.

23. ANTT Caixa 7336, Cepilha 312, Doc. 10 Pedro II to Luís I, Rio, October 23, 1864; AGP XL - 1 D. Isabel to Gaston, count d'Eu, São Cristóvão, October 15, 1865.

24. "Joies et tristesses."

25. AGP XLI - 4 Gaston, count d'Eu, to Marguerite d'Orléans, Petrópolis, October 22, 1864; AGP XXXVIII - 1 Pedro II to D. Isabel, Rio, November 4, 1864.

26. AGP unnumbered Countess of Barral to D. Isabel, [Rio,] October 22, 1864.

27. AGP XXXVIII - 1 Pedro II to D. Isabel, Rio, October 29, 1864; AGP unnumbered Countess of Barral to D. Isabel, [Rio,] October 30, 1864.

28. Passage dated November 3 in João Batista Calógeras to Lucille Calógeras, Rio, October 28, 1864, in Antônio Gontijo de Carvalho, *Um Ministério visto por dentro* (Rio de Janeiro, 1959), 116.

29. AGP XL - 2 D. Isabel to Pedro II, [Petrópolis,] October 30, 1864; AGP XL - 3 D. Isabel to D. Teresa Cristina, [Petrópolis,] November 5, 1864.

30. AGP XL - 2 D. Isabel to Pedro II, [Petrópolis,] November 8, 1864.

31. Passage dated December 18 in João Batista Calógeras to Lucille Calógeras, Botafogo, [Rio,] December 11, 1864, in A. G. de Carvalho, *Ministério*, 161; AGP XL - 2 D. Isabel to Pedro II, Petrópolis, December 17, 1864.

32. AGP XLI - 1[1] Gaston, count d'Eu, to Pedro II, Petrópolis, October 20, 1864.

33. AGP XL - 2 D. Isabel to Pedro II, [Petrópolis,] December 20, 1864; AGP XL - 1 Passage dated August 8 in D. Isabel to Gaston, count d'Eu, São Cristóvão, August 7, 1865.

34. AGP XL - 3 D. Isabel to D. Teresa Cristina, Petrópolis, December 17, 1864; AGP XL - 2 D. Isabel to Pedro II, Petrópolis, December 19, 1864.

35. AGP XXIX - 1 François, prince of Joinville, to Pedro II, Claremont, [England,] February 21, 1865. "Ladylike" is in English.

36. RA QVJNL Entry for February 21, 1865, in Queen Victoria's journal.

37. AGP XL - 3 D. Isabel to D. Teresa Cristina, Claremont, [England,] April 9, 1865. D. Leopoldina suffered a miscarriage on May 2, 1865.

38. AGP XL - 3 D. Isabel to D. Teresa Cristina, Vienna, May 2, 1865.

39. AGP XL - 2 D. Isabel to Pedro II, Vienna, May 2, 1865.

40. AGP XL - 2 D. Isabel to Pedro II, Claremont, [England,] May 20, 1865.

41. AGP XL - 2 D. Isabel to Pedro II, Laranjeiras, July 31, 1865.

42. AGP XLI - 3 Gaston, count d'Eu, to D. Isabel, Laranjeiras, July 22, 1865. The envelope is addressed: "To my much loved Isabel on the occasion of my departure for the province of Rio Grande do Sul. Delivered 1/8/865." In 1863, William Banting had published in England *A Letter on Corpulence, Addressed to the*

Public, the first popular diet book, of which 50,000 copies were sold or given away.

43. AGP XL - 1 D. Isabel to Gaston, count d'Eu, São Cristóvão, August 1, 1865; Passages dated August 2, 3, 1865, "at 2 and half," August 3, 1865, "at 10 in the evening," and August 9, 1865, August 11, 1865, Passage dated September 24, in September 22, 1865, October 9, 1865, and October 20, 1865.

44. AGP XL - 1 Passage dated August 5 in D. Isabel to Gaston, count d'Eu, São Cristóvão, August 1, 1865, August 7, 1865, August 12, 1865, August 25, 1865, October 1, 1865, October 20, 1865.

45. AGP XL - 1 Passage dated August 2 in D. Isabel to Gaston, count d'Eu, São Cristóvão, August 1, 1865; Passage dated October 8 in October 7, 1865; October 13, 1865.

46. AGP XL - 1 D. Isabel to Gaston, count d'Eu, São Cristóvão, September 18, 1865. The paper wrapping containing the hair is endorsed by the count d'Eu: "Isabel's hair cut on 18/9/864 and sent to me in the Pr. of R. G. do Sul."

47. AGP XLI - 3 Gaston, count d'Eu, to D. Isabel, Au camp devant Uruguayana, September 11, 1865.

48. AGP XLI - 1 Gaston, count d'Eu, to Louis, duke of Nemours, River Uruguay, September 25, 1865.

49. AGP XXXVIII - 3 Pedro II to D. Teresa Cristina, Pelotas, October 26, 1865; AGP XLI - 3 Gaston, count d'Eu, to D. Isabel, Desterro, Santa Catarina, November 6, 1865.

Chapter 4, pages 83–119

1. "Joies et tristesses"; AGP XL - 1 Passage dated August 12 in D. Isabel to Gaston, count d'Eu, São Cristóvão, August 11, 1865, September 28, 1865.

2. AGP XL - 4 D. Isabel to Louis, duke of Nemours, Laranjeiras, February 5, 1867.

3. AGP XL - 4 D. Isabel to Louis, duke of Nemours, São Cristóvão, September 3, 1865; Laranjeiras, February 5, 1867; Gaston, count d'Eu, to Mme. Bernard de Lagrave, Laranjeiras, August 5, 1866, quoted in Alberto Rangel, *Gastão d'Orléans (o ultimo conde d'Eu)* (São Paulo, 1935), 127.

4. AGP XLI - 1[1] Gaston, count d'Eu, to Pedro II, [Laranjeiras,] July 5, 1867.

5. AGP XL - 2 D. Isabel to Pedro II, Petrópolis, January 21 and February 3, 1868; AGP XL - 1 Passage dated September 27 in D. Isabel to Gaston, count d'Eu, São Cristóvão, September 17, 1869.

6. AHMI I - DBM - 6.4.865. - PI. B. c. 1-27 Pedro II to the countess of Barral, undated, [Rio, December 7 or 8, 1865,] printed in R. Magalhães Jr., *D. Pedro II e a condessa de Barral*, 56.

7. AGP XLI - 1 Gaston, count d'Eu, to Louis, duke of Nemours, Petrópolis, December 22, 1867.

8. AGP XLI - 1 Gaston, count d'Eu, to Louis, duke of Nemours, Laranjeiras, March 11, 1867 (quoted in A. Rangel, *Gastão d'Orléans*, 160); AGP XL - 2 D. Isabel to Pedro II, Petrópolis, November 19, 1867; AGP XL - 3 D. Isabel to D. Teresa Cristina, Laranjeiras, December 16, 1867.

9. AHMI I - DBM - 8.1.867. - PI. B. c. 1-27 Pedro II to the countess of Barral, Rio, December 23, 1867, printed in R. Magalhães Jr., *D. Pedro II e a condessa de Barral*, 56. The printed text misreads the word "calorosa" (hot) as "chuvosa" (rainy).

10. AGP XL - 2 D. Isabel to Pedro II, Petrópolis, January 24, 1868.

11. AGP XLI - 3 Gaston, count d'Eu, to D. Isabel, Bagé, Rio Grande do Sul, October 17, 1865.

12. AGP XL - 1 D. Isabel to Gaston, count d'Eu, São Cristóvão, August 25, 1865.

13. Gaston, count d'Eu, to Mme. Bernard de Lagrave, Laranjeiras, August 5, 1866, quoted in A. Rangel, *Gastão d'Orléans*, 127. The ellipsis before the word "novels" appears in the original letter.

14. AGP XL - 1 Passage dated October 8 in D. Isabel to Gaston, count d'Eu, São Cristóvão, October 7, 1865.

15. AGP unnumbered Countess of Barral to D. Isabel, undated [Paris, May 20, 1867].

16. AGP XLI - 1 Gaston, count d'Eu, to Louis, duke of Nemours, Laranjeiras, January 3, 1868.

17. AGP XL - 3 D. Isabel to D. Teresa Cristina, Aguas Virtuosas da Campanha, September 9, October 10 and 23, 1868.

18. AGP XL - 3 D. Isabel to D. Teresa Cristina, Aguas Virtuosas da Campanha, September 20, 1868; AGP XL - 2 D. Isabel to Pedro II, Aguas Virtuosas da Campanha, September 7 and 9, October 2, 1868.

19. AGP XL - 2 D. Isabel to Pedro II, Aguas Virtuosas da Campanha, October 10, 1868.

20. AGP XL - 2 D. Isabel to Pedro II, São Cristóvão, August 3, 1866.

21. AGP XL - 4 D. Isabel to Louis, duke of Nemours, Laranjeiras, February 5, 1867.

22. AGP XL - 3 D. Isabel to D. Teresa Cristina, Aguas Virtuosas da Campanha, September 20, 1868.

23. AGP XLI - 1 Gaston, count d'Eu, to Louis, duke of Nemours, [Petrópolis,] February 5, 1869 (quoted in A. Rangel, *Gastão d'Orléans*, 206).

24. AGP XL - 3 D. Isabel to D. Teresa Cristina, Petrópolis, February 16 and 20, 1869; AGP XL - 2 D. Isabel to Pedro II, Petrópolis, February 20, 1869.

25. AHMI POB Cat. A Maço 104 Doc. 9358 D. Isabel to Pedro II, Petrópolis, February 22, 1869. The sentence beginning, "Can they have unanimously . . . ," was added by D. Isabel as an interlining.

26. "The Three Fishers," in Charles Kingsley, *Life and Works*, v. 16: *Poems* (London, 1902), 252.

27. AGP XLI - 3 Gaston, count d'Eu, to D. Isabel, Laranjeiras, March 29, 1869.

28. AGP XL - 1 D. Isabel to Gaston, count d'Eu, São Cristóvão, March 30, 1869.

29. AGP XL - 1 Passage dated October 2 in D. Isabel to Gaston, count d'Eu, São Cristóvão, September 30, 1869.

30. AGP XL - 1 Passage dated July 2 in D. Isabel to Gaston, count d'Eu, São Cristóvão, July 1, 1869; September 17, 1869, passage dated October 2 in September 30, 1869. The novel by the count of Gobineau was *L'Abbaye de Typhaines*. The count of Paris, Gaston d'Orléans's first cousin, had recently published *Les associations ouvrières en Angleterre (Trade Unions)*.

31. AGP XL - 1 Passage dated July 14 in D. Isabel to Gaston, count d'Eu, São Cristóvão, July 1, 1869, passage dated September 6 in August 30, 1869.

32. AGP XL - 1 Passage dated July 14 in D. Isabel to Gaston, count d'Eu, São Cristóvão, July 1, 1869, passage dated September 28 in September 17, 1869.

33. AGP XL - 1 D. Isabel to Gaston, count d'Eu, February 21, 1869; AGP XL - 4 D. Isabel to Louis, duke of Nemours, São Cristóvão, April 9, 1869; AGP XLI - 3 Gaston, count d'Eu, to D. Isabel, Quartel Geral em Pirayu, Paraguay, June 13, 1869.

34. AGP XL - 1 Passage dated December 29 in D. Isabel to Gaston, count d'Eu, São Cristóvão, December 21, 1869.

35. AGP XLI - 1[1] Gaston, count d'Eu, to Pedro II, March 4, 1870.

36. AGP XL - 1 D. Isabel to Gaston, count d'Eu, São Cristóvão, at 9. $^{1/2}$ p.m., March 15, 1870.

37. AGP XLI - 3 Gaston, count d'Eu, to D. Isabel, Quartel Geral em Vila do Rosario, Paraguay, March 12, 1870; AGP XLI - 30 Gaston, count d'Eu, to Jules Gauthier, Petrópolis, February 26, 1873.

38. AGP XL - 3 D. Isabel to D. Teresa Cristina, Petrópolis, December 13, 1872.

39. AGP XLI - 1 Gaston, count d'Eu, to Louis, duke of Nemours, Laranjeiras, June 22, 1870.

40. AGP XLI - 30 Gaston, count d'Eu, to Jules Gauthier, Petrópolis, June 17, 1876.

41. AGP XLI - 3 Gaston, count d'Eu, to D. Isabel, Quartel Geral em Pirayu, Paraguay, July 14, 1869, Quartel Geral em Vila do Rosario, Paraguay, March 12, 1870. The book was *Mémoires de Mme. de Motteville sur Anne d'Autriche et sa cour*, 4 vols., published at Paris in 1844.

42. AGP XLI - 30 Gaston, count d'Eu, to Jules Gauthier, Petrópolis, March 28, 1877.

43. AGP XL - 3 D. Isabel to D. Teresa Cristina, Laranjeiras, July 26, 1870; Pernambuco, August 28, 1870.

44. AGP XLI - 5 Gaston, count d'Eu, to the countess of Barral, Cannes, March 15, 1890; AGP XLI - 1¹ Gaston, count d'Eu, to Pedro II, Bushy Park, London, January 7, 1871.

45. AGP XL - 4 D. Isabel to Louis, duke of Nemours, Meran, Austria, February 16, 1871.

46. AGP XL - 3 D. Isabel to D. Teresa Cristina, Meran, Austria, February 17, 1871.

47. AGP XXXVIII - 2 Pedro II to Gaston, count d'Eu, Petrópolis, March 23, 1871. Pedro II, when writing to the count, referred to the empress as "your mother."

48. AGP XL - 1 Passage dated July 2 in D. Isabel to Gaston, count d'Eu, São Cristóvão, July 1, 1869; Passage written in July 1872 in Cristiano B. Ottoni, *Autobiographia* (Rio de Janeiro, 1908), 183–84.

49. Instituto Histórico e Geográfico Brasileiro, Rio de Janeiro (hereafter IHGB), Arquivo do barão de Cotegipe (hereafter BC), Lata 892, Pasta 150 José Bento da Cunha Figueiredo to João Maurício Wanderley, baron of Cotegipe, n. p., March 13, [1871]; Passage written in late July 1872 in C. B. Ottoni, *Autobiographia*, 194.

50. Pedro II, *Conselhos à regente* (Rio de Janeiro, 1958), 1.

51. Ibid., 60.

52. AGP XL - 3 D. Isabel to D. Teresa Cristina, Laranjeiras, August 27, 1866.

53. AGP XL - 2 D. Isabel to Pedro II, Laranjeiras, June 4, 1871.

54. AGP XL - 4 D. Isabel to Louis, duke of Nemours, Laranjeiras, June 26, 1871.

55. AGP XL - 2 D. Isabel to Pedro II, Laranjeiras, September 4, 1871.

56. AGP XL - 2 D. Isabel to Pedro II, Laranjeiras, March 6, 1872.

57. AGP XL - 2 D. Isabel to Pedro II, Laranjeiras, August 27, 1871; AGP unnumbered Countess of Barral to D. Isabel, [Paris,] November 7, 1871.

58. AGP XL - 2 D. Isabel to Pedro II, Petrópolis, February 4, 1872.

59. AGP XL - 2 D. Isabel to Pedro II, Petrópolis, March 6, 1872.

Chapter 5, pages 121–158

1. José Antônio Soares de Sousa, *A vida do visconde de Uruguay (1807–1866) (Paulino José Soares de Sousa)* (São Paulo, 1937), 45. Emphasis added.

2. AGP XL - 1 Passage dated October 8 in D. Isabel to Gaston, count d'Eu, São Cristóvão, October 7, 1865.

3. Francisca, princess of Joinville, to Pedro II, Mount Lebanon, London, June 18, 1870, original in AGP and quoted in L. L. Lacombe, *Isabel*, 181.

4. AGP XL - 3 D. Isabel to D. Teresa Cristina, Laranjeiras, June 21, 1871; AGP XLI - 1¹ Gaston, count d'Eu, to Pedro II, Laranjeiras, August 5, 1871.

5. AGP XLI - 1 Gaston, count d'Eu, to Louis, duke of Nemours, Laranjeiras, January 22, 1867.

6. "Sacred Heart, devotion to," *New Catholic Encyclopedia* (New York, 1967), XII: 818–19.

7. AGP XLI - 3 Gaston, count d'Eu, to D. Isabel, Devant Uruguayana, October 2, 1865; AGP XL - 3 D. Isabel to D. Teresa Cristina, Meran, Austria, February 17, 1871.

8. AGP XL - 2 D. Isabel to Pedro II, Petrópolis, January 5, 1871 [*sic*, 1872]; February 4, 1872.

9. AGP XL - 4 D. Isabel to Louis, duke of Nemours, Petrópolis, February 20, 1872; AGP XL - 3 D. Isabel to D. Teresa Cristina, Petrópolis, December 13, 1872.

10. AGP XL - 2 D. Isabel to Pedro II, Grand Hôtel de Londres, Paris, May 18, 1873; AGP XLI - 1[1] Gaston, count d'Eu, to Pedro II, Paris, May 23, 1873.

11. AGP XL - 3 D. Isabel to D. Teresa Cristina, Grand Hôtel de Londres, Paris, October 19, 1873. On the shrine at Lourdes and the Marian apparitions from 1830 to 1900, see Ralph Gibson, *A Social History of French Catholicism, 1789–1914* (London, 1989), 145–51.

12. AGP XLI - 1[1] Gaston, count d'Eu, to Pedro II, Hotel Royal Danieli, Venice, November 27, 1873, Paris, January 19, 1874; AGP XL - 2 D. Isabel to Pedro II, Hotel Royal Danieli, Venice, December 2, 1873.

13. AGP XL - 2 D. Isabel to Pedro II, rue de Berri, Paris, March 7 and 18, 1874.

14. AGP XXXVIII - 2 Pedro II to Gaston, count d'Eu, Petrópolis, February 18, 1874.

15. AGP XL - 2 D. Isabel to Pedro II, rue de Berri, Paris, May 17, 1874.

16. AGP XLI - 30 Gaston, count d'Eu, to Jules Gauthier, Laranjeiras, August 8, 1876.

17. AGP XLI - 30 Gaston, count d'Eu, to Jules Gauthier; AHMI POB Cat. B Maço 38 Doc. 1058 Entry in D. Teresa Cristina's diary for July 26–28, 1874; AGP XL - 3 D. Isabel to D. Teresa Cristina, Petrópolis, July 26, 1875; "Joies et tristesses."

18. Pedro II to count of Gobineau, Rio, August 14, 1874, printed in Georges Raeders, ed., *D. Pedro II e o conde de Gobineau (correspondencias ineditas)* (São Paulo, 1938), 477.

19. Countess of Barral to Pedro II, Petrópolis, September 13, 1874, original in AGP and printed in Condessa de Barral, *Cartas*, 86; AGP XL - 2 D. Isabel to Pedro II, Petrópolis, October 18, 1874.

20. AGP XL - 2 D. Isabel to Pedro II, Petrópolis, November 5, 1874, March 15, 1875.

21. AGP XL - 1 D. Isabel to Gaston, count d'Eu, São Cristóvão, October 15, 1875; D. Isabel and countess of Barral to D. Teresa Cristina, Petrópolis, Novem-

ber 28, 1874, original in AGP and printed in Condessa de Barral, *Cartas*, 99; AGP XL - 2 D. Isabel to Pedro II, Petrópolis, June 1, 1875.

22. R. Gibson, *French Catholicism*, 265, 266.

23. AGP XL - 2 D. Isabel to Pedro II, Grand Hôtel du Louvre, Bagnères de Luchon, August 31, 1873; AGP XLI - 1[1] Gaston, count d'Eu, to Pedro II, Hôtel de Castille, Niles [?], October 25, 1873.

24. Biblioteca Nacional, Rio de Janeiro, Coleção Tobias Monteiro (hereafter BNRJ TM), Armário 25, Pac. 25 Pedro II to Luís Alves de Lima, duke of Caxias, [Rio,] September 19, 1875.

25. AGP XLI - 1 Gaston, count d'Eu, to Louis, duke of Nemours, Petrópolis, January 27, 1875.

26. AGP XL - 1 D. Isabel to Gaston, count d'Eu, Petrópolis, April 5, May 26, June 10, 1875.

27. AGP XLI - 1 Gaston, count d'Eu, to Louis, duke of Nemours, Petrópolis, July 26, São Cristóvão, August 2, 1875.

28. AGP XL - 1 D. Isabel to Gaston, count d'Eu, Petrópolis, June 11, 1875.

29. AGP XLI - 1 Gaston, count d'Eu, to Louis, duke of Nemours, [Petrópolis,] September 6, 1875.

30. AGP XLI - 1[1] Gaston, count d'Eu, to Pedro II, Petrópolis, October 14, 1875; AGP XLI - 30 Gaston, count d'Eu, to Jules Gauthier, Petrópolis, October 28, 1875.

31. "Le docteur Depaul au Brésil," *Le Figaro*, December 1, 1875.

32. AGP XLI - 1 Gaston, count d'Eu, to Louis, duke of Nemours, Petrópolis, November 22, 1875 (cited in L. L. Lacombe, *Isabel*, 188).

33. AGP XL - 2 D. Isabel to Pedro II, Petrópolis, November 21, 1875, December 29, 1875; AGP XLI - 30 Gaston, count d'Eu, to Jules Gauthier, Petrópolis, May 13, 1876. The first use of "Baby" is in a letter to her father of November 25, 1875.

34. PRO FO 13 Brazil Correspondence v. 517 George B. Mathew, minister, to the earl of Derby, foreign secretary, No. 100 Political (Confidential), Rio, November 22, 1876; IHGB BC Lata 955 Pasta 17 Undated memorandum (written about 1882) by João Maurício Wanderley, baron of Cotegipe.

35. AGP XL - 2 D. Isabel to Pedro II, Paço da Cidade, April 14, 1876. She was replying to a letter he had written to her on the steamer bound for the United States.

36. AGP XL - 2 D. Isabel to Pedro II, Paço da Cidade, April 14, 1876; AGP XL - 1 D. Isabel to Gaston, count d'Eu, Petrópolis, March 16, March 17, 1877.

37. AHMI POB Cat. A Maço 175 Doc. 7792 Memorandum by Pedro II in a notebook with marbled covers, printed in R. Magalhães Jr., *D. Pedro II e a condessa de Barral*, 161; PRO FO 13 Brazil Correspondence v. 517 George B. Mathew, minister, to the earl of Derby, foreign secretary, No. 100 Political (Confidential), Rio, November 22, 1876.

38. AGP XLI - 30 Gaston, count d'Eu, to Jules Gauthier, Rio, October 12, 1876.

39. PRO FO 13 Brazil v. 517 George B. Mathew, minister, to the earl of Derby, foreign secretary, Rio, No. 100 Political (Confidential), Rio, November 22, 1876; AGP XLI - 1 Gaston, count d'Eu, to Louis, duke of Nemours, Rio, November 6, 1876 (cited in A. Rangel, *Gastão d'Orléans*, 326).

40. AGP XL - 1 D. Isabel to Gaston, count d'Eu, Paço da Cidade, September 15, September 19, September 20, 1876; AGP XLI - 30 Gaston, count d'Eu, to Jules Gauthier, Rio, October 12, 1876.

41. AGP XLI - 1 Gaston, count d'Eu, to Louis, duke of Nemours, Petrópolis, April 11, 1876; AGP XLI - 30 Gaston, count d'Eu, to Jules Gauthier, Petrópolis, May 13, October 12, 1876.

42. AGP XLI - 5 Gaston, count d'Eu, to the countess of Barral, Paço da Cidade, Rio, October 4, 1876.

43. AGP XLI - 5 Gaston, count d'Eu, to the countess of Barral, Petrópolis, January 11, 1877; AGP XLI - 30 Gaston, count d'Eu, to Jules Gauthier, Petrópolis, September 14, 1875.

44. AGP XLI – 5 Gaston, count d'Eu, to the countess of Barral, Paço da Cidade, October 4, 1876, Petrópolis, January 12, 1877.

45. AGP XL - 1 D. Isabel to Gaston, count d'Eu, Petrópolis, March 16, 1877, May 17, 1877; AGP XL1 - 1[1] Gaston, count d'Eu, to Pedro II, Petrópolis, June 2, 1877.

46. IHGB BC Lata 892 Pasta 150 Antônio da Costa Pinto e Silva to João Maurício Wanderley, baron of Cotegipe, n. p., May 31, 1877.

47. AGP XL - 2 D. Isabel to Pedro II, Petrópolis, June 10, 1877.

48. AGP XLI - 1[1] Gaston, count d'Eu, to Pedro II, Palácio Isabel, Rio, July 5, 1877; AGP XL - 2 D. Isabel to Pedro II, Rio, July 22, 1877.

49. PRO FO 13 Brazil v. 526 G. A. Walker, consul, to the earl of Derby, foreign secretary, Consular No. 36, British Consulate, Pernambuco, August 29, 1877; AGP XLI - 1 Gaston, count d'Eu, to Louis, duke of Nemours, Laranjeiras, September 29, 1877 (cited in A. Rangel, *Gastão d'Orléans*, 331).

50. AGP XLI - 1 Gaston, count d'Eu, to Louis, duke of Nemours, Laranjeiras, August 30, 1877 (cited in A. Rangel, *Gastão d'Orléans*, 334–35); AGP unnumbered Countess of Barral to Gaston, count d'Eu, Hôtel des Trois Rois, Bâle à Zurich, July 28, 1877.

51. AGP XLI - 1 Gaston, count d'Eu, to Louis, duke of Nemours, Petrópolis, November 29, 1877.

52. AGP XLI - 1 Gaston, count d'Eu, to Louis, duke of Nemours, Laranjeiras, September 29, 1877.

53. AGP XLI - 5 Gaston, count d'Eu, to the countess of Barral, November 29, 1877.

54. AGP XLI - 5 Gaston, count d'Eu, to the countess of Barral, Petrópolis, September 29, November 29, 1877.

55. AGP XLI - 1 Gaston, count d'Eu, to Louis, duke of Nemours, Laranjeiras, January 30, 1878.

56. AGP XL - 2 D. Isabel to Pedro II, Paris, February 23, 1879.

57. AGP XL - 2 D. Isabel to Pedro II, Hôtel d'Albe, Paris, June 8, 1878.

58. AGP XL - 2 D. Isabel to Pedro II, 27 rue de la Faisanderie, Paris, October 30, 1879.

59. AGP XLI - 1[1] Gaston, count d'Eu, to Pedro II, Paris, October 31, 1879; Pedro II to the countess of Barral, Rio, December 22, 1879, printed in R. Magalhães Jr., *D. Pedro II e a condessa de Barral*, 294.

60. AGP XLI - 1[1] Gaston, count d'Eu, to Pedro II, Orléans, February 10, 1879, Villers-sur-Mer, [France,] September 2, 1880.

61. AGP XLI - 5 Gaston, count d'Eu, to the countess of Barral, [Paris,] December 30, 1880.

62. AGP XL - 1 D. Isabel to Gaston, count d'Eu, 27 rue de la Faisanderie, Paris , January 27, 1881; AGP XL - 2 D. Isabel to Pedro II, 27 rue de la Faisanderie, Paris, April 7, 1881.

63. Countess of Barral to D. Teresa Cristina, Paris, August 8, 1881, original in AGP and printed in Condessa de Barral, *Cartas*, 179.

Chapter 6, pages 159–198

1. Lisa Tiersten, "Marianne in the Department Store: Gender and the Politics of Consumption in Turn-of-the-Century Paris," Geoffrey Crossick and Serge Jaumin, eds., *Cathedrals of Consumption: The European Department Store, 1850–1939* (Aldershot, England, 1999), 116.

2. AGP XL - 1 D. Isabel to Gaston, count d'Eu, 27 rue de la Faisanderie, Paris, February 6, 1881.

3. *Gazeta Academica* (Bahia) 2 (August 1886): 166–77, cited in June E. Hahner, *Emancipating the Female Sex: The Struggle for Women's Rights in Brazil, 1850–1940* (Durham NC, 1990), 62, 239.

4. AGP XL - 1 D. Isabel to Gaston, count d'Eu, Paço Isabel, September 25, 1882; Isabelle, comtesse de Paris, *Tout m'est bonheur* (Paris, 1978), 53.

5. AGP XLI - 5 Gaston, count d'Eu, to the countess of Barral, Petrópolis, February 5, 1882.

6. AGP XL - 1 D. Isabel to Gaston, count d'Eu, Paço Isabel, May 25, 1882.

7. AGP XLI - 1 Gaston, count d'Eu, to Louis, duke of Nemours, Rio, September 2, 1884.

8. AGP XL - 4 D. Isabel to Louis, duke of Nemours, Petrópolis, December 22, 1881.

9. AGP XL - 2 D. Isabel to Pedro II, Petrópolis, June 15, 1883.

10. AGP XLI - 5 Gaston, count d'Eu, to the countess of Barral, Rio, January 14, 1884; AGP XL - 4 D. Isabel to Louis, duke of Nemours, Petrópolis,

December 22, 1881, March 18, 1882, Rio, August 13, 1883, Petrópolis, December 16, 1883; Comtesse de Paris, *Bonheur*, 59.

11. AGP XL - 4 D. Isabel to Louis, duke of Nemours, Petrópolis, March 18, 1882.

12. AGP XL - 4 D. Isabel to Louis, duke of Nemours, Petrópolis, September 1, 1886.

13. Diary entry for August 3, 1882, in Roberto Mendes Gonçalves, *Um diplomata austríaco na côrte de São Cristóvão (à margem do diário do barão de Hubner) Brasil—Uruguai—Argentina de 1882* (Rio de Janeiro, 1976), 46–47.

14. AHMI POB Cat. A Maço 196 Doc. 8891 Copy of Gaston, count d'Eu, to Antônio Martins Pinheiro Filho, Petrópolis, March 9, 1886.

15. J. F. McMillan, *France and Women*, 53.

16. See the classic discussion of the term in Carroll Smith-Rosenberg, "Female World of Love and Ritual: Relations between Women in Nineteenth-Century America," *Signs* 1, n. 1 (Autumn 1975): 1–30.

17. Interview with Amanda Doria, baroness of Loreto, on November 15, 1922, in M. Monteiro, "A Familia Imperial," 82.

18. AGP XLI - 5 Gaston, count d'Eu, to the countess of Barral, Petrópolis, January 2, 1882, Rio, August 16, 1884.

19. The original diary is held in AGP XL - 2. The text relating to São Paulo province has been published, with copious and very useful notes, the quotation being from that work; see Ricardo Gumbleton Daunt, ed., *Diário da princesa Isabel (excursão dos condes d'Eu à província de S. Paulo em 1884)* (São Paulo, 1957), 35.

20. AGP XL - 4 D. Isabel to Louis, duke of Nemours, Desterro, Santa Catarina, December 25, 1884.

21. Diary entry for November 15, 1884, in R. G. Daunt, *Diário*, 32.

22. AHMI I - DLC - 7.4.886 - Orl. c. 1 Gaston, count d'Eu, to Ambrósio Leitão da Cunha, baron of Marmoré, Rio, April 7, 1886; AHMI POB Cat. A Maço 196 Doc. 8885 Baron of Marmoré to the count d'Eu, Rio, April 9, 1886.

23. AGP XLI - 1 Gaston, count d'Eu, to Louis, duke of Nemours, Rio, September 2, 1884.

24. AGP XLI - 5 Gaston, count d'Eu, to the countess of Barral, Rio, September 9, 1886; Pedro II to the countess of Barral, Petrópolis, January 7, 1887, in Condessa de Barral, *Cartas*, 257.

25. Countess of Barral to Pedro II, Villa des Caroubiers, Nice, February 24, 1887, original in AGP and printed in Condessa de Barral, *Cartas*, 264.

26. AGP XL - 2 D. Isabel to Pedro II and D. Teresa Cristina, São Cristóvão, July 2, 1887.

27. AHMI POB Cat. A Maço 199 Doc. 9030 Untitled narrative by D. Isabel, dated by her "Dezembro de 1888" (hereafter cited as "Memorandum of December 1888"); AGP XLI - 5 Gaston, count d'Eu, to the countess of Barral, Rio, July 14, 1887.

28. AGP XLI - 1 Gaston, count d'Eu, to Louis, duke of Nemours, São Cristó-vão, August 11, 1887.

29. Memorandum of December 1888; AGP XL - 2 D. Isabel to Pedro II and D. Teresa Cristina, Paço Isabel, December 3, 1887.

30. AGP XL - 5 D. Isabel to the countess of Barral, Petrópolis, January 11, 1888; D. Isabel's letter is written entirely in French; IHGB BC Lata 960 Pasta 28 Memorandum entitled "Conferencia com S. A. (Paço Isabel) em 14 de janeiro de 1888" (hereafter cited as "Conferencia").

31. "Conferencia."

32. Ibid.; Memorandum of December 1888.

33. AGP XL - 5 D. Isabel to the countess of Barral, São Cristóvão, Febru-ary 22, 1888. The letter is written in Portuguese.

34. Memorandum of December 1888; AGP XL - 2 D. Isabel to Pedro II and D. Teresa Cristina, São Cristóvão, March 14, 1888.

35. Memorandum of December 1888.

36. *Organizações e programas ministeriais: Regime parlamentar no império*, 2d ed. (Rio de Janeiro, 1962), 240.

37. Memorandum of December 1888. The portion of the original Portuguese text translated here is written in a cryptic and diffuse style, very difficult to trans-late directly into English. The ellipsis after the word "undertaking" appears in D. Isabel's text.

38. AGP XL - 2 D. Isabel to Pedro II and D. Teresa Cristina, São Cristóvão, March 14, 1888.

39. AGP XLI - 1 Gaston, count d'Eu, to Louis, duke of Nemours, São Cristó-vão, August 23, 1888.

40. BNRJ TM Armário 32 Pacote 95 Handwritten note by Tobias Monteiro, headed "Chegado do I. em 88. Ideia abdicação." Following the words "frame of mind," the note also contains the phrase "(It is clear that there was a desire to obtain the abdication immediately.)". The count d'Eu's letter of August 23, 1888, confirms that Pedro II refused to entertain the proposal.

41. AGP XLI - 1 Gaston, count d'Eu, to Louis, duke of Nemours, Petrópolis, November 12, 1888.

42. Rodrigo Melo Franco de Andrade, *Rio Branco e Gastão da Cunha* (Rio de Janeiro, 1953), 198.

43. João Capistrano de Abreu to José Maria da Silva Paranhos Júnior, future baron of Rio Branco, Rio, December 23, 1887, in José Honório Rodrigues, ed., *Correspondência de Capistrano de Abreu* (Rio de Janeiro, 1954), 1: 119; João Carlos de Sousa Ferreira to François Picot, Rio, February 10, 1889, in *1° Centenario do Jornal do Comércio, 1827–1927* (Rio de Janeiro, 1928), 200.

44. Georges Clemenceau, *Le "justice" du sexe fort* (Paris, 1907), quoted in J. F. McMillan, *France and Women*, 228.

45. "A sociedade no Rio de Janeiro: A princeza imperial (continuação)," *Gazeta da Tarde*, March 12, 1886. This article was one of a series ostensibly written by a

European diplomat and originally published in a Saint Petersburg newspaper but in fact concocted by the *Gazeta da Tarde*'s own staff.

46. Ibid.

47. "A sociedade no Rio de Janeiro: O conde d'Eu (conclusão da quarta carta)," *Gazeta da Tarde*, March 26, 1886.

48. AGP XLI - 5 Passage dated May 21 in Gaston, count d'Eu, to the countess of Barral, Petrópolis, May 14, 1889; João Carlos de Sousa Ferreira to François Picot, Rio, March 28, 1889, in *1° Centenario*, 203.

49. AGP XLI - 5 Passage dated May 21 in Gaston, count d'Eu, to the countess of Barral, Petrópolis, May 14, 1889.

50. AGP XLI - 5 Gaston, count d'Eu, to the countess of Barral, Petrópolis, May 28, 1889.

51. AGP XLI - 5 Gaston, count d'Eu, to the countess of Barral, Petrópolis, June 7, 1889.

52. AGP XL - 1 D. Isabel to Gaston, count d'Eu, Tijuca, Rio, August 18, 1889; João Carlos de Sousa Ferreira to François Picot, Rio, August 28, 1889, in *1° Centenario*, 210.

53. AGP XLI - 5 Gaston, count d'Eu, to the countess of Barral, Petrópolis, February 5, 1889.

54. João Carlos de Sousa Ferreira to François Picot, Rio, September 13, 1889, in *1° Centenario*, 213.

55. AGP XLI - 1 Gaston, count d'Eu, to Louis, duke of Némours, Paço Isabel, October 17, 1889 (cited in A. Rangel, *Gastão d'Orléans*, 385).

56. AHMI POB Cat. A Maço 207 Doc. 9413 "Memoria para meus filhos." This narrative, written by D. Isabel in draft form late in November, is printed in Raymundo Magalhães Jr., *Deodoro: A espada contra o império*, 2 vols. (Rio de Janeiro, 1957), 2: 396–403. The passage quoted is on p. 396.

57. R. Magalhães Jr., *Deodoro*, 2: 396.

58. Ibid.; D. Luiz de Orléans-Bragança, *Sob o cruzeiro do sul: Brasil—Argentina—Bolivia—Paraguay—Uruguay* (Montreux, Switzerland, 1913), 9.

59. R. Magalhães Jr., *Deodoro*, 2: 396.

60. Ibid., 398.

61. *Jornal do Comércio*, November 17, 1889, printed in L. L. Lacombe, *Isabel*, 261.

62. D. Luiz de Orléans-Bragança, *Sob o cruzeiro do sul*, 9–10.

63. R. Magalhães Jr., *Deodoro*, 2: 399, 400.

Chapter 7, pages 199–234

1. Patricia Vertinsky, *The Eternally Wounded Woman: Women, Doctors and Exercise in the Late Nineteenth Century* (Manchester, England, 1990), 89.

2. R. Magalhães Jr., *Deodoro*, 2: 395, 396.

3. Ibid.

4. Ibid., 2: 402.

5. AHMI POB Cat. A Maço 207 Doc. 9413 Note written in French by D. Isabel, (quoted in translation in L. L. Lacombe, *Isabel*, 265).

6. R. Magalhães Jr., *Deodoro*, 2: 401.

7. Gaston, count d'Eu, to the countess of Barral, *Alagoas*, November 27, 1889, printed in "A deposição do Imperador e a viagem para o exílio," *AnMI* 16 (1955): 238.

8. R. Magalhães Jr., *Deodoro*, 2: 401. The flag flown by the *Alagoas*, while traveling from Rio to São Vicente, was an improvisation, copying the stars and the stripes of the U.S. flag, but using yellow and green. "Our flag" was the flag of the Brazilian Empire.

9. Ibid., 400–401; AGP XL - 2 D. Isabel to Pedro II, Bordo do vapor *Alagoas*, December 2, 1889.

10. *Gazeta de Portugal*, December 8, 1889, reproducing interview in *Novidades*, December 7, 1889.

11. IHGB Lata 658 Livro 6 Manuscript entitled "Notas de Viagem" of Amanda Doria, baroness of Loreto (hereafter cited as "Notas de Viagem"), entry for December 29, 1889.

12. AGP XLI - 1 Gaston, count d'Eu, to Louis, duke of Nemours, Lisbon, January 7, 1890.

13. P. Calmon, *Pedro II*, 3: 1048–1049; AHMI POB Cat. B Maço 37 Doc. 1057 (hereafter cited as "Pedro II's diary"), entry for January 15, 1890.

14. "Notas de Viagem," entry for January 25, 1890.

15. Ibid. Entries for January 28 and 30, 1890.

16. Ibid. Entry for February 8, 1890; Pedro II's diary, entry for February 4, 1890.

17. Pedro II's diary, entry for February 11, 1890.

18. Ibid. Entry for February 16, 1890.

19. AGP XLI - 5 Gaston, count d'Eu, to the countess of Barral, Cannes, March 15, 1890.

20. M. Monteiro, "A Familia Imperial," 82.

21. Pedro II's diary, entry for September 10, 1890.

22. AHMI I - DMM - 1889/96 - I. c. 1-21 D. Isabel to the count of Mota Maia, undated [Versailles, September 10 or 11, 1890].

23. Pedro II's diary, entry for October 5, 1890.

24. Ibid. Entry for October 3, 1891; AGP XL - 1 D. Isabel to Gaston, count d'Eu, Vichy, August 12, 1891.

25. AGP XLI - 5 Gaston, count d'Eu, to the countess of Barral, Cannes, March 15, 1890; Pedro II's diary, entry for August 4, 1891.

26. AHMI I - DED - 1866/899 - I.B. c. 1-40 D. Isabel to Adelaide Taunay, Versailles, January 18, 1891; Pedro II's diary, entries for April 10, May 13, 1891.

27. Pedro II's diary, entries for August 16, 20, 21, and 22, 1891, and September 12, 1891; AGP XL - 1 D. Isabel to Gaston, count d'Eu, Vichy, August 16 and 22, 1891.

28. Pedro II's diary, entry for November 13, 1891.

29. João Carlos de Sousa Ferreira to François Picot, Rio, December 28, 1889, in *1° Centenario*, 216.

30. IHGB, Coleção Visconde de Ouro Preto (hereafter OP), Lata 427, Doc. 19, Draft of an appeal to D. Isabel, dated "Rio, da Nbo de 1892."

31. IHGB OP Lata 427 Doc. 19 Draft of an appeal to D. Isabel, dated "Rio, da Nbo de 1892," and D. Isabel to Srs. Ouro Preto, Lafayette, and João Alfredo, Boulogne-sur-Seine, December 4, 1892.

32. Universidade Federal de Pernambuco, Recife, Coleção João Alfredo (hereafter UFP JA), D. Isabel to João Alfredo Correia de Oliveira, Boulogne-sur-Seine, December 4, 1892. The 1824 Constitution had created a fourth branch of the government, *o poder moderador* (the regulating power), entrusted to the emperor.

33. UFP JA D. Isabel to João Alfredo Correia de Oliveira, Boulogne-sur-Seine, December 4, 1892.

34. AGP XL - 1 D. Isabel to Gaston, count d'Eu, Luchon, September 4, 1894.

35. AHMI I - DED - 1866/889 – I.B. c. 1-40 D. Isabel to Adelaide Taunay, Dinard, September 11, 1893; AHMI I - DVC - 30.3.867 - I.B. bi. 1-4 D. Isabel to the viscountess of Lajes, Saint Gervais, August 30, 1896, Boulogne-sur-Seine, October 4, 1902.

36. *Discours prononcé par Mgr. de la Ville Rabel Archevêque de Rouen aux obsèques de S. A. I. et R. Madame la Comtesse d'Eu en l'église Notre-Dame d'Eu le 18 Novembre 1921* (Eu, France, n. d.), 6.

37. Arquivo do Museu Histórico Nacional, Rio de Janeiro, Coleção Loreto, D. Isabel to Amanda Doria, baroness of Loreto, cited in L. L. Lacombe, *Isabel*, 273.

38. Comtesse de Paris, *Bonheur*, 55.

39. AGP XLI - 5 Gaston, count d'Eu, to the countess of Barral, Petrópolis, February 9, 1889.

40. Comtesse de Paris, *Bonheur*, 19.

41. UFP JA D. Isabel to João Alfredo Correia de Oliveira, April 8, 1904, printed in P. Calmon, *Isabel*, 323.

42. D. Luíz de Orléans-Bragança, *Sob o cruzeiro do sul*, 6.

43. IHGB OP Lata 427 Doc. 19 D. Isabel to the Diretório Monarquista, Château d'Eu, November 9, 1908; printed in D. Carlos Tasso de Saxe-Coburgo e Bragança, "O ramo brasileiro da casa da Bragança: Apontamentos genealógicos," *Anais do Museu Histórico Nacional* 18 (1968): 105.

44. AHMI I - DLC - 7.4.886 - Orl. c. 1-18 Gaston, count d'Eu, to Ambrósio Leitão da Cunha, baron of Marmoré, Boulogne-sur-Seine, September 17, 1895; "Joies et tristesses."

45. UFP JA D. Isabel to João Alfredo Correia de Oliveira, August 11, 1914, printed in P. Calmon, *Isabel*, 334, where the year is misstated as "1911"; Comtesse de Paris, *Bonheur*, 53, 54.

46. Comtesse de Paris, *Bonheur*, 52, 53.

47. Ibid., 57, 59.

48. D. Luíz de Orléans-Bragança, *Sob o cruzeiro do sul*, 28.

49. Comtesse de Paris, *Bonheur*, 60; AGP XL - 4 D. Isabel to Louis, duke of Nemours, Meran, Austria, February 16, 1871.

50. AMHI POB Cat. A. Maço 204 Doc. 9354 D. Isabel to Gaston, count d'Eu, Boulogne-sur-Seine, November 30, 1918.

51. IHGB Coleção Baronesa de Loreto Lata 299 Pasta 19 Gaston, count d'Eu, to Amanda Doria, baroness of Loreto, Boulogne-sur-Seine, July 31, 1919; AGP XL - 1 D. Isabel to Gaston, count d'Eu, Eu, January 5, 1921.

52. AGP XLI - 3 Gaston, count d'Eu, to D. Isabel, Hôtel Avenida, Lisbon, December 12, 1920, and four letters of later date.

53. *Discours prononcé*, 6; IHGB Coleção Baronesa de Loreto Lata 299 Pasta 19 Gaston, count d'Eu, to Amanda Doria, baroness of Loreto, Castello d'Eu, November 19, 1921.

Chapter 8, pages 235–249

1. Sewell, "Theory," 10.

2. Ibid., 10, 15, 20.

3. Ibid., 21.

4. Jeanne H. Block, *Sex Role Identity and Ego Development* (San Francisco, 1984), 8–9; Carolyn G. Heilbrun, *Writing a Woman's Life* (New York, 1988), 20–21.

5. Undated draft document, in D. Teresa Cristina's handwriting, entitled "Attributes of the Governess," original in AHMI POB and printed in L. L. Lacombe, "Educação," 250.

6. AGP unnumbered Countess of Barral to D. Isabel, [Paris,] November 23, 1865.

7. J. H. Block, *Sex Role Identity*, 249; AGP XL 2 D. Isabel to Pedro II, Laranjeiras, September 4, 1871.

8. AGP XI - 30 Gaston, count d'Eu, to Jules Gauthier, Petrópolis, May 13, 1876.

9. Ester de Lemos, *D. Maria II (a rainha e a mulher) no centenário da sua morte* (Lisbon, 1954), 201; AGP XL - 2 D. Isabel to Pedro II, 27 rue de la Faisanderie, Paris, March 23, 1880.

10. Memorandum of December 1888.

11. IHGB BC Lata 955 Pasta 17 Undated memorandum (written about 1882) by João Maurício Wanderley, baron of Cotegipe.

12. AGP XL - 2 D. Isabel to Pedro II, São Cristóvão, March 14, 1888.

13. Comtesse de Paris, *Bonheur*, 28.

14. BNRJ TM Armário 32 Pacote 96 Typewritten note headed, "Disse-me a Baronesa de Loreto em Março de 1917—Poços de Caldas."

ANNOTATED BIBLIOGRAPHY

Barman, Roderick J. *Citizen Emperor: Pedro II and the Making of Brazil, 1825–1891.* Stanford, 1999.

> The most recent study in English of D. Isabel's father, analyzing his personality, his activities, and his influence on the formation of a public and political culture of Brazil as a nation-state. Discusses his relationships with the women in his life (stepmother, wife, daughters, mistresses, and friends) but is written very much from a masculine viewpoint. Can be used to supplement and explain the context of this study of D. Isabel.

Barral, Condessa de (Luísa Margarida Portugal de Barros). *Cartas a suas magestades 1859–1890.* Rio de Janeiro, 1977.

> Transcribes the surviving letters written to D. Isabel's parents by the woman who was from 1856 to 1864 *aia* (supervisor) to the princess and her sister. Because of her intelligence and charm, the countess served, more than did D. Teresa Cristina, as a role model and guide for D. Isabel during childhood and adolescence. The friendship thus created survived and flourished until the countess's death in 1891. A number of the letters were written jointly by the countess and D. Isabel. The passages written by the princess are indicative of her personality. Does not transcribe all the jointly written letters.

Bernardes, Maria Thereza Caiuby Crescenti. *Mulheres de ontem? Rio de Janeiro, século XIX.* São Paulo, 1989.

> Lack of coherence and conceptual sophistication does not lessen this work's value as an attempt to identify the names and record the working lives of women who were active as writers and educators in Rio de Janeiro in the imperial period. Not well developed

or systematic, it lacks both a knowledge of the imperial period and an ability to probe deeply into the topic.

Besse, Susan K. *Restructuring Patriarchy: The Modernization of Gender Inequality in Brazil, 1914–1940*. Chapel Hill, NC, 1996.
The study's first chapter provides a succinct and forceful overview of the position of women in Brazil prior to 1914. The author's Marxist viewpoint stresses the economic factors that produced a patriarchal social system and sees this system as the cause for the subordinate position of women.

Borges, Dain. *The Family in Bahia, Brazil, 1870–1945*. Stanford, 1992.
The standard work in English studying the transition in Brazil from the traditional family to the modern family, using the state of Bahia as its example. Focuses on the practices of middle and upper sectors of society, practices not necessarily representative of Bahian society as a whole. Elucidates the context of an important stage—marriage—in the life course of most women, specifically of most upper-class women, living in Brazil during D. Isabel's lifetime.

Calmon, Pedro. *A princesa Isabel "a redentora."* São Paulo, 1941.
This book, written some twenty years after D. Isabel's death, provided the first full account of her life. Unusual in treating a woman as worthy of a biography, the work is limited by the narrow range of sources consulted and by the author's deliberate avoidance of any systematic analysis of D. Isabel's character and her actions. It embodies what might be termed the standard historiographical approach to the princess and reflects traditional gender attitudes.

Del Priore, Mary, and Carla Bassanezi, eds. *História das Mulheres no Brasil*. São Paulo, 1997.
This multiauthored survey of women and their place in the history of Brazil is quite variable in quality, in part because of the lack of primary research and conceptual innovation in a number of the contributions. The article most relevant to D. Isabel's life, "Mulher e família burguesa," by Maria Angela D'Incao, exemplifies these problems. The contributions by Miridan Knox Falci and Joana Maria Pedro on women in the northeast and the far south engage more closely with their topics and provide interesting insights on upper-class women in these areas.

Graham, Sandra Lauderdale. *House and Street: The Domestic World of Servants and Masters in Nineteenth-Century Rio de Janeiro*. Cambridge, England, 1988.

> A very clear, systematic study of the settings in which women, both employers and servants or slaves, existed in Rio de Janeiro during the late imperial period. The author shows how little urbanization and modernization had altered traditional structures both of gender and of employment. The absence of materials on individual life histories makes the study very much written from the outside.

Hahner, June E. *Emancipating the Female Sex: The Struggle for Women's Rights in Brazil, 1850–1940*. Durham, NC, 1990.

> This useful study investigates the long, laborious campaign to secure civil and political rights for Brazilian women. Makes clear how little had been achieved in the period before the overthrow of the Empire in 1889 and shows that women fared no better under the new Republican regime. A pioneering study that builds on the author's initial articles on the subject, the work identifies the topics that need further investigation in depth.

Heilbrun, Carolyn G. *Writing a Woman's Life*. New York, 1988.

> This perceptive study, full of original insights and telling phrases, is indispensable preliminary reading for anyone (particularly if male) who wishes to write the life story of a woman. The author seeks to show how the biographer can contribute to freeing women, their lives, their expectations, and their language from the power and control that men until very recently possessed. The work's single weakness lies in its emphasis on cultural action, thus underestimating the important role played by men's control of material resources in maintaining female subordination.

Karasch, Mary. *Slave Life in Rio de Janeiro, 1808–1850*. Princeton, NJ, 1987.

> This finely produced book takes the reader into the world of slaves in the capital of Brazil during the years prior to D. Isabel's birth. Although not addressing directly the role of gender among the slaves themselves, the work is very conscious of gender differences and gives space and attention to the experience of slave women in respect to their work, personal lives, and relations with the free world.

Lacombe, Lourenço L. *Isabel a princesa redentora (biografia baseada em documentos inéditos)*. Petrópolis, 1989.
> The only full biography of D. Isabel to have been published thus far. Based on the private papers of the imperial family, the study is most thorough on D. Isabel's childhood and young adulthood, but inexplicably the author failed to make use of the letters D. Isabel exchanged with the countess of Barral, her *aia* and friend in adulthood. D. Isabel's later life, in particular the thirty years (1889–1921) of exile in France, are treated in an increasingly summary fashion. The author is not comfortable with gender issues and avoids any close analysis of the role played by gender in D. Isabel's life and outlook.

Levi, Darrell E. *The Prados of São Paulo, Brazil: An Elite Family and Social Change, 1840–1930*. Athens, GA, 1987.
> Designed to be a case study set within "the new Brazilian family history," this work provides useful information about a leading *fazendeiro* (planter) family in the coffee area of southern Brazil. In conceptual terms, the book is little changed from its origins as a 1973 dissertation, which drew heavily upon Gilberto Freyre's interpretation of imperial Brazil and relied upon the idea of "modernization" as its principal theoretical prop.

Matos, Maria Izilda S. de, and Maria Angélica Soler, eds. *Gênero em debate: Trajetória e perspectivas na historiografia contemporânea*. São Paulo, 1997.
> This short collection of articles is significant for its attempt to introduce Brazilians to the concept of gender, the value of gender as a tool for studying and understanding the past, and the ways in which gender can be employed in Brazilian history. It surveys the French- and English-language theoretical literature on gender. Given their brevity, the individual essays are necessarily more overviews than studies in depth, but the work is noteworthy as a pioneering effort on the subject.

Mattoso, Katia M. de Queirós. *Família e sociedade na Bahia do século XIX*. São Paulo, 1988.
> Focusing on the city of Salvador, rather than Bahia as a whole, this study provides a precise and illuminating analysis of the nature of family structure as shaped by the law, racial beliefs, and social prac-

tices. Although the place of women is not neglected, the work pays little attention to gender issues as such. The study runs parallel to and should be used in conjunction with Eni de Mesquita Samara's study of the family in São Paulo.

_____. *To Be a Slave in Brazil, 1550–1888.* Trans. Arthur Goldhammer. New Brunswick, NJ, 1986.

An accessible and graphically written account of slave life in Brazil or, more accurately, in Bahia state, this work gives agency to slaves in respect to their daily lives. It is oblivious to the fact that gender differences existed among slaves, just as much as they did among free people. It does not consider what the impact of gender was in the realm of work, personal life, and life strategies.

McMillan, James F. *France and Women, 1789–1914: Gender, Society and Politics.* London, 2000.

A systematic overview of the place of women in French society that explains the reasons why, in a nation-state that adopted "equality" as one of its goals, women were denied both political and social rights and why feminism developed so slowly. Since France served as the model for Brazilian elite society and since D. Isabel herself spent a quarter of her life between 1864 and 1889 in France and lived in exile there from 1889 to 1921, the work provides excellent background information for understanding her as a woman.

Paris, Isabelle, comtesse de. *Tout m'est bonheur.* Paris, 1978.

Written by D. Isabel's eldest granddaughter, born in 1911, this account gives in its first three chapters a child's perception of her paternal grandparents' personalities and their life at the château d'Eu and the villa at Boulogne-sur-Seine, during the Great War and its aftermath. The work's value lies in the writer's closeness to her grandparents, for whom she was a reminder and almost a reincarnation of their own daughter, born dead in 1873.

Pedro, Joana Maria. *Mulheres honestas e mulheres faladas: Uma questão de classe.* Florianópolis, 1994.

Presents copious and revealing evidence on attitudes toward and the lives of women, particularly those at the top end of society, in the town of Desterro, renamed Florianópolis in 1895, in southern

Brazil from about the 1870s into the 1920s. The author postulates but does not demonstrate a direct relationship between political conditions, at first disorder and then stability, and the position of women. The work demonstrates how much printed and manuscript materials can reveal about women and gender attitudes but, as a study, it would profit from a more developed theoretical structure.

Rangel, Alberto. *Gastão d'Orléans (o ultimo conde d'Eu)*. São Paulo, 1935.

Designed to rehabilitate the count d'Eu and his role in public affairs during the imperial period, this biography is both deferential and conventional in its handling of the count's character and life. It is useful mainly for the factual information it provides and for the copious quotations it contains from the count's letters to his father and to his former tutor. The work pays a minimum of attention to D. Isabel and avoids any analysis of the couple's relationship.

Rose, Phyllis. *Parallel Lives: Five Victorian Marriages*. New York, 1983.

Written to prompt its readers "to question how the presumption of marriage, the fiction of marriage, has affected the shape of their lives," this book is a percipient and stimulating study of the lives of five literary couples who lived in Great Britain during the nineteenth century. The work vividly demonstrates that "the shifting tides of power between a man and a woman joined, presumably, for life" are a central part of gender relations. The work is a model as to how gender biography should be written.

Samara, Eni de Mesquita. *As mulheres, o poder e a família: São Paulo, século XIX*. São Paulo, 1989.

Studies the family structure in parts of São Paulo city in the early nineteenth century, based on the 1836 census records and wills for the city from 1800 to 1860. Much narrower in scope than the title claims, the work does not develop its findings as far as it might in conceptual terms. Nonetheless, it is valuable for the insights it does offer.

Schwartz, Lilia Moritz. *As barbas do imperador: D. Pedro II, um monarca nos trópicos*. São Paulo, 1998.
Informative study of the imagery, both contemporary and subsequent, surrounding D. Isabel's father that served to create the perception of the man and his rule still hegemonic in Brazil. Reveals the extent to which the emperor dominated the public sphere, seeing D. Isabel as an extension of himself. Particularly useful for the numerous contemporary images it reproduces of the princess, the count d'Eu, and their children.

Scott, Joan Wallach. *Gender and the Politics of History*. New York, 1988.
This collection of previously published articles is notable for "Gender: A Useful Category of Historical Analysis," pp. 28–50. This study has established itself as the primary statement of gender as an abstract category and has served as a catalyst for the adoption by historians of gender as an analytical tool.

Silva Dias, Maria Odila Leite da. *Power and Everyday Life: The Lives of Working Women in Nineteenth-Century Brazil*. Trans. Ann Frost. New Brunswick, NJ, 1995.
First published in 1984 as *Quotidiano e poder em São Paulo no século XIX*, this work discusses the lives, above all the working lives, of ordinary women in the town of São Paulo. Particularly strong on the lives of street vendors, both slave and free, who formed an essential sector in the economy. Also points to the racial tensions existing within the servant class. Regrettably, the poor quality of the translation makes the text far less accessible and effective in English than it could be.

Tasso de Saxe-Coburgo e Bragança, D. Carlos. "O ramo brasileiro da casa da Bragança: Apontamentos genealógicos." *Anais do Museu Histórico Nacional* 18 (1968): 7–209.
A useful source for tracing the ramifications of D. Isabel's family connections through her parents and her husband. The data make plain the multiple links that bound the princess during her life to the dynasties, both reigning and deposed, of Europe. The family paintings and photographs reproduced in the article provide excellent visual information on the imperial family.

Viana Lyra, Maria de Lourdes. "Isabel de Bragança, uma princesa imperial." *Revista do Instituto Histórico e Geográfico Brasileiro*, v. 158 (January-March 1997): 83–131.

> This study focuses on D. Isabel's public role as the three-time regent of Brazil during the 1870s and 1880s, showing how little attention historians have given to the princess. Drawing on published materials, the article undertakes a careful evaluation of the background to D. Isabel's regencies and her conduct of the government at those times. The study tries to place D. Isabel in the context of politics and to assess her role in the trajectory of the imperial regime.

Vieira, Hermes. *A princêsa Isabel no cenário abolicionista do Brasil*. São Paulo, 1941.

> This extravagantly overwritten work seeks to rehabilitate the posthumous reputation of D. Isabel by presenting her as an exemplary woman devoted to doing good and always anguished by the existence of slavery. The book's willingness to see religion as a central factor in D. Isabel's life and its profuse transcription of documents give the study some value, but the princess is never more than a stock figure. In 1989, a revised edition, with a new title, *Princesa Isabel: Uma vida de luzes e sombras*, appeared. The prose style is more direct, many of the banalities removed, and most of the document transcriptions deleted. Despite the addition of some fresh materials, the work remains unchanged in its basic approach to D. Isabel.

Viotti da Costa, Emilia. *The Brazilian Empire: Myths and Histories*. Rev. ed. Chapel Hill, NC, 2000.

> The first edition of this work, published in 1985, contained no mention of D. Isabel and indeed very little about women. Its framework of analysis did not take into account gender, although the author is a woman. The revised edition includes a new chapter entitled "Patriarchalism and the Myth of the Helpless Woman in the Nineteenth Century." The evidence produced, the author's discussion of it, and her conclusions simply do not support the viewpoint presented in the chapter title. The approach to questions of gender is very much driven by a traditional Marxist slant.

INDEX

Italic page numbers indicate an illustration; an "f" after a number indicates a continuation on the next page, and an "ff" on the next two pages.

Latin American Silhouettes
Studies in History and Culture

William H. Beezley and
Judith Ewell
Editors

Volumes Published

Brian Loveman and Thomas M. Davies, Jr., eds., *The Politics of Antipolitics: The Military in Latin America*, 3d ed., revised and updated (1996). Cloth ISBN 0-8420-2609-6 Paper ISBN 0-8420-2611-8

Dianne Walta Hart, *Undocumented in L.A.: An Immigrant's Story* (1997). Cloth ISBN 0-8420-2648-7 Paper ISBN 0-8420-2649-5

William H. Beezley and Judith Ewell, eds., *The Human Tradition in Modern Latin America* (1997). Cloth ISBN 0-8420-2612-6 Paper ISBN 0-8420-2613-4

Donald F. Stevens, ed., *Based on a True Story: Latin American History at the Movies* (1997). Cloth ISBN 0-8420-2582-0 Paper ISBN 0-8420-2781-5

Jaime E. Rodríguez O., ed., *The Origins of Mexican National Politics, 1808–1847* (1997). Paper ISBN 0-8420-2723-8

Che Guevara, *Guerrilla Warfare*, with revised and updated introduction and case studies by Brian Loveman and Thomas M. Davies, Jr., 3d ed. (1997). Cloth ISBN 0-8420-2677-0 Paper ISBN 0-8420-2678-9

Adrian A. Bantjes, *As If Jesus Walked on Earth: Cardenismo, Sonora, and the Mexican Revolution* (1998; rev. ed., 2000). Cloth ISBN 0-8420-2653-3 Paper ISBN 0-8420-2751-3

A. Kim Clark, *The Redemptive Work: Railway and Nation in Ecuador, 1895–1930* (1998). Cloth ISBN 0-8420-2674-6 Paper ISBN 0-8420-5013-2

Louis A. Pérez, Jr., ed., *Impressions of Cuba in the Nineteenth Century: The Travel Diary of Joseph J. Dimock* (1998). Cloth ISBN 0-8420-2657-6 Paper ISBN 0-8420-2658-4

June E. Hahner, ed., *Women through Women's Eyes: Latin American Women in* *Nineteenth-Century Travel Accounts* (1998). Cloth ISBN 0-8420-2633-9 Paper ISBN 0-8420-2634-7

James P. Brennan, ed., *Peronism and Argentina* (1998). ISBN 0-8420-2706-8

John Mason Hart, ed., *Border Crossings: Mexican and Mexican-American Workers* (1998). Cloth ISBN 0-8420-2716-5 Paper ISBN 0-8420-2717-3

Brian Loveman, *For la Patria: Politics and the Armed Forces in Latin America* (1999). Cloth ISBN 0-8420-2772-6 Paper ISBN 0-8420-2773-4

Guy P. C. Thomson, with David G. LaFrance, *Patriotism, Politics, and Popular Liberalism in Nineteenth-Century Mexico: Juan Francisco Lucas and the Puebla Sierra* (1999). ISBN 0-8420-2683-5

Robert Woodmansee Herr, in collaboration with Richard Herr, *An American Family in the Mexican Revolution* (1999). ISBN 0-8420-2724-6

Juan Pedro Viqueira Albán, trans. Sonya Lipsett-Rivera and Sergio Rivera Ayala, *Propriety and Permissiveness in Bourbon Mexico* (1999). Cloth ISBN 0-8420-2466-2 Paper ISBN 0-8420-2467-0

Stephen R. Niblo, *Mexico in the 1940s: Modernity, Politics, and Corruption* (1999). Cloth ISBN 0-8420-2794-7 Paper (2001) ISBN 0-8420-2795-5

David E. Lorey, *The U.S.-Mexican Border in the Twentieth Century* (1999). Cloth ISBN 0-8420-2755-6 Paper ISBN 0-8420-2756-4

Joanne Hershfield and David R. Maciel, eds., *Mexico's Cinema: A Century of Films and Filmmakers* (2000). Cloth ISBN 0-8420-2681-9 Paper ISBN 0-8420-2682-7

Peter V. N. Henderson, *In the Absence of Don Porfirio: Francisco León de la Barra*

and the Mexican Revolution (2000).
ISBN 0-8420-2774-2

Mark T. Gilderhus, *The Second Century: U.S.-Latin American Relations since 1889* (2000). Cloth ISBN 0-8420-2413-1
Paper ISBN 0-8420-2414-X

Catherine Moses, *Real Life in Castro's Cuba* (2000). Cloth ISBN 0-8420-2836-6
Paper ISBN 0-8420-2837-4

K. Lynn Stoner, ed./comp., with Luis Hipólito Serrano Pérez, *Cuban and Cuban-American Women: An Annotated Bibliography* (2000). ISBN 0-8420-2643-6

Thomas D. Schoonover, *The French in Central America: Culture and Commerce, 1820–1930* (2000). ISBN 0-8420-2792-0

Enrique C. Ochoa, *Feeding Mexico: The Political Uses of Food since 1910* (2000). ISBN 0-8420-2812-9

Thomas W. Walker and Ariel C. Armony, eds., *Repression, Resistance, and Democratic Transition in Central America* (2000). Cloth ISBN 0-8420-2766-1   Paper ISBN 0-8420-2768-8

William H. Beezley and David E. Lorey, eds., *¡Viva México! ¡Viva la Independencia! Celebrations of September 16* (2001).
Cloth ISBN 0-8420-2914-1
Paper ISBN 0-8420-2915-X

Jeffrey M. Pilcher, *Cantinflas and the Chaos of Mexican Modernity* (2001).
Cloth ISBN 0-8420-2769-6
Paper ISBN 0-8420-2771-8

Victor M. Uribe-Uran, ed., *State and Society in Spanish America during the Age of Revolution* (2001). Cloth ISBN 0-8420-2873-0   Paper ISBN 0-8420-2874-9

Andrew Grant Wood, *Revolution in the Street: Women, Workers, and Urban Protest in Veracruz, 1870–1927* (2001). ISBN 0-8420-2879-X

Charles Bergquist, Ricardo Peñaranda, and Gonzalo Sánchez G., eds., *Violence in Colombia, 1990–2000: Waging War and Negotiating Peace* (2001).
Cloth ISBN 0-8420-2869-2
Paper ISBN 0-8420-2870-6

William Schell, Jr., *Integral Outsiders: The American Colony in Mexico City, 1876–1911* (2001). ISBN 0-8420-2838-2

John Lynch, *Argentine Caudillo: Juan Manuel de Rosas* (2001).
Cloth ISBN 0-8420-2897-8
Paper ISBN 0-8420-2898-6

Samuel Basch, M.D., ed. and trans. Fred D. Ullman, *Recollections of Mexico: The Last Ten Months of Maximilian's Empire* (2001). ISBN 0-8420-2962-1

David Sowell, *The Tale of Healer Miguel Perdomo Neira: Medicine, Ideologies, and Power in the Nineteenth-Century Andes* (2001).
Cloth ISBN 0-8420-2826-9
Paper ISBN 0-8420-2827-7

June E. Hahner, ed., *A Parisian in Brazil: The Travel Account of a Frenchwoman in Nineteenth-Century Rio de Janeiro* (2001). Cloth ISBN 0-8420-2854-4
Paper ISBN 0-8420-2855-2

Richard A. Warren, *Vagrants and Citizens: Politics and the Masses in Mexico City from Colony to Republic* (2001).
ISBN 0-8420-2964-8

Roderick J. Barman, *Princess Isabel of Brazil: Gender and Power in the Nineteenth Century* (2002).
Cloth ISBN 0-8420-2845-5
Paper ISBN 0-8420-2846-3

Stuart F. Voss, *Latin America in the Middle Period, 1750–1929* (2002).
Cloth ISBN 0-8420-5024-8
Paper ISBN 0-8420-5025-6

Lester D. Langley, *The Banana Wars: United States Intervention in the Caribbean, 1898–1934*, with new introduction (2002). Cloth ISBN 0-8420-5046-9   Paper ISBN 0-8420-5047-7